Ralph Ellison

Twayne's United States Authors Series

Warren French, Editor

University College of Swansea, Wales

TUSAS 582

RALPH ELLISON
©*photo by Bern Schwartz*

Ralph Ellison

Mark Busby

Texas A&M University

Twayne Publishers
A Division of G. K. Hall & Co. • Boston

Ralph Ellison
Mark Busby

Copyright 1991 by G. K. Hall & Co.
All rights reserved.
Published by Twayne Publishers
A division of G. K. Hall & Co.
70 Lincoln Street
Boston, Massachusetts 02111

Copyediting supervised by Barbara Sutton.
Book production by Gabrielle B. McDonald.
Book design by Barbara Anderson.
Typeset in Garamond by Graphic Sciences Corporation of Cedar Rapids, Iowa.

First published 1991.
10 9 8 7 6 5 4 3 2 1

The paper used in this publication meets the minimum requirements
of American National Standard for Information Sciences—Permanence
of Paper for Printed Library Materials, ANSI Z39.48-1984. ∞™

Printed and bound in the United States of America.

Library of Congress Cataloging-in-Publication Data

Busby, Mark.
    Ralph Ellison / Mark Busby.
        p.   cm. — (Twayne's United States authors series ; TUSAS 582)
    Includes bibliographical references (p.   ) and index.
    ISBN 0-8057-7626-5 (alk. paper)
    1. Ellison, Ralph—Criticism and interpretation.   I. Title.
    II. Series.
    PS3555.L625Z6   1991
    818'.5409—dc20   90-28501
                                                                                    CIP

For Linda and Josh

Contents

Preface
Acknowledgments
Chronology

Chapter One
Coming from the Territory: Geography, Biography,
and Fate   1

Chapter Two
From Propaganda to Art: Early Stories   22

Chapter Three
A Twentieth-Century Masterpiece:
Invisible Man   39

Chapter Four
The Actor's Shadows: Ellison's Literary
Antecedents   65

Chapter Five
The Jagged Grain: Later Stories, the Second
Novel   93

Chapter Six
The Mellow Bugler: Ellison's Nonfiction   120

Chapter Seven
Ellison's Achievement and Influence   140

Notes and References   145
Selected Bibliography   155
Index   164

Preface

The purpose of this book is to examine not just Ralph Ellison's only novel, *Invisible Man*, now recognized as an American classic, but his whole career. My thesis is that Ellison's regional background, especially his southwestern frontier childhood, profoundly affects his work. As a young African American growing up on the frontier, Ellison imbibed the frontier spirit—the promise that all things are possible and the awareness that language can make men and women free. For Ellison the frontier also represents the border area, where various cultural forces come together to create a new synthesis. Thus, amalgamation, assimilation, and cultural syncretism characterize his work. The American frontier looks both ways: west toward freedom and chaos, east toward restriction and tradition. Just as the southwestern jazz musician learned to improvise against and within the tradition, so Ellison's archetypical artist strives to achieve freedom within restriction or, to use an oxymoronic phrase, restricted freedom. Ordered chaos, visible darkness, traditional individuality, antagonistic cooperation: all characterize Ralph Ellison's complex worldview drawn from his experience on the frontier where cultural minglings flourished.

The significance of Ellison's southwestern past and other details of his life and work are the subject of chapter 1. Ellison's family had gone to the territory for freedom and opportunity, and Ellison had grown up in an atmosphere of hope and possibility in a rich culture whose values permeated his life. In the second chapter I examine Ellison's stories written before *Invisible Man* from his early political, leftist beginnings through stories set in Oklahoma to his mature stories written shortly before he began his first novel.

Chapter 3 concentrates on *Invisible Man*, particularly the importance of frontier mythology in the novel. Chapter 4 concerns one of the most important areas of Ellison scholarship: the various influences on and allusions in *Invisible Man*. By amalgamating themes, images, and techniques from European, American, and African American cultures, Ellison has synthesized and promoted the elements he values. Similar concerns recur in chapter 5, which focuses on the stories published after *Invisible Man*, particularly the eight Hickman stories from the still unpublished second novel. Ellison's nonfiction—his two collections, *Shadow and Act* and *Going to the Territory*, as well as uncollected nonfiction—is the subject of chapter 6. This study concludes by summarizing Ellison's life and work and discussing his influence on his contemporaries.

Throughout his career, Ellison has questioned and challenged the disparity between the beckoning ideals and limiting reality of the American dream, especially for ethnic groups too often denied the space to achieve it. But in a number of significant ways, Ellison's life and work highlight sustaining elements of the dream that the territory ahead continues to represent in the American imagination.

Acknowledgments

To acknowledge all who have affected this book, I must go a long way back, over 20 years. As a student at East Texas State University, I met Jim Byrd, whose enthusiasm for African American literature in general and Ralph Ellison in particular initially got me and my friend and fellow student James Gray started. Like Ellison's narrator, James spent some time in the business world before he returned to school and finished a master's thesis on Ralph Ellison's early stories. When I began this project, James Gray generously loaned me a big book bag of materials he had collected in his research; I owe him many thanks for his friendship and help.

I also thank Warren French for encouraging me in this project after a chance meeting in New Orleans; students in the Black Education Program at the University of Colorado and students at Texas A&M for expanding my understanding of Ellison; Dale Knobel, director of the Honors Program at Texas A&M University for research funds; Larry Mitchell and the Department of English and the Interdisciplinary Group for Historical Literary Study at Texas A&M for support; my friend and colleague Larry Reynolds for reading the manuscript; Josh Busby for his enthusiasm; and Linda Busby, once again, for being my best editor.

Chronology

1914 Ralph Waldo Ellison born 1 March in Oklahoma City.

1920 Attends Frederick Douglass School in Oklahoma City.

1933 Goes to Tuskegee Institute to study music.

1936 Moves to New York City to study sculpture and raise money to return to school.

1937 Attends mother's funeral in Dayton, Ohio; stays seven months hunting; returns to New York; meets Richard Wright; publishes first book review in *New Challenge*.

1938 Joins Federal Writers' Project.

1939 Publishes first short story, "Slick Gonna Learn."

1942 Edits *Negro Quarterly*.

1943 Joins Merchant Marine.

1945 Receives Rosenwald Grant; begins *Invisible Man*.

1946 Marries Fanny McConnell.

1952 Publishes *Invisible Man*.

1953 Receives National Book Award and Russwurm Award.

1955 Lives in Rome.

1958 Begins Hickman stories; teaches at Bard College.

1960 Publishes first Hickman story, "And Hickman Arrives."

1964 Publishes *Shadow and Act*; teaches at Rutgers and Yale universities.

1965 *Invisible Man* selected as most distinguished post–World War II novel in *Book Week* poll.

1967 Fire in summer home destroys 368 pages of Hickman manuscript.

1969 Receives Medal of Freedom.

1970 Becomes Albert Schweitzer Professor of Humanities at New York University; awarded the Chevalier de l'Ordre des Artes et Lettres by André Malraux, minister of cultural affairs in France.

1975 Elected to American Academy of Arts and Letters.

1986 Publishes *Going to the Territory*.

Chapter One

Coming from the Territory: Geography, Biography, and Fate

In the Territory

In 1975 a branch library on Northeast 23d Street in Oklahoma City was dedicated and named the Ralph Waldo Ellison Library. It is a fitting monument to one of Oklahoma's most celebrated sons, for Ralph Ellison has come to be recognized as one of the world's most distinguished men of letters, and his outlook has been affected by his Oklahoma past. Ellison has often recalled Heraclitus' axiom that geography is fate and also noted that "where Frederick Jackson Turner's theory of the frontier has been so influential in shaping our conception of American history, very little attention has been given to the role played by geography in shaping the fate of Afro-Americans."[1] The effect of geography on Ellison's fate is apparent from his dramatic emphasis on varied geographical experiences—from Oklahoma to Alabama to New York.

Geography influences his writing so completely that the symbolic values of the three primary locations where he spent his life provide a metaphor that permeates his work: thesis/antithesis=synthesis. His southwestern background provided him with freedom and possibility; the South offered restriction and limitation; the North allowed a mature synthesis. Writing requires constant interaction with the shadow of the past—with one's geography and history—to produce the synthesis of art, which, Ellison emphasizes, imagination offers: "As I say, imagination itself is *integrative,* a matter of making symbolic wholes out of parts."[2]

Ralph Waldo Ellison was born in Oklahoma City on 1 March 1914, the son of Lewis Alfred and Ida Millsap Ellison. All four grandparents had been slaves. His mother grew up on a White Oak, Georgia, plantation, and his father was from Abbeville, South Carolina, before he became a soldier and served in Cuba, the Philippines, and China, fighting in the Boxer Rebellion there. After operating a candy kitchen in Chattanooga, Tennessee, and then a restaurant, Lewis Ellison became a construction foreman, and it was that job that brought his family to Oklahoma. There they settled in a rooming house on First Street on Oklahoma's east side, and Ellison's father went into business selling ice and coal.

The Ellisons and other African Americans left the South to raise their families on the Oklahoma frontier because they sought better conditions for their children. Once settled, they fought hard to keep segregationist laws, like those in Texas, out of the Oklahoma constitution. Oklahoma, unlike Texas and Arkansas, had no tradition of slavery. Added to this history was a sense of connection between native Americans, who constituted a significant proportion of Oklahoma's population, and African Americans. Whereas the South, Ellison noted in an interview with Hollie West, embodied its slave past in "buildings, patterns of movement about the cities, in manners, in signs, in monuments," the traditions of the Oklahoma frontier were in the "attitudes and memories of individuals."[3] Fortunately, Ellison's geographical fate was to be born in Oklahoma, where the experience of "Southwestern blacks differs from that of *Southeastern* blacks" (*GT*, 43). In Oklahoma, Ellison noted, "the atmosphere of the place there was a sense that you had to determine your own fate, and that you had a chance to do it" (West, 12)—that the world was possibility.

Ellison and his boyhood friends acted out positive aspects of the American frontier belief in a free and open territory. This frontier experience of the world as possibility, contradicted by his later oppressive experience, has been central to Ellison's imaginative attempts to confront the reality of a seemingly free world that actually provides restraints: "One thing is certain, ours was a chaotic community, still characterized by frontier attitudes . . . which [encourage] the individual's imagination—up to the moment 'reality' closes in upon him—to range widely and, sometimes, even to soar."[4]

He refers to himself and his friends growing up there as "frontiersmen" who looked to a variety of heroic models: "Gamblers and scholars, jazz musicians and scientists, Negro cowboys and soldiers from the Spanish-American and First World Wars, movie stars and stunt men, figures from the Italian Renaissance and literature" (*SA*, xv–xvi). In fact, he and his friends thought of themselves as Renaissance men, noting that "it was no more incongruous . . . for young Negro Oklahomans to project themselves as Renaissance Men than for white Mississippians to see themselves as ancient Greeks or noblemen out of Sir Walter Scott" (*SA*, xvii). These young, black frontiersmen thought that they "were supposed to be whoever we would and could be and do anything and everything which other boys did, and do it better" (*SA*, xvii).

Ellison retained his youthful Renaissance man ideal, as well as the Oklahoma emphasis on freedom and possibility, throughout his education at

Tuskegee Institute and into his writing experience: "I managed, by keeping quiet about it, to cling to our boyish ideal during three years in Alabama, and I brought it with me to New York, where it not only gave silent support to my explorations of what was then an unknown territory, but served to mock and caution me when I became interested in the communist ideal. And when it was suggested that I try my hand at writing, it was still with me" (*SA*, xviii). After living in New York City for over 40 years, Ellison acknowledged that his southwestern past remained vivid for him: "I dream constantly of Oklahoma City. My childhood is there. And, as you known, you tend to dream, can't help dreaming, of your early experiences and of the people you first knew. . . . As a result, my early life stays fresh."[5]

One important part of Ellison's past is his name. Having been named for Ralph Waldo Emerson led to complex and confusing questions of identity. He has recalled the humor that revolved around "a small brown nubbin of a boy carrying around such a heavy moniker" (*SA*, 152). Much later, after he had written *Invisible Man,* he learned that his father had named him for Emerson and hoped his son would be a poet. When Ralph was three, his father died in an accident.[6]

To support Ralph and his younger brother, Herbert, Ellison's mother, called "Brownie" by her friends, worked at various jobs as a domestic and as stewardess of the Avery Chapel Afro-Methodist Episcopal church. Because the minister had his own home, Ellison's family moved into the parsonage, where Ellison found a number of books. Soon, because of the people's frontier aggressiveness, more books were available. After a black Episcopal priest was told it was illegal for blacks to use a local library, he challenged the law and discovered no law existed, only custom, whereupon the whites opened rooms for a black library in the Slaughter Building, appointed a librarian, and stocked the rooms with books. Ellison's mother also often brought home magazines such as *Vanity Fair* and *Literary Digest* from houses she cleaned. He was especially intrigued by articles about Stravinsky and Picasso and the world beyond Oklahoma.

Ellison became a voracious and eclectic reader, beginning with fairy tales, then junior fiction, westerns, detective stories, the Haldeman Julius Blue books, and the Harvard Classics available from a friend whose parents had received a "New England" education by white teachers who came to the Southwest after the Civil War (*SA*, 155). His interest in the frontier continued; he read James Fenimore Cooper's *The Last of the Mohicans* 10 times.[7] Shaw, Maupassant, *Jude the Obscure,* and *Wuthering Heights* also attracted his attention, and in grade school, his teacher, Mrs. L. C. McFarland, introduced him to the New Negro movement of the 1920s. He read Langston

Hughes, Countee Cullen, Claude McKay, James Weldon Johnson, and others who excited him about "the glamour of Harlem" (*SA,* 159).

Ellison's understanding of the power of narrative was expanded by the tales from a rich oral tradition that he heard while working at Randolph's Drugstore on "Deep Second Street," the heart of the black community; at Halley Richardson's shoeshine parlor; at the churches, schoolyards, barbershops, and cotton-picking camps; and while selling newspapers or collecting bottles for bootleggers. He listened intently to stories of buried treasure; headless horsemen; Jesse James; black outlaws, cowboys, and marshals; former slaves who became Indian chiefs; and other stories from the Southwest.

Initially Ellison was drawn to music as the artistic medium toward which he devoted his energy, primarily because of the diverse, extensive music program at the Frederick Douglass School in Oklahoma City, which he attended for all 12 years. After a next-door neighbor, Mr. Mead, taught him the fundamentals of the brass alto horn, his mother bought him a used cornet, and he joined the school band at age eight. Mrs. Zelia N. Breaux, the music teacher, provided him advanced musical training, including a music appreciation course with recordings, classes on harmony and musical form, a marching and concert band, glee clubs, an orchestra, and a chorus, and each year she directed an operetta.[8] As a member of the band, Ellison played "military music, the classical marches, arrangements of symphonic music, overtures, snatches of opera" (*SA,* 11). He also sang classical religious music and Negro spirituals. On May Day at the celebrations at the Western League Ball Park he heard Irish jigs and Scottish flings.

As Ellison's formal interest in music grew, he received private lessons in trumpet and symphonic composition from Ludwig Hebestreit, conductor of the Oklahoma City Orchestra and band director at Classen High School, in exchange for cutting Hebestreit's lawn. From Hebestreit, Ellison learned much about the lives of Beethoven, Wagner, and Schumann and set a personal goal of composing a symphony by age 26.

None of Ellison's formal training was in jazz, still considered a vernacular form, yet jazz permeated his world and became central to his work. Ellison often lay awake listening to the music of such local bands as the Blue Devils Orchestra at the nearby jazz hall. Although Mrs. Breaux did not encourage her pupils to learn jazz, she influenced them by bringing jazz musicians to the Aldridge Theater, which she managed. Among the important Oklahoma City musicians of the time were Oran "Hot Lips" Page, Edward Christian (the brother of Charlie Christian, famed jazz guitarist), Harry Youngblood, "Little Willie" Lewis, Edward "Crack" McNeal, Lawrence "Inky" Williams, Ermuel "Bucket" Coleman, Buster Smith, and Jimmy

Rushing (who became one of Ellison's lifelong friends), all of them players with the Blue Devils. William "Count" Basie was also a member of the band for a while before he gained fame.[9]

The Blue Devils' name suggests depression and the blues and also refers to people who cut barbed wire fences during cattle country range wars and had an outlaw connotation (Welburn, 7). Their music demonstrated freedom within discipline, one of Ellison's continuing themes, and their style became a fundamental part of American jazz: "The Southwestern rhythm and that great freedom within discipline that you first heard in Count Basie's band was swiftly incorporated into Benny Goodman and most of the white big bands. . . . 'Swing' was generated in the Southwest and quickly took over. . . . In it the presence of the blues was more obvious, as were the kinds of improvisation" (Welburn, 14).

While Mrs. Breaux influenced Ellison's musical interests, her father, Dr. Inman Page, the principal at Douglass, oversaw his academic pursuits. A former slave, Dr. Page was an 1877 graduate of Brown University, where he had been selected class orator. In a 1979 address at Brown, Ellison recalled Dr. Page's reading of St. Paul's Epistles during daily chapel exercises, as well as Dr. Page's stern remonstrance after catching Ellison in horseplay during chapel. Like Dr. Page, other teachers at Douglass brought extensive academic training to Oklahoma; Ellison studied Latin for four years with a teacher who also knew Greek and Hebrew.

Although music was Ellison's primary interest in school, his emphasis on being a Renaissance man led him to other pursuits, including playing both tackle and running back on the football team. Another interest led to an experience that perhaps indicates the importance of electricity and radios as images in Ellison's work. When he was a young boy, his family lived in a white middle-class neighborhood while his mother was custodian for some apartments. Looking for some ice cream cartons used as tuning coils for building radios, he met a white boy named Hoolie looking for the same objects. Hoolie helped Ellison break racial barriers and also taught Ellison the importance of approaching the "intricacies of electronics with such daring" and being "intellectually aggressive" (*SA,* 5).

From Hoolie and from a variety of other influences, Ellison developed an ingrained sense of American democracy. There were numerous examples of people from Oklahoma whose achievements and intelligence took them beyond the seeming limitations of their environment. J. D. Randolph, for example (ironically named for Jefferson Davis), owned the rooming house where the Ellisons lived when Ralph was born, and he became a substitute grandfather for him. Randolph was the custodian to the law library at the

Oklahoma State Capitol. When he was about 11, Ellison assisted Randolph in the law library by sweeping and dusting. He soon realized that numerous legislators regularly asked Jeff's opinion of the law, and he further understood the irony and injustice of Mr. Randolph's position, for he "knew that Mr. Randolph appeared to possess a surer grasp of law than certain of the legislators, and my youthful sense of justice led me to see his exclusion from the profession as an act of injustice" (*GT,* 322). Another important Oklahoma influence was Roscoe Dunjee, editor of the *Black Dispatch.* Ellison met Dunjee at Randolph's Drugstore, where Ellison was a soda jerk and delivery boy. Ellison also sold Dunjee's papers while walking barefoot along the streets. Dunjee's editorials about "the historical background of the black struggle" were an important part of Ellison's education (West, 14).

Ellison won a scholarship from the state of Oklahoma (a device for keeping minority students out of state colleges) and decided to study music at Tuskegee Institute in Tuskegee, Alabama, after he learned that Tuskegee's choir, directed by William L. Dawson, had opened Radio City Music Hall.[10] Before he could attend, Ellison had to buy the required trumpet and get to Alabama. As a part-time elevator operator making eight dollars a week in the depth of the depression, he could not raise money for transportation, so he turned to a family friend named Charlie who regularly rode the rails for advice.

In June 1933 Ellison began hoboing to Tuskegee and soon found himself affected by the Scottsboro boys affair. At the Decatur, Alabama, railroad yards, he was taken off a freight train by railroad detectives who ordered him and 40 or 50 other hoboes to line up by the tracks during the Scottsboro boys' trial. Fearing that he too might become a victim, Ellison saw an opening when others being herded from the train began running, and he too ran "far closer to the ground that I had ever managed to do as a high school football running back" (*GT,* 325). The experience, especially the "fear, the horror and sense of helplessness before legal injustice," remained a vivid memory.

In the South

Tuskegee had been founded in 1881 by Booker T. Washington, who set forth the early principles of vocational education that were central to Tuskegee's mission. In his famous Atlanta Exposition Address of 1895, he stated, "Cast down your bucket where you are," meaning that blacks should accept the limited opportunity prescribed by the white world and learn the trades open to black people: "It is at the bottom of life we must begin, and not at the top."[11] (Washington would become an important figure in Ellison's writing. The narrator in *Invisible Man* quotes from Washington's speech during his address after the battle royal, and it is clear that the narrator's college, as well as Dr. Bledsoe, Homer Barbee, and other characters and events, are drawn from Ellison's experience at Tuskegee.)

By the time Ellison arrived at Tuskegee in 1933, however, it had moved far from Washington's original conception of a trade school modeled on his alma mater, Hampton Institute. Washington had created the school from a shanty and through wily determination turned it into a prosperous institution by cultivating white benefactors and by developing a canny public relations program. In his published works and speeches he lavished praise on his benefactors and optimistically told them what they wanted to hear. In *Up from Slavery*, published in 1901, he lamented the existence of the Ku Klux Klan and called the time of their existence during Reconstruction the South's "darkest period." But he went on to assert that "today there are no such organizations in the South, and the fact that such ever existed is almost forgotten by both races. There are few places in the South now where public sentiment would permit such organizations to exist" (Washington, 64). In 1923, however, just eight years after Washington's death, the Klan protested hiring black workers for the proposed veterans' hospital, and some 100 Klansmen marched on Tuskegee.[12]

Washington personally selected his successor, Major Robert Russa Moton, who became president in 1915 and served until he retired in 1935, during Ellison's junior year. During Ellison's first semester, Moton delivered a speech in the chapel in which he recalled being summoned to Washington's deathbed. According to the *Tuskegee Messenger,* Washington had transferred his power to Moton and told him, "Major, don't forget Tuskegee" (O'Meally 1980, 16).

Although the atmosphere of accepting limitation that Washington created continued at the school, the course of study had changed considerably over the years, and when Ellison arrived, Tuskegee had a strong liberal arts component and an especially impressive music department headed by composer and choir director William L. Dawson. Ellison and the other students majoring in music were required to practice for 3 hours a day on a major instrument and 1 hour a day on a minor instrument and to take classes in conducting, harmony, solfeggio (sight singing and ear training), music appreciation, counterpoint, composition, and instrumentation, as well as English, modern languages, physical education, and psychology (O'Meally 1980, 18).

Another important influence was music teacher Hazel Harrison, head
of Tuskegee's piano department and a highly respected concert pianist
who had studied with Ferruccio Busoni in Berlin until forced to return to
the United States during Hitler's rise to power. A friend of Sergei
Prokofiev, Percy Grainger, and Egon Petri, Harrison demanded the highest standards, and from her Ellison learned of "the little man at Chehaw
Station" (a railroad stop near Tuskegee), by which she meant the existence
of high critical standards in unexpected places. Harrison's concept of high
democratic standards had a direct impact on Ellison, and indirectly, she
also affected the shape of Ellison's literary career, for through her Ellison
met Alain Locke when the author visited Harrison in Tuskegee in 1936.
Later through Locke, Ellison met Langston Hughes and, through Hughes,
Richard Wright.

A class that had a particularly negative effect on Ellison was sociology,
primarily because of its textbook, *Introduction to the Science of Sociology,*
by white sociologists Robert Park and Ernest W. Burgess. He was outraged when he read, "The Negro is, by natural disposition, neither an intellectual nor an idealist, like the Jew; nor a brooding introspective, like
the East Indian; nor a pioneer and frontiersman, like the Anglo-
Saxon. . . . He is, so to speak, the lady among the races."[13] "This conten-
tion," Ellison later noted wryly, "the Negro instructor passed blandly
along to us without even bothering to wash his hands, much less his teeth"
(*SA,* xx). Throughout his career, Ellison has expressed continued antipa-
thy for sociological approaches to race, often pointing to sociologist-
politician Daniel Patrick Moynihan's concept of benign neglect as the
product of spurious sociological conclusions.

Ellison's literary training at Tuskegee was more informal than formal.
Still, he dedicated *Shadow and Act* to Morteza Drexel Sprague, the head of
the English department, calling him a "dedicated dreamer in a land most
strange." On his own, Ellison read T. S. Eliot's *The Waste Land* and was
"caught up in a piece of poetry which moved me but which I couldn't reduce to a logical system" (*GT,* 39). The poem, he decided, was similar to
jazz because the jazz musician, like Eliot, had to know the tradition out of
which he worked but also had to improvise on that tradition (*GT,* 40). He
also concluded that Eliot's "range of allusion was as mixed and as varied as
that of Louis Armstrong" (*SA,* 160). When he asked Sprague about the
poem, Sprague told him how to find Eliot's sources and the criticism he
needed to understand the poem (Kostelanetz, 39). Reading Eliot's appended notes and studying Eliot's sources had a profound effect: "That
really was a beginning of my literary education and, actually, it was the be-

ginning of my transformation (or shall we say, metamorphosis) from a would-be composer into some sort of novelist" (*GT*, 40).

Working part time in the college library, he first read modernists such as Ezra Pound, Gertrude Stein, Sherwood Anderson, Ford Madox Ford, James Joyce, F. Scott Fitzgerald, and Ernest Hemingway and then turned to nineteenth-century writers Herman Melville and Mark Twain, as well as to influential works by Karl Marx and Sigmund Freud (Hersey 1987, 301).[14] "Books which seldom, if ever, mentioned Negroes," he noted "were to release me from whatever 'segregated' idea I might have had of human possibilities." He quickly adapted to studying writing after the time spent learning music. "It was absolutely painless," he commented, "because it involved no deadlines or credits" (*SA*, 160).

Ellison maintained his Renaissance man ideal at Tuskegee; not only did he study music and read widely, but he also began studying sculpture with Eva Hamlin, an art professor. She recognized his talent, encouraged his work, and later, when he left for New York, gave him a letter of introduction to a black sculptor in Harlem, Augusta Savage (O'Meally 1980, 25). As a further extension of his abilities, Ellison began writing poetry there. In fact, his first published work was a poem about a friend with appendicitis who died of peritonitis after being refused admittance at a white hospital (Hersey 1987, 301). Still, writing was not yet a serious enterprise: "Rather it was a reflex of reading, an extension of a source of pleasure, escape and instruction" (*SA*, xii).

All of his experiences in the South were especially important, particularly as they contrasted with those of his Southwestern past. Oklahoma was not free from racial discrimination, though, for Ellison had grown up in a jim crow world where Governor "Alfalfa Bill" Murray was a notorious racist. Ida Ellison worked throughout her life to break down the restrictions, and, Ellison recalls, there was never a time that he was not aware of "her overt and explicit concern with political conditions" (Hersey 1987, 288). In fact, during his sophomore year at Tuskegee, she was jailed several times for breaking a segregated housing ordinance in Oklahoma City. However, the major difference between Oklahoma and Alabama was the atmosphere: "The education which goes on outside the classrooms, which goes on as they walk within the mixed environment of Alabama, teaches children that they should not reach out for certain things. Much of the education that I received at Tuskegee (now, this isn't quite true of Oklahoma City) was an education away from the uses of the imagination, away from the attitudes of aggression and courage. . . . You did not do certain things because you might be destroyed" (*GT*, 65).

Ironically, much of the restriction came from the black community. Safety demanded the loss of individuality: "The pre-individualistic black community discourages individuality out of self-defense. Having learned through experience that the whole group is punished for the actions of the single member, it has worked out efficient techniques of behavior control" (*SA*, 90). Young African Americans in the South, Ellison concluded, had to learn to "annihilate the impulses" of individuality. The black southern community, Ellison noted, represented the "psychological dynamics" to which Booker T. Washington applied the "crabs in a basket" metaphor: if one tried to crawl out, the others pulled him back in (*GT*, 297).

North toward Harlem

Ellison left the South by chance. At the end of his junior year, he discovered that confusion about his scholarship left him without money for school, so he left for New York City to seek funds to complete his senior year and to study sculpture with Augusta Savage. After arriving in New York on 5 July 1936, he took a room at the Harlem Annex of the YMCA. The next morning when he went across the street for breakfast, he recognized Alain Locke, whom he had met just a few weeks earlier in Tuskegee. Boldly he approached Locke and asked if he remembered him, and Locke answered, "Why of course I do" (*GT*, 200). Locke introduced him to Langston Hughes, but Ellison, who had read Hughes's poetry in school in Oklahoma, had already recognized him from photographs. When the conversation turned to poetry, Ellison asked Hughes if he knew Richard Wright, whose poems, "I Have Seen Black Hands" and "Between the World and Me," Ellison had recently read.[15] Hughes not only knew Wright, but he knew that Wright would soon be moving to New York to work in the Harlem bureau of the *Daily Worker* and to edit a magazine, *New Challenge*. Hughes wrote to Wright about Ellison, and Wright in turn sent Ellison a card, which Ellison has kept, that read, "Dear Ralph Ellison, Langston Hughes tells me that you're interested in meeting me. I will be in New York," and told him how to get in touch when he arrived (*GT*, 201; also Hersey 1987, 301). Ellison's relationship with Wright, discussed more fully in chapter 4, has been one of the most important and complex relationships of his life.

At the breakfast meeting with Locke and Hughes, Hughes introduced another writer's work that would be important to Ellison: André Malraux. Hughes was carrying copies of Malraux's *Days of Wrath* and *Man's Fate* and asked Ellison to return them for him but suggested that he could read them beforehand (Hersey 1987, 301). Malraux's fiction and aesthetic philosophy would also become important to Ellison.

Ellison worked at the Harlem YMCA as a waiter and counterman for vacationing workers and soon found other ways to support himself during the depression—as a barman, a freelance photographer, and a file clerk and receptionist for the psychiatrist Harry Stack Sullivan. While he was filing the case histories of Sullivan's patients, Ellison, with a renewed interest in modern psychology, reread Freud. His plans to study sculpture with Augusta Savage had to be altered. Tied up with a Work's Progress Administration (WPA) art project, Savage could not take another pupil. With Locke's and Hughes's help, Ellison studied with Harlem artist Richmond Barthe for about a year, until he decided his skills as a sculptor were limited (O'Meally 1980, 29–30).

In his spare time, he began to see the city, especially its cultural attractions, and to enjoy "the many forms of social freedom that were unavailable to me in Alabama" (*GT,* 147). He found it "dreamlike" to be in New York and initially thought of it as one of the freest American cities; however, he soon discovered that the restrictions of the South existed in New York as well. The difference was that the South's clear signals of segregation were not obvious in New York, forcing one to discover them. Ellison thought of himself, ironically, as "having to enact, touch-and-go, the archetypical American role of pioneer" as he faced a new land and mapped a new territory (*GT,* 148).

From Music to Literature

At first Ellison's interest in music continued, but he discovered the difficulty of getting work in New York during the depression, especially since he had no money to join the union. He did have one public performance—playing trumpet for a modern dance performance conducted by Alex North and danced by North's wife, Anna Sokolow (Hersey 1987, 94)—and he studied composition with Wallingford Reigger, but it soon became clear that writing was his medium. Once he decided to write, he put down the horn and refused to go to concerts for fear of being diverted from writing.

Ellison's mother died in 1937. After falling off a porch, she went to a black physician, who without x-raying her, decided that she had arthritis. Some weeks later she died of tuberculosis of the hip. Ellison called the physician's act "immoral and life destructive" (Hersey 1987, 93) and has often used the experience, which caused him much bitterness, as an example of how important it is for one to learn one's craft. He went to Dayton, Ohio, for her funeral and stayed seven months. There he extended his literary study while he and his brother, Herbert, sustained themselves by hunting quail and selling them to General Motors officials. He has often been quoted as saying that he learned how to shoot by reading Hemingway: "At night I practiced writing and studied Joyce, Dostoievsky, Stein and Hemingway. Especially Hemingway; I read him to learn his sentence structure and how to organize a story. I guess many young writers were doing this, but I also used his description of hunting when I went into the fields the next day. I had been hunting since I was eleven but no one had broken down the process of wing-shooting for me and it was from reading Hemingway that I learned to lead a bird. When he describes something in print, believe him; believe him even when he describes the process of art in terms of baseball or boxing; he's been there" (*SA*, 169–70).

On his return to New York, Ellison's friendship with Wright dedicated him to the craft to which the Renaissance man from Oklahoma would devote the rest of his life. Ellison began to hang around the office of the *Daily Worker*, where Wright worked. They talked about literature and writing, and Ellison read the manuscript of *Uncle Tom's Children*. Ellison, who at the time had written only classroom assignments and a few poems, was in awe of the accomplished writer. Still, Wright seemed interested in discussing his ideas with someone of a similar background. Recognizing Ellison's keen interest in literature, Wright asked him to write a book review for *New Challenge*, and Ellison reviewed Waters Edward Turpin's novel *These Low Grounds* for the fall 1937 issue. Except for an earlier college poem, this review was Ellison's first publication, and it marked his formal transition from musician to writer.

Wright challenged him further. Needing a story for the next issue of *New Challenge*, Wright turned to Ellison and said, "You talk well about stories. Why don't you try" (Hersey 1987, 301). In response, Ellison wrote a story based on his hoboing experiences, "Hymie's Bull." Ellison still has the original galley proofs of the story, but the magazine folded before the story was published.

He continued writing book reviews for a number of journals such as *New Masses, Direction,* and the *Negro Quarterly,* publishing over 20 signed reviews and literary essays between 1937 and 1944 and numerous unsigned ones and political and social essays. In 1939 he began a novel, *Slick Gonna Learn,* a section of which became his first published story in 1939. His second story, "The Birthmark," appeared in *New Masses* on 2 July 1940. These two early stories, concerned with police brutality, reflect the leftist ideology that influenced Ellison at the time. From 1940 to 1944 he published six more stories—three set in Oklahoma that use two young black characters, Buster and Riley, and three stories that demonstrate Ellison's maturation—"In a Strange Country," "Flying Home," and "King of the Bingo Game."

At the WPA

Ironically the depression had a positive effect on blacks. Government programs begun to pull America out of the depression were especially important for advancing the opportunities of blacks, because "during that period a lot of Negroes had the opportunity to work in WPA at clerical jobs and so on, so that for us the Depression represented in many ways a lunge forward. We were beneficiaries of the government's effort toward national recovery" (*GT,* 294). Ellison finds this result "a very *blues,* or tragicomic thing to say" because a "gift of freedom arrived wrapped in the guise of a disaster." He explains, "It is ironic, but no less true, that the most tragic incident of our history, the Civil War, was a disaster which ended American slavery" (*GT,* 204).

When Ellison returned to New York, he worked for the Federal Writers' Project from 1938 to 1942 and had a number of experiences that affected his writing and his outlook on life. His position gave him time to concentrate on writing as a craft and to work on his own as well.[16] His major assignment was a book to be titled *Negroes in New York.* Another project, headed by B. A. Botkin, was to collect folklore such as children's rhymes, games, and songs. Along the way he interviewed many older people and got them to tell him stories, usually by approaching them informally and beginning to tell stories to get them started. One of the most important effects on his writing was to develop a technique "that captured the idiom rather than trying to convey the dialect through misspellings."[17]

He also picked up phrases and images that appear in his creative work. For example, in 1939 he interviewed Lloyd Green, a Pullman porter who had come north 25 years before. Green emphasized that he was not a New Yorker by saying, "I'm in New York, but New York ain't in me" (Banks, 250). Mary Rambo advises the narrator in *Invisible Man,* "Don't let this Harlem git you. I'm in New York, but New York ain't in me, understand what I mean? Don't git corrupted."[18]

Another important interviewee was Leo Gurley, who told Ellison a story about Sweet-the-Monkey, a black man who outwitted the whites, in Florence, South Carolina: "Sweet could make hisself invisible. You don't believe it? Well here's how he done it. Sweet-the-monkey cut open a black cat and took out its heart. Climbed up a tree backwards and cursed God. After that he could do anything. The white folks would wake up in the morning and find their stuff gone. He cleaned out the stores. He cleaned out the houses. Hell, he even cleaned out the damn bank! He was the boldest black sonofabitch ever been down that way. And couldn't nobody do nothing to him. Because they couldn't never see im when he done it" (Banks, 244)

While he worked for the WPA, Ellison also found time to spend at the offices of *Negro Quarterly,* a "Review of Negro Life and Culture," begun by Angelo Herndon. Herndon wanted a managing editor and asked Ellison to take the job, promising the same salary as he received at the WPA. Ellison resigned from the Federal Writers' Project in 1942 to become managing editor of *Negro Quarterly.* He worked there for almost a year, but the money was irregular, and the journal ceased publication (Hersey 1987, 304).

Ellison also did freelance writing and covered one of the significant events of the early 1940s, a riot in Harlem in 1943, which he reported for the *New York Post.* After an incident in a bar involving a New York policeman, a black soldier, and the soldier's wife and mother, Harlem erupted in a riot that lasted for a day and a night. Many white businesses from 110th Street to 145th Street in Harlem were looted, burned, and destroyed. The riot serves as the partial basis for the apocalyptic climax in *Invisible Man* (Geller, 153).

From Merchant Mariner to *Invisible Man*

After unsuccessfully trying to enlist in the U.S. Navy band and then deciding that he did not want to be in a jim crow army, Ellison joined the Merchant Marine in 1943 and served as a cook until 1945. At sea Ellison could concentrate on his writing and then return home for significant amounts of time before going out again. On one layover in 1944 Ellison met Fanny McConnell through a mutual friend who knew that both of them were interested in books. They planned a blind date and arranged to meet in front of Frank's Restaurant on 125th Street by identifying the colors of his coat and her dress. Fanny was born in Louisville, Kentucky, reared in Pueblo, Colorado, and Chicago, and educated at Fisk University in Nashville (where she worked for James Weldon Johnson) and at the University of Iowa. After graduation she had organized a small theater group in Chicago and then moved to New York and went to work for the Urban League (Anderson 1976, 105; Hersey 1987). They were married in 1946.[19]

While in the Merchant Marines, Ellison worked on a novel set in a German prisoner-of-war camp. His main character, a black American pilot appointed camp leader because of his rank, achieves enormous power over other American prisoners, many of them white southerners. In a fellowship application to the Julius Rosenwald Fund, now part of the Richard Wright Archive at Yale University, Ellison explained the novel's purpose: to explore "what type of democratic relationships are necessary for a highly conscious Negro to function with white men and at the same time exercise the fullest potentialities of his personality."[20] In introductory comments to the Thirtieth-Anniversary Edition of *Invisible Man,* Ellison summarized the main character's conflict: "Having to choose between his passionate rejection of both native and foreign racisms while upholding those democratic values which he held in common with his white countrymen, my pilot was forced to find support for his morale in his sense of individual dignity and in his newly awakened awareness of human loneliness. . . . Therefore he had either to affirm the transcendent ideals of democracy and his own dignity by aiding those who despised him, or accept his situation as hopelessly devoid of meaning; a choice tantamount to rejecting his own humanity."[21]

Ellison tried to work on the prison camp novel on his next voyage in the winter of 1944 during the Battle of the Bulge as he served on a ship taking war supplies across the North Atlantic. The ship's water supply had become contaminated with rust, and when it reached Le Havre, Ellison had a kidney infection and was depressed. Because his condition worsened on the return trip, "ailing in kidney and in art," he took sick leave as the war wound down in the summer of 1945 and went with Fanny to John and Amelia Bates's farm in Waitsfield, Vermont, to write and to recuperate.[22]

Setting up his typewriter in the open doorway of a large old barn there, he struggled with his prison camp novel. He found that "creatures from Afro-American fables—Jack-the-Rabbit and Jack-the-Bear—blended in my mind with figures of myth and history" (Ellison, "Message") about whom he had been reading in Lord Raglan's *The Hero* and distracted him from his novel. "Images of incest and murder, dissolution and rebirth whirled in my head," he recalled. In such a state, he sat at the typewriter and suddenly typed what were to become the first words of his novel: "I am an invisible man." Starting to destroy the page, he then reread it and began to wonder what kind of voice would speak such words:

And suddenly I could hear in my head a blackface comedian bragging on the stage of Harlem's Apollo Theatre to the effect that each generation of his family was becoming so progressively black of complexion that no one, not even its own mother, had ever been able to see the two-year-old baby. The audience had roared with laughter, and I recognized something of the same joking, in-group, Negro Ameri-

can irony sounding from my rumpled page. Slowly, like an image surfacing from
the layers of an exposed Polaroid exposure, a shadow of the speaker arose in my
mind and I grasped at his range of implication. (Ellison, "Message")

When Ellison returned to his one-room ground floor apartment on St.
Nicholas Avenue in New York City, he found himself preoccupied with the
voice and continued to work on the novel in Beatrice and Francis
Steegmuller's eighth-floor apartment at 608 Fifth Avenue while his friends
were abroad. There he kept "businessman's hours," taking the elevator up
early and leaving late.

By then Fanny had become executive director of the American Medical
Center for Burma, an organization that promoted the work of Dr. Gordon
S. Seagrave, the "Burma Surgeon." Ellison supplemented Fanny's regular
salary by building high-fidelity audio systems and selling book reviews, articles, short stories, and photographs. Additionally, his Rosenwald grant was
renewed, and he received monthly support from art patron Mrs. J. Caesar
Guggenheimer (Ellison, "Introduction," ix–xi).

Ellison worked on *Invisible Man* for seven years. Before finishing it, he
signed a contract with Frank Taylor, who showed portions of the manuscript
to the editor of the English magazine *Horizon,* Cyril Connolly, who published the battle royal chapter as "Invisible Man" in the October 1947 issue.
The same section appeared in America in 1948 in *Magazine of the Year.*
These circumstances, Ellison explains, account for "the 1947 and 1948
copyright dates that have caused confusion for scholars" (Ellison, "Introduction," xxi). The Prologue was published in the January–February issue of
Partisan Review, shortly before the novel appeared in April 1952.

Initial reviews of *Invisible Man,* particularly those by white reviewers,
were generally very favorable. For a first novel by a relatively unknown
writer, the book received extensive coverage with reviews by a number of established authors and reviewers: Saul Bellow in *Commentary* (June 1952),
Richard Chase in *Kenyon Review* (Autumn 1952), Irving Howe in *Nation*
(10 May 1952), R. W. B. Lewis in *Hudson Review* (Spring 1953), Wright
Morris in the *New York Times Book Review* (13 April 1952), Orville
Prescott in the *New York Times* (16 April 1952), Delmore Schwartz in *Partisan Review* (May–June 1952), Anthony West in the *New Yorker* (31 May
1952), and others. Bellow called it a "book of the very first order, a superb
book . . . tragicomic, poetic, the tone of the very strongest sort of creative
intelligence." Prescott proclaimed that it "blazes with authentic talent."
West described it as "an exceptionally good book" with "robust courage."
Most of the reviews pointed to the book's universality. Webster Schott in

the *Kansas City Star* (31 May 1952) praised it as "one of the best novels yet written by an American Negro . . . concerned with themes which are . . . universal rather than racial."
Not all of the comments were favorable. Some reviewers criticized the style for wordiness, "artiness," and obscurity and the tone for melodrama or hysteria. Schott found it "burdened with cloudy passages and harmed by occasional inconsistencies." Robert Langbaum in *Furioso* (Fall 1952) attacked the novel vigorously as "positively irritating" and full of "literary affectation."
African American reviews were more mixed. Langston Hughes in *New York Age* (28 February 1953) called the novel "deep, beautifully written, provocative and moving." Alain Locke in *Phylon* (March 1953) praised its psychological realism and called the novel the third peak in the development of Negro fiction after *Cane* and *Native Son.* Henry F. Winslow in the *Crisis* (June–July 1952) noted Ellison's "rare gift of weaving with masterful story-telling ability the rich texture of atmospheric reality." Other black reviewers were less positive. J. Saunders Redding in *Afro-American* (6 May 1952) found a disparity between the stylistic and thematic elements of the novel, suggesting that it is like using a steam shovel "to dig a compost pit for a kitchen garden." Even harsher attacks came from the Left. Lloyd L. Brown in *Masses and Mainstream* (June 1952), Abner W. Berry in *Daily Worker* (1 June 1952), and John O. Killens in *Freedom* (June 1952) expressed Marxist positions and blasted the novel. Berry called the novel "439 pages of contempt for humanity, written in an affected, pretentious and otherworldly style to suit the king-pins of world white supremacy" and said that it shows contempt toward blacks. Killens asserted that "Negro people need Ralph Ellison's *Invisible Man* like we need a hole in the head or a stab in the back" and called it "a vicious distortion of Negro life."

From Accolades to the Academy

The negative responses were decidedly in the minority, however, and *Invisible Man* and Ralph Ellison soon began to receive numerous awards and recognition. In 1953 Ellison received the Russwurm Award, the Certificate of Award from the *Chicago Defender,* and the National Book Award, whose citation from the jury (Martha Foley, Irving Howe, Howard Mumford Jones, and Alfred Kazin) read: "With positive exuberance of narrative gifts, he has broken away from the conventions and patterns of the tight 'well-made' novel. Mr. Ellison has the courage to take many literary risks, and he has succeeded with them."[23] In 1954 he won a Rockefeller Foundation Award and was selected to give a lecture tour in Germany and to lecture at the Salzburg Seminar in Austria. He received Prix de Rome Fellowships from the American Academy of Arts and Letters and lectured and toured Italy with the U.S. Information Agency in 1955 and 1956. From 1958 to 1961 Ellison taught Russian and American literature at Bard College. He served as Alexander White Visiting Professor at the University of Chicago in 1961 and then as visiting professor of writing at Rutgers and a fellow in American studies at Yale from 1962 to 1964. He was selected Gertrude Whittall Lecturer at the Library of Congress and delivered the Ewing Lectures at UCLA in January and April 1964. He has also taught African American folklore, creative writing, and literature at Columbia, Fisk, Princeton, Antioch, and Bennington. From 1970 to 1980 Ellison was the Albert Schweitzer Professor of Humanities at New York University.

Under Siege

In the 1960s and 1970s Ellison was attacked on several fronts. A decade after *Invisible Man*'s publication, Ellison's publisher was suggesting that the next novel, sections of which began appearing in 1960, would soon be ready. The literary world speculated about why the author of a successful first novel had not yet finished a second one. Comparisons were made to first novelists who could not take early success, such as Thomas Heggen, author of *Mr. Roberts,* and Ross Lockridge, author of *Raintree County.* But the most sustained and significant attacks accused Ellison of not calling loudly enough for social change.

The first important attack came from a white critic, Irving Howe, who in comparing Ellison and Baldwin with Richard Wright found the two younger writers lacking in social protest. In a long essay, "Black Boys and Native Sons," in *Dissent* (Autumn 1963), Howe chastised both Baldwin and Ellison for avoiding the social protest that characterized Richard Wright's *Native Son.* Ellison subsequently answered Howe with two essays in the *New Leader,* collected under the single title "The World and the Jug" in *Shadow and Act* (1964), a collection of essays, reviews, and interviews written between 1942 and 1964. The essays in *Shadow and Act* are important for revealing Ellison's background, particularly the effect of his Oklahoma past, his interest in music, and his knowledge of classic American literature, as well as his defense against Howe's charges.

Howe's attack, however, was mild compared to those Ellison received from black militants as the 1960s wore on.[24] Because Ellison remained staunchly integrationist, militants during the growth of the "black is beauti-ful" and black aesthetic movements denigrated Ellison and labeled him an Uncle Tom. A *Negro Digest* survey of important black writers in 1968 ranked Ellison fourth, with Richard Wright designated as the "most impor-tant black American writer of all time" (Walling, 127). At Oberlin in 1969, Ellison was jeered by black students, and, James Alan McPherson notes, "One girl said to him: " 'Your book doesn't mean anything because in it you're shooting down Ras the Destroyer, a rebel leader of black people.' "[25]

Ellison also found himself outside the majority of black intellectuals' consensus about the Vietnam War. While most black leaders such as Mar-tin Luther King, Jr., opposed the war, Ellison supported it and President Lyndon Johnson, for complex reasons. Kostelanetz concluded that Ellison defended America's involvement "less out of patriotic enthusiasm than tragic necessity" after Ellison told him, "I don't see us withdrawing from the war. . . . We have certain responsibilities to the Vietnamese and the struc-ture of power in the world. It's too bad, but that's the way it is" (Kostelanetz 1969, 55).

Ellison's southwestern past also contributed to his support for Johnson. In "The Myth of the Flawed White Southerner," Ellison acknowledged that while many black intellectuals recoiled from Johnson because of his "style and accent," Ellison's Oklahoma background led him to "listen to the indi-vidual intonation, to *what* was said as well as to *how* it was said" (*GT,* 80–81). Ellison believed he saw beneath the surface of Johnson's style and appearance and concluded that the president was maligned and misunder-stood. In actuality, Ellison thought, Johnson had "knocked the pins out of the great structure of racism in this country" (Kostelanetz, 54).

Johnson valued Ellison's support and awarded him the Medal of Free-dom in 1969. Despite the attacks, Ellison maintained a high profile and ac-cepted numerous public appointments. He served as vice-president of the American PEN club and the National Institute of Arts and Letters, trustee of the Citizens' Committee for Public Television and the John F. Kennedy Center in Cambridge, and member of the National Council on the Arts and the Carnegie Commission on Educational Television. Other awards contin-ued as well. In 1964 Tuskegee awarded Ellison an honorary doctorate in hu-mane letters, and he has received honorary degrees from Rutgers, Michigan, Williams, Harvard, and Wesleyan. In 1970 André Malraux, who greatly influenced Ellison's work, serving as the minister of cultural affairs in France, awarded Ellison the Chevalier de l'Ordre des Artes et Lettres.

The Second Novel?

Ellison's failure to publish a second novel has given rise to a number of questions. Since 1960 he has published eight excerpts of the work in progress in such varied publications as *Noble Savage, Quarterly Review of Literature,* and *Massachusetts Review.* These eight stories total almost 150 pages of prose already in print, and Ellison's friends who have seen the manuscript suggest that it was over 20 inches thick in 1982.[26] The central question remains: Why has he not yet published the novel?

The complex answer involves several possibilities. First, real-world chaos began to mirror Ellison's fictional world, which focused on a political assassination. In 1963 John Kennedy's assassination shook the world, Malcolm X was killed in 1965, and Robert Kennedy and Martin Luther King were assassinated in 1968. These events led Ellison to reexamine his work: "One of the things which really chilled me—slowed down the writing—was that eruption of assassinations, especially the first. Because, you see, much of the mood of this book was conceived as comic. Not that the assassination was treated comically, but there is humor involved, and that was rather chilling for me, because suddenly life was stepping in and imposing itself upon my fiction. . . . I know that it led me to try to give the book a richer structuring, so that the tragic elements could contain the comic and the comic the tragic, without violating our national pieties" (Hersey 1987, 290). In November 1967 a fire in his Pittsfield, Massachusetts, home in the Berkshires destroyed 368 pages of manuscript and further interrupted his progress. Others suggest that Ellison has not completed the second novel because he is a perfectionist who continues to polish. One friend told Richard Kostelanetz, "Ralph is insanely ambitious. He actually writes quickly, but won't release this book until he is sure that it is the greatest American novel ever written" (Kostelanetz 1969, 46).

Coming Back

Despite the attacks of the sixties and seventies and despite the fact that he has published only one novel, in the eighties Ellison moved to the forefront of American literature. A number of African American literary theorists published sophisticated works about black literature, including Ellison's. Additionally, when arguments about expanding the American canon dominated discussion, Ellison was often pointed to as a black writer who must be included. Ellison was elected to the American Academy of the Arts and Letters in 1975, awarded the Langston Hughes medallion for contribution in arts and letters by City College of New York in 1984, and was presented the National Medal of Arts in 1985. A second essay collection, *Going to the Territory*, was published in 1986 and contains Ellison's essays written from 1964 to 1985, as well as some essays left out of *Shadow and Act*. As an indication of the renewed interest in Ellison's work, five books on Ellison were published in 1988 and 1989.

Coming from the territory where his geographical fate was to develop frontier attitudes about freedom, possibility, and amalgamation, Ralph Ellison has charted new frontiers in American literature. Although he seemed to burst upon the American scene in 1952, actually his writing apprenticeship lasted over a decade.

Chapter Two

From Propaganda to Art: Early Stories

During his fiction writing apprenticeship from 1939 to 1944, Ellison published eight short stories. The first two were political protests that grew out of his relationship with Richard Wright and such journals as *New Masses*. Although he acknowledged his early work had a persuasive purpose, he never believed he was writing "the official type of fiction" and has refused to accept that he wrote from a narrowly leftist viewpoint: "I wrote what might be called propaganda—having to do with the Negro struggle—but my fiction was always trying to be something else; something different even from Wright's fiction. I never accepted the ideology which the *New Masses* attempted to impose on writers" (*GT,* 294). Ellison tried to move these stories beyond limited naturalism, but they offer only glimpses of the concerns of the mature writer. Set in the South where Ellison had experienced limitation, they concentrate on human constraints and racial tension.

In his next three stories—"Afternoon," "Mister Toussan," and "That I Had the Wings"—Ellison abandoned the narrowly political, returned to his southwestern past, and created two young boys, Buster and Riley, whose adventures in Oklahoma draw from black southwestern folklore. Although their stories are told against a background of racial injustice and bigotry, foremost in them is the two boys' sense of hope and possibility, particularly as they build imaginatively on southwestern and African American folklore. They are a black Huck Finn and Tom Sawyer, ready to shape their experiences into exciting adventures. Restrictions on them are apparent, but these come primarily through the adults who supervise them.

By returning imaginatively to the Southwest, Ellison created stories about the power of the human imagination to reach beyond limits, an important theme in his later work as well. In the Southwest the frontier myth of freedom and possibility inspires the boys, but they often find themselves confronted by older blacks conditioned by a slave past. Through humor, wit, and verbal games, Buster and Riley assert their own identities and resist being straitjacketed by others' definitions of reality. These are initiation stories in which the boys learn to test the boundaries of their limitations— sometimes to soar and sometimes to fall and fail.

In his mature stories—"In a Strange Country," "Flying Home," and "King of the Bingo Game"—Ellison concentrates on the themes of racial identity and alienation and uses African American folk materials in a unique stylistic combination of irony and symbolism. Together these eight stories demonstrate how Ellison shaped his experiences in the Southwest, the South, and the North and began to move toward his mature artistic vision. When Ellison went South to Alabama, he found a much more restricted society than Oklahoma, and his earliest stories examine that authoritarian world.

Early Political Stories

"Slick Gonna Learn" "Slick Gonna Learn," published in *Direction* in September 1939, was identified as being from "an Unpublished First Novel."[1] In an "Author's Synopsis" of the events in the novel prior to the published section, Ellison explains what leads up to the present action. Set in the South, the story concerns the title character's response to being laid off from his job just as his pregnant wife requires medical care. To try to get money, Slick enters a crap game and loses his last two dollars. He appeals to the local pimp, Bostic, for five dollars. Bostic refuses but suggests that Slick's wife might earn him the money: " 'If it's good enough to marry, it's good enough to sell' " (10). Slick attacks him and breaks "a rigidly enforced taboo" (10) by striking a white policeman who arrives. He then "loses his power to act" (10) and waits to be taken to jail.

The published story begins at this point and concerns three related episodes in which Slick expects one particular outcome, only to have his expectations reversed. First, Slick is taken to court and taunted by a white judge who stereotypes him: " 'Leave it to the niggers to have kids' " (11). Expecting punishment, Slick is released because the judge apparently wants to shield reporters, on hand to cover a strike, from any evidences of racial conflict. In the second episode, as Slick leaves court, angry white policemen planning revenge force him into their car. At the moment the police assault Slick, a car radio call directs them to proceed to a riot at the Hopkins plant. They kick him out of the car, take a few random shots, and leave him battered and bruised by the roadside. Thus, in deus ex machina fashion, Slick is saved by the union workers.

In the third episode Slick is picked up by a white union man, identified by "a row of buttons on his cap," who kindly gives him a ride. The scene recalls the opening of John Steinbeck's *The Grapes of Wrath,* published the same year, as the driver tells Slick, " 'I don't usually pick up riders, lose my job if I did. But hell! a man is still a man and it's nasty as hell tonight' " (16). Expecting ill treatment by a white man, Slick is surprised by the man's benevolence. As they approach the city, Slick sees how "the light of the city broke the blackness in a million shimmering glints" and is confused: "He turned and watched the man bent over the steering wheel, studying his face and tried to connect him with the experiences of the day as the truck roared through the rain to the city" (16).

As Robert O'Meally observes, this story follows a clear political thesis drawing from Ellison's associations with Marxism and Richard Wright. Slick learns elements of the class struggle; the events are caused by his lost job. He also learns that answers to problems will come from the union. But elements also suggest Ellison's desire to move beyond propaganda, particularly the stylistic devices that emphasize Slick's growing impotence and alienation. Interestingly, one of the devices to suggest fragmentation is synecdoche; characters often see only part of the scene. At times, the imagery is quite effective. When Slick leaves the courtroom, he follows "the blue back away from the dull illumination of the desk lamp" (11). Later in the car with the police, he sees "a flame and a face drawing on a cigarette." These suggestive synecdoches and Ellison's concern with consciousness move the story beyond the limitations of protest fiction.

"The Birthmark"   "The Birthmark," written in a harshly naturalistic style, is the story of the lynching of a young black man named Willie. The police have told Willie's brother and sister, Matt and Clara, that Willie has been run over by a car, and they are brought to the scene to identify the body. When they arrive, buzzards—birds that reappear in Ellison's fiction—circle slowly, "black shapes against the still, blue air" (16). The body has been covered by the brightly colored comic pages from the newspaper. As Leonard Deutsch notes, "The motif of Negro life as part of a stark and unreal comic-book world" becomes a significant one in *Invisible Man.*[2] When Matt moves the papers to look for the birthmark that was below Willie's navel, they discover that Willie has been castrated. Willie's literal castration is Matt's figurative one: "Matt went weak. He felt as though he had been castrated himself" (16). Clara's response suggests the heavy-handedness of Ellison's political theme. She cries out that Willie was lynched and charges Matt with complicity for refusing to band together to protest lynchings: " 'They asked us last month to sign a piece of paper saying we wanted things like this to stop and you were afraid. Now look at my brother, he's laying there looking like something ain't even human' " (16).

More didactic than "Slick Gonna Learn," "The Birthmark" foreshadows later stylistic and thematic concerns. Besides the buzzard and comics imagery and the theme of impotence and castration, Ellison uses suggestive color imagery. The title, perhaps ironically influenced by the Hawthorne story with the same title, refers to black skin indelibly given at birth, never to be removed. The blue police uniforms and blue sky become intertwined. Edith Schor points to the symbolic significance: "Blue is specific evil; it is the color of the policeman's shirt and the judge's eyes [in "Slick Gonna Learn"], but it quickly takes on a larger meaning in the color of the sky]. Color symbolism is used for the conditions of existence against which the drama of the human mind, from ignorance to vision, is played in the symbolism of dark and light."[3]

Buster and Riley Stories

"Afternoon" "Afternoon" tracks Buster and Riley as they lazily spend a summer afternoon in Oklahoma walking down an alley, talking about the humming high-voltage line and bootleggers, and using an apple as a baseball. Throughout the insignificant events of the afternoon, Buster and Riley test seeming limitations. When Buster asserts that he can break a glass insulator on an electric pole, Riley demonstrates Ellison's humorous and ironic use of color imagery by calling him "fulla brown" and challenges him. Buster, drawing eclectically from a pantheon of heroes, says that he will throw like "ole Lou Gehrig" throwing out runners at first base and immediately breaks the insulator.

Wandering lazily down the alley, they muse about rumors of bootleggers forced to pour their contraband into the toilet during a police raid. Ellison identifies the Oklahoma setting when Buster laughs at the thought that "all the fish in the Canadian River was drunk" (30). The largest east-west tributary in Oklahoma, the Canadian passes through the center of Oklahoma City. Later Oklahoma is reemphasized when the boys sit and listen to the "thump, thump, thump of oil wells pumping away to the south" (31).

As they continue their walk, the two boys begin to chant a raffish folk rhyme. Ellison had collected children's rhymes as part of his WPA project, and this is the first story in which he uses these rhymes to suggest aspects of his characters, exuberant adolescents who respond to the world as any other youthful boys would given their circumstances and background. Verbal playfulness is one characteristic.

As Ellison described himself and his friends as being black Huck Finns, so Buster and Riley recall Twain's characters. Walking along the alley, they see and smell a dead cat, and the superstition that characterizes Huck, Tom, and Jim's relationship enters. "You'd better spit on it, else you'll have it for supper," (31) Buster suggests. As they pass the "maggot ridden body," they spit on it and walk on down the alley. Besides echoing Twain, the maggot-filled cat and Riley's "fulla brown" comment introduce subtly the suggestions of death and decay that contrast with the images of life and possibility in the next experience. As Buster and Riley leave behind the cat's stench, they immediately see an apple tree, and Buster suggests that they get some apples. The more pragmatic Riley, however, cautions: " 'Naw, theyll give you the flux. They too green' " (31). Thus, as he has done throughout his career, Ellison builds this early story on duality.

Although the apples are too green to eat, they do not resist the boy's imaginative power of transformation: an apple becomes a baseball. Buster, like pitcher "School-boy Rowe," smashes the apple into a pole. Riley, in a phrase that recalls Ellison's bird hunting in Dayton and Hemingway's influence, remarks that the apple " 'come apart like when you hit a quail solid with a shotgun' " (32).

Finally, they wander back to Buster's house, a clean, grey cottage. As they get close, Buster begins to feel guilty for not having come home sooner, since he was supposed to help his mother wash and hang clothes. When she asks him where he has been and he tells her he went to Riley's, Buster's mother responds angrily. Although Buster knows that he is partially responsible for her anger, he also understands that her emotions are affected by her relationship with whites. He thinks: "She was like this whenever something went wrong with her and the white folks" (35).

Undertones of racial conflict surface when Riley tries to console Buster by telling him he ought to be glad that he does not have a father like his who is " 'so mean he hates hisself' " (36) because of his treatment by whites. Riley recalls how his father once tried to beat him until his mother stopped him, saying that she would not allow her son to be treated like "no slave." Musing about the future, they both decide that they will be like black heavyweight boxer Jack Johnson, who unlike the maggot-ridden cat in the alley, is "fast as a cat." Sitting quietly, the boys watch a "black and yellow wasp" as it disappears inside its "grey, honeycomb-like nest" and think of Johnson. This concluding coda quietly brings the story to an end, but the image of the wasp in its nest suggests a quiet power ready to be released.

O'Meally finds this story a "departure for the author in that it has no clear political brunt" and suggests that Ellison "seems to have decided that his naturalistic stories, concentrating on the brutalities of existence and on the moment of violent confrontation, missed some vital aspects of life as he himself had lived it." O'Meally downplays the story's undercurrent of racial conflict but notes that the boys' names "announce their sturdiness and high-spiritedness" and points out that they are "aware of social injustices; but they test the values of their society and dare it *not* to make a place for them" (O'Meally 1980, 60–63). Schor concludes that "Afternoon" is concerned with "the internalization of a slave psychology" as it affects "the complex question of Negro identity." Although she finds the boys' assertiveness and self-confidence admirable, she faults the story for being unrealistic because it concludes "with the romantic assumption that the boys can grow up and retain their innocence and transform it into adult assertive power" (Schor, 50–51).

Leonard Deutsch reads the story as overwhelmingly positive. Buster and Riley are the "antithesis of the youthful invisible man" because of their self-confidence and pride in their folk heritage and African American heroes: "Not at all confused about their identities, Riley and Buster are on the sure path to manhood" (Deutsch 1973, 55). Indeed, Buster and Riley are positive characters who emphasize individuality and freedom, but they are also Ellison's initiates growing aware of the limitations of others' definitions of reality.

"Mister Toussan"   Ellison's second Buster and Riley story emphasizes the boys' imaginative power, particularly their use of folklore to create a sense of identity as they confront restriction. As in "Afternoon," Ellison presents a dual conflict between the boys and the bigotry of the white world, on the one hand, and, on the other, restrictions reinforced by older black figures who attempt to transmit a slave mentality. These imaginative, full-of-life African American southwesterners, however, resist limitations and use their verbal skills to lead them beyond restrictions. By framing the story in folk rhymes, which begin and end the story, Ellison stresses the importance of folklore in the boys' development. The initial rhyme is provided by Ellison, but Riley chants the last one, suggesting the progression from general to specific application.

The story itself is a frame-tale, as Buster and Riley tell their version of the history of Toussaint L'Ouverture, the black folk hero who led Haitian slaves against Napoleon's soldiers. As the story begins, Buster and Riley have been reprimanded by a white man, Mr. Rogan, for trying to take cherries from his tree, and he now sits on a rocking chair on his porch in the heat to keep away these "little nigguhs." Ironically the trees are filled with birds that take the cherries and are unmolested by the old man. Noting sarcastically that mockingbirds are getting the cherries, Riley concludes, "Man, I tell you white folks ain't got no sense" (19).

As the boys sit on the porch, they hear behind them the clatter of Riley's mother's sewing machine as she sews for whites and the sound of her voice as she sings the old spiritual, "All God's Chillun":

> I got wings, you got wings,
> All God's chillun got a-wings
> When I get to heaven gonna put on my wings
> Gonna shout all ovah God's heaven.

Spirituals with the promise of heavenly reward were an integral part of the submission of slaves. Religion's pledge that earthbound suffering would be compensated by eternal bliss eased slaves' misery. As Schor notes, Riley's mother brought that concept into postslavery times: "She brings into the machine age the hope of heavenly reward—wings in a future life—as recompense for bondage on earth. The spiritual that once served to make the condition of forced submission bearable is not part of the social pattern of voluntary submission" (Schor, 53).

For Buster and Riley, however, restriction and resignation breed contempt. The wings of the song and of a passing butterfly lead Riley to ask Buster what he would do if he had wings, and Buster replies that he would go up north, maybe to Chicago, New York, or "Deetroit," or "anywhere else colored is free" (19).

As their imaginations take them to worlds beyond, Buster's mention of Africa leads to a discussion of Africans' laziness. At first Buster reveals the influence of white stereotyping by calling Africans "the most lazy folks in the whole world . . . just black and lazy!" (19). But when Riley challenges him, Buster recalls a story his teacher told him of "one of them African guys named Toussan what she said whipped Napoleon" (19). Buster then relates and creates a tale about "sweet Papa Toussan," an African from "Hayti," who taught the "peckerwoods" a lesson. In another comment on limitations imposed by a white world, Buster notes that the "Toussan" story, like many told by his "good ole teacher," is not provided in the history books.

Along the way both boys get entranced by the rhythm of their storytelling, and their language becomes the verbal gamesmanship of call and response that characterizes black religious services:

"Toussan was clean. . . ."

". . . He was a good, clean mean," said Riley.

"Aw, man, he was sooo-preme," said Buster. (20)

Although Riley had never heard the story, he takes it up and adds to it. But at the height of their story, Riley's mother calls out and tells them to quieten down: " 'White folks say we tear up a neighborhood when we move in it and you-all out there jus' proving them to be true.' "(20). The boys' spirits, however, have been bolstered by their retelling—and embellishing of—the story of a black man with strength to overcome white oppression. As a result, they plan a new assault on old man Rogan's cherries.

Marcus Klein, in an early confused reading (he has Riley telling Toussaint's story and Rogan with a shotgun), faults the story for a lack of correspondence between the "manner and the purported subject," saying that Ellison had trouble adapting myth and ritual to his work.[4] Although Schor partially shares Klein's judgment, finding the story "dramatically incomplete," she sees similarities with *Invisible Man* because the story "implies that the nature of reality is not an imposed absolute but is man-made. Here we have an early version of a basic theme of *Invisible Man*. The boys, in their jam session, create a story that humanizes the world, that brings it down to man's size" (Schor, 57). O'Meally finds no fault with "Mr. Toussan," concluding that it is "tightly woven and powerful . . . the finest of the Buster-Riley stories" (O'Meally 1980, 63). Indeed, "Mr. Toussan" consolidates and foreshadows numerous ideas important to Ellison: conflict with imposed versions of reality, the power of language and the imagination, the strength of folklore to bolster cultural identity, and the use of wings as a metaphor for imagination and freedom.

"That I Had the Wings"   The third Buster and Riley story first appeared in *Common Ground* in 1943. Like the two previous stories, it concerns the theme of the boys' initiation into awareness of the complex ways of freedom and restriction in their world. As before, restriction comes from racial limitations imposed by whites on blacks and a slave mentality accepted by older blacks who pass it on to the next generation. Ellison repeats the imagery of wings and again compares his characters and Mark Twain's.

The story begins with Riley's watching a mother robin teaching her young to fly. The young robin hesitates until the mother flies to another tree. Without the mother's hovering, the young robin tries to fly, suggesting that the young must test their ability without adult coaxing. Soon the reader learns that Riley cannot leave his own yard because the day before he had

climbed the church roof to catch some pigeons and had fallen. Consequently his Aunt Kate, who replaces Riley's mother as the figure of authority, has restricted him to the yard. Older than Riley's mother, Aunt Kate,
"born way back in slavery times," also echoes the various aunts and surro-
gate mothers with whom Huck and Tom Sawyer contend—Aunts Sally
and Polly and the Widow Douglass. The story also echoes Twain in that
Riley concludes that he will have nothing to do with the adult's Holy
Ghost: " 'Well, all I know is the Holy Ghost sho must hurt bad, cause
everybody gits to cryin and cuttin the fool. . . . I don't like nothin yuh have
to cry over before yuh kin feel good' " (33). Similarly, Huck Finn rejected
Miss Watson's idea of heaven.

Bored staying in the yard and not restricted like Riley, Buster decides to
leave. To make him stay, Riley, in "sudden inspiration," improvises upon an
old rhyme:

> If I was the President
> Of these United States
> Said if I was the President
> Of these United States
> I'd eat good chocolate candy bars
> An swing on the White House gates—
> Great—God a-mighty, man—
> I'd swing on them White House gates![5]

His Aunt Kate hears him and angrily scolds him for "takin the Lawd's
name in vain" and for "talkin bout bein the President," asking him: "Whut
yuh think would happen to yo po ma if the white folks wuz to hear she wuz
raisin up a black chile whuts got no better sense than to talk about bein President?"(31) She tells them they should sing "some a the Lawd's songs,"
such as one about having "the wings of-vah dove" (31). Riley is momentarily
cowed but then concludes that Aunt Kate is too old to understand his de-
sires. He then parodies one of Aunt Kate's favorite songs: "Amazin' grace,
how sweet the sound. A bull frog slapped his granma down."

The boys begin to discuss the chickens in the yard, and Riley declares
that he would like to be like Ole Bill, the rooster who controls the roost.
They begin to mythologize Bill, giving him heroic attributes by comparing him to one of Ellison's favorite figures, Louis Armstrong, and then to
Joe Louis. They next decide to try to get Ole Bill to fly but give up and
decide to parachute baby chickens from the garage roof. The plan is for
Buster to drop the chicks from the roof and for Riley to catch them before

they reach the ground. As Riley is about to catch the chicks, Aunt Kate yells angrily at him and causes him to feel impotent and unable to act, "poised, like a needle caught between two magnets" (37). Consequently the baby chicks fall to the ground and are killed. Aunt Kate reminds him that she had earlier cautioned him about his actions and declares: " 'The Lawd's gonna punish yuh in hell-fire for that. . . . Someday yuh remember them words an moan an cry' " (37), causing Riley to conclude that she has "done put a curse on him" (37).

To add injury to this insult, before Riley can get out of the chicken pen, Ole Bill charges and spurs him: "He saw with tear-filled eyes the bright red stream against the brown where the spur had torn his leg." Marcus Klein, noting Ellison's use of the castration theme in "The Birthmark" and *Invisible Man,* sees Ole Bill's attack as a symbolic castration and concludes that Riley has entered the black world of limited possibility (Klein; 99). But the rest of the story provides indications that Riley will rise to test the limitations again. When he fell from the church the day before, Riley was unabashed by the failure, calling his impulse to extend the boundaries of possibility similar to what causes "them white guys to jump outa them airplane in them parachutes" (32). His reaction indicates that "That I Had the Wings" is a blues story. The blues, as Robert Bone notes, "begin with personal disaster. They speak of flooded farmlands and blighted crops, of love betrayed and lovers parted, of the black man's poverty and the white man's justice. For the blues are a poetic confrontation of reality. They are a form of spiritual discipline, a means of transcending the painful conditions with which they deal. The crucial feature of the blues response is the margin of freedom it proclaims. . . . Within limits there is always choice and will."[6] Ellison makes it clear in *Shadow and Act* that the blues are an integrative force, speaking "to us simultaneously of the tragic and the comic aspects of the human condition and they express a profound sense of life shared by many Negro Americans precisely because their lives have combined these modes" (250).

Not only is "That I Had the Wings" a blues story, but it includes recognizable blues forms within it. As James Gray points out, the specific form that Riley uses when he improvises on Aunt Kate's spirituals is a blues form.[7] In *A Popular History of Music,* Carter Harman, defines elements of blues: "The blues was a vocal lament with undercurrents of humor, usually (but not always) in slow, draggy tempo. The singer improvised three lines of verse: the first two, identical in words and similar in melody; the third, a kind of answer in rhyme."[8] Harman uses W. C. Handy's "St. Louis Blues" as an example: "I hate to see that evenin' sun go down / I hate to see that

evenin' sun go down / 'Cause my baby done left this town." Riley's improvised lines that cause Aunt Kate anguish early in the story follow the same
pattern:

> If I was the President
> of these United States
> Said if I was the President
> of these United States
> I'd eat good chocolate candy bars
> An swing on the White House gates.

Seasoned Stories of 1944

The three stories Ellison published in 1944, combined with the Buster
and Riley stories, demonstrate the richness and complexity of this writer's
vision. The later stories demonstrate significant differences in characterization and style from the previous ones. Ellison now concentrates on young
adults rather than boys, and these stories illustrate his grappling with conflicting emotions of patriotism for and alienation from America during
World War II. Stylistically they combine realism, myth, folklore, and passages usually called surrealistic that characterize *Invisible Man,* a style recognizably Ellisonian. One of the major elements of that style, the surrealism, is
perhaps influenced by Ellison's Oklahoma past.

Surrealism is generally associated with the movement in France in the
1920s headed by André Breton, who was strongly influenced by Freud.
More recently, the term *magical realism,* usually associated with South
American writers, has been applied by Wayne Ude to North American fiction characterized by "the style of prose romance, with its heightened yet
commonplace diction; its loose, informal syntax; its strong, dark rhythms
and sounds; its use of juxtaposition and metaphor; its lack of concern for
surface coherence in the presence of deeper coherence."[9] As Ude notes, there
are two North American sources of this style: the romance novels of
Hawthorne, Melville, Poe, and Faulkner, and native American culture.
Ellison has often noted his debt to nineteenth-century American writers as
well as the connections between African Americans and native Americans on
the Oklahoma frontier, and one of his later stories "A Coupla Scalped Indians," makes the connection directly with surrealism—or magical realism.

"In a Strange Country" In the introduction to the thirtieth anniversary edition of *Invisible Man,* Ellison points out the similarity between the novel and two early stories, "In a Strange Country" and "Flying Home":

> During the same period [as "Flying Home"] I had published yet another story in which a young Afro-American seaman, ashore in Swansea, South Wales, was forced to grapple with the troublesome "American" aspects of his identity after white Americans had blacked his eye during a wartime blackout on the Swansea street called Straight (no, his name was *not* Saul nor did he become a Paul!). But here the pressure toward self-scrutiny came from a group of Welshmen who rescued him and surprised him by greeting him as a "Black Yank" and inviting him to a private club, and then sang the American National Anthem in his honor. Both stories were published in 1944, but now in 1945 on a Vermont farm, the theme of a young Negro's quest for identity was reasserting itself in a far more bewildering form. (xiv)

Taking its title from Hemingway's "In Another Country," a story about a wounded American who learns from an experience in a foreign country, "In a Strange Country"[10] concerns a young African American merchant marine, Parker, who is beaten by a group of white American soldiers shortly after landing in Wales. The story begins in a Welsh pub where Parker has been taken by the Welshmen who rescued him. Parker's eye begins to swell shut and disturb his vision, but Mr. Catti and other Welshmen try to make him feel comfortable. They invite him to a private club where different singers perform. As they listen to the music, Mr. Catti tells Parker that although the singers are from different places, "When we sing, we are Welshmen" (43). Finding it difficult to see, Parker has begun to listen carefully to the music, and that leads to a realization: "Parker smiled, aware suddenly of an expansiveness that he had known before only at mixed jam sessions. When we jam, sir, we're Jamocrats! He liked these Welsh. Not even on the ship, where the common danger and the fighting union made for a degree of understanding, did he approach white men so closely" (43).

The singers perform the "Welsh National Anthem," "God Save the King," the "Internationale," and then close the evening with "The Star-Spangled Banner," in Parker's honor. Giving up the feelings of alienation and estrangement he felt since the beating, Parker senses his identity as an American, a "black Yank" as the Welshmen call him. He suddenly sings, almost involuntarily, and "with dreamlike wonder" thinks: "For the first time in your whole life . . . the words are not ironic" (44).

Here Ellison emphasizes Parker's complex sense of identity and suggests an ironic reading of the title. Parker's normal feeling is "the familiar and hateful emotion of alienation" (42). After the beating, he first feels a "blind rage" that ebbs into "a smoldering sense of self-hate and ineffectiveness" (41). But Parker is an intelligent and educated man who recognizes that the Welsh are a minority among the English majority; he calls them "a different breed; even from the English" (41). In his stream of consciousness he begins to think of Othello, only to correct himself: "And remember what they did to Othello. *No, he did it to himself. Couldn't believe in his woman, nor in himself*" (43). Parker's strange country is his own altered consciousness where the epiphanic vision leads to an affirmation of himself as a black Yank who no longer feels only self-hate, alienation, and irony.

The story explores familiar Ellison themes of a search for identity in racially complex experience and the disparity between traditional American ideals of democracy and brotherhood and the reality of racism. Ellison also uses images of sight and blinding lights, as well as music and blues riffs on language. Parker grows in understanding as his literal sight becomes limited by his swelling eye. Despite Parker's alienation and estrangement, however, Ellison provides clues to Parker's potential. Like Buster and Riley before him and the narrator of *Invisible Man* to follow, Parker uses language imaginatively and humorously. He puns on *democrat,* transforming it into *Jamocrat,* and when he goes with Catti to hear the music, he wonders if he will hear *"Massa's in de—Massa's in de Old Cold Masochism!"* (42). Improvisational, creative punning is a trait of the Ellison hero.

"Flying Home" "Flying Home," perhaps Ellison's most successful short story, brings together several of his themes, images, and techniques: themes of isolation, estrangement, racial strife, initiation, and search for identity; bird, wing, and flying imagery; laughing, judgmental men; and framing, myth, folklore, and distorted, surreal—or magical realism—passages. Moreover, the story demonstrates how Ellison differs from other modernists in the use of myth.[11] Other modernists use myth to lift their works toward a universal and timeless plane; Ellison couples myth with black folklore to historicize his work.

The story draws from a specific historical event that concerned Ellison during World War II: "A Negro air school had been established at Tuskegee during the war, apparently as a sop to civil libertarians. Its pilots never got out of training. The school became a sufficient issue for Judge Hastie to resign from the War Department in protest over it" (Klein, 102–13). In this story a black pilot trainee, Todd, is attempting to correct a dangerous maneuver when he hits a buzzard, crash lands in a field, and breaks his ankle. An old black "peasant" sharecropper, Jefferson, sends his son for help and then tells the pilot two folktales. The first is a story about seeing two buzzards arising from a horse's carcass, and the second, cataloged by folklorists as early as 1919 as the "Colored Man in Heaven" tale,[12] is about a black angel who was expelled from heaven because of his pride. The second story offends Todd, who thinks Jefferson is mocking him. During this time Todd recalls his childhood fascination with flying.

When Dabney Graves, the white man who owns the farm arrives, he has Todd straitjacketed because "you all know you cain't let the nigguh git up that high without his going crazy."[13] As he begins to be taken away, Todd suddenly realizes his own pride has estranged him from his roots, "And it was as though he had been lifted out of his isolation, back into the world of men" (270).

Although Todd is from "up north," the title refers to his perceived return to his racial history. Earlier he had thought condescendingly how different he was from all that Jefferson represents: "He felt cut off from them by age, by understanding, by sensibility, by technology and by his need to measure himself against the mirror of other men's appreciation" (257). And he feels humiliated that he must be identified racially with Jefferson: "Humiliation was when you could never be simply yourself, when you were always a part of this old black ignorant man" (256).

Jefferson's stories indicate he is one of Ellison's wise fools, like Jim Trueblood, Peter Wheatstraw, and the narrator's grandfather in *Invisible Man*. Ostendorf mistakenly thinks that Jefferson tells his stories naively, just to pass the time (Ostendorf 1976, 195), but the old sharecropper understands the political ramifications of Todd's position. When Jefferson asks Todd why he wants to fly, Todd replies to himself, "Because it makes me less like you," and aloud, "It's as good a way to fight and die as I know" (258). Jefferson knowingly responds, "But how long you think before they gonna let you all fight?" Then Jefferson subtly communicates to Todd that he sees him as a "jimcrow" black man, by telling him that his son calls buzzards "jimcrows." Like the jim crow laws that institutionalized segregation and forced black people to accept separate and unequal treatment, Todd is a "jimcrow" pilot, allowed only to fly an "advanced trainer" in a separate and unequal air force. He is a buzzard feeding on the dead horse of bigotry by allowing himself to be a symbol.

Susan L. Blake, in an article critical of Ellison's use of African American folklore, points to implications of the buzzard imagery:

The buzzard is a common figure in black folklore, representing sometimes the black person scrounging for survival, sometimes his predators, and always the precariousness of life in a predatory society. . . . Representing not only the black man, Todd, but the Jim Crow society, they symbolize the destructiveness of both. Todd thinks of himself as a buzzard. . . . But there is also a clear analogy between him and the horse's carcass. . . . He is being devoured by both the Jim Crow society and his own shame at blackness. Todd (*Tod* "death") is, in trying to destroy old Jefferson, also feeding on his own dead self.[14]

Jefferson's second folktale is even more pointed; he tells how he once went to heaven and flew so well that he was given a "parachute and a map of the state of Alabama" and expelled. But while he was there, "I was the flyinest sonofabitch what ever hit heaven!" (262). It is a story of pride, and Todd recognizes its import, feeling "such an intense humiliation that only great violence would wash it away" (262).

Todd's alienation from Jefferson disappears after Graves, who represents "all the unnamed horror and obscenities that he had ever imagined," kicks him in the chest and straitjackets him. At that moment, like the conclusion of Hawthorne's "My Kinsman, Major Molineux," "hot, hysterical laughter tore from his chest" (269). Sensing that Graves, who "done killed enough of us," (267) might kill Todd, Jefferson and his son sidetrack the white man into concern for the plane and take Todd away.

As they leave, the story ends with a powerfully affirmative image of transformation, one that consolidates the story's themes and images from myth and folklore. Todd looks up at a flying buzzard and "like a song within his head he heard the boy's soft humming and saw the dark bird glide into the sun and glow like a bird of flaming gold" (270). Joseph Trimmer points out in one of the best commentaries on this story:

This transformation of the buzzard into the "bird of flaming gold" ties together the various symbolic patterns which have been at work in the story. Todd, like Icarus, has tried to fly too close to the sun, and his fall has taught him conceit. But like Adam's, Todd's fall can be seen as fortunate for it eventually occasions his salvation. The Daedalus figure, Jefferson, has taught his "son" the error of his ways. That error is not so much in aspiration—the story certainly does not counsel acceptance of jimcrow—but in the method and motive of aspiration.[15]

The mythic comparisons—Todd/Icarus/Adam, Jefferson/Daedalus, Buzzard/Phoenix—combined with African American folklore presented in the style of magical realism all mark the mature Ralph Ellison. "Flying Home" also demonstrates a sophisticated attitude toward black characters who have had to live with racism. In his Buster and Riley stories, Ellison often presents older characters like Riley's mother or Aunt Kate as negative figures who attempt to impose a slave mentality on the two boys. Often Buster and Riley draw from African American folklore and their frontier assertiveness to affirm their identities, but they often reject older blacks who have been there before them. With Todd and Jefferson, however, Ellison achieves the balance between affirmation and denial. Jefferson, like Louis Armstrong and Jim Trueblood, has learned to use his creative powers to assert self in the face of forces that deny it. In this sense, the title "Flying Home" resonates with meaning for both author and character.

"King of the Bingo Game" Ellison's last 1944 story looks both backward and forward in Ellison's career. Like the early stories and unlike the other two 1944 stories, this one ends pessimistically. In some ways it resembles "Slick Gonna Learn" in that the main character, in stress because his wife needs medical attention, discovers the world is based on chance and luck. It is the first Ellison story concerning a young black man from the South who discovers a lack of community support after the great migration north.

This story concerns a nameless young man who desperately needs money for his critically ill wife, Laura. Unable to get a job because he has no birth certificate, he hopes to win money offered as a sales promotion at a local movie theater. To win the prize of $36.90, he must first win a bingo game and then cause an electrically controlled wheel to land on the appropriate (and ironic) number—double zero. By playing five cards, he gets his chance at the wheel, but feeling such exhilaration at being in control of something, he cannot let loose of the power line. The button that controls the wheel is connected by a wire, and as the main character holds it, he feels immense power and identity, yelling "This is God!" and decides that he has been "reborn" as "The-man-who-pressed-the-button-who-held-the-prize-who-was-the-King-of-Bingo" (277). Finally, as he is dragged off the stage to the hoots of the audience, the wheel lands on the winning number.

Ellison here combines several related images that indicate control. The film itself is a complex metaphor for this young man's existential position. As he watches the movie, he gets caught up in the suggested humanity of the actors, but he realizes that he is merely looking at two-dimensional images projected upon a flat screen. The same thing will happen every time he watches the film's white beam: "It was strange how the beam always landed right on the screen and didn't mess up and fall somewhere else. But they had it all fixed. Everything was fixed."[16] This conclusion causes him to recall a dream he had about walking down a railroad track as a boy. As he runs to get off the track, he looks back and sees "with terror that the train had left the track and was following him right down the middle of the street, and all the white people laughing as he ran screaming . . ." [Ellison's ellipsis] (272). The twirling projection reel and the indomitable train wheel connect with the whirling wheel of fortune, a rather obvious image of the wheel of life. All of these images recall one of the most memorable scenes of modern man caught in forces of mechanical change: Charlie Chaplin on the turning gears in his 1936 film about power, racism, and control, *Modern Times.*[17]

Another recurring image is a thin, black line. In *Invisible Man,* Tod Clifton makes the Sambo dolls dance by using invisible black thread.[18] The story's nameless character thinks of himself as being "like a long thin black wire that was being stretched and wound upon the bingo wheel" (276). While the cord gives him identity and control, it also limits him since he can run only to its end and cannot let go. (Running returns throughout the novel.) In this moment of rebirth the black line also suggests the umbilical cord, like the wire connected to the narrator's stomach in the machine scene in *Invisible Man.*

Themes of control and freedom are central to *Invisible Man,* as are the images of light and electricity. Also central to the story is the search for identity as the unnamed narrator lacks a birth certificate to validate his being. While the pessimistic conclusion looks back to earlier stories, "King of the Bingo Game" foreshadows the universal applications of these Ellison concerns as they reappear in the novel. Certainly on one level the story is about "the namelessness, the invisibility, or lack of identity experienced by the black American" and "the suppression of Blacks in an indifferent white America."[19] But it is also about the universal existential position of twentieth-century men and women who feel themselves alone in a world controlled by large mechanical forces and by mere chance.

When *Invisible Man* appeared in 1952, some readers thought it seemed to have been written by an unknown writer who miraculously produced a work out of nowhere. These eight stories written prior to the novel demonstrate, however, that Ralph Ellison tested his limits as a writer; began to examine the themes, images, and techniques that characterize his work; and learned his craft as he moved steadily toward *Invisible Man.*

Chapter Three
A Twentieth-Century Masterpiece: *Invisible Man*

Invisible Man is probably the most important and influential American novel since World War II, and, arguably, the most important twentieth-century American novel, the *Moby Dick* of the twentieth century. Tony Tanner calls *Invisible Man* "seminal for subsequent American fiction."[1] Zbigniew Lewicki concludes that it "is more than the most important black novel in America, or even 'one of the greatest post-war American novels.' It is a book that signifies the end of one literary tradition and the arrival of another."[2] The concept of invisibility has entered American vocabulary, much as have those of babbittry and catch-22.

Selected by critics as the most distinguished single work published since World War II in a 1965 *Book Week* poll and a 1978 *Wilson Quarterly* poll, *Invisible Man* has returned to the forefront of American critical thought as the century draws to a close. After attacks by proponents of the black aesthetic at the end of the sixties and the beginning of the seventies, the novel suffered a brief period of eclipse. But critical discussions of the making and unmaking of the American canon have reemphasized its importance. African American literary theorists who apply varieties of European literary theories to African American literature have also underscored Ellison's stature. He is now firmly in the American canon; the major American literature anthologies used in college literature classes include a selection from Ellison. The novel's significance is also demonstrated by the increasing number of book-length works on it and on Ellison.

The novel's strength derives from Ellison's integrative imagination. He draws from classical works in the European tradition, major works in the American canon, African American literature and folklore, native American mythology, children's games and rhymes, and his own experience—in short, from wherever his imagination leads him. These varied influences will be discussed in the next chapter; the focus in this chapter is on the neglected significance of frontier mythology drawn from Ellison's southwestern past.[3] Despite the fact that most of *Invisible Man* is set in Harlem, the narrative relies on frontier imagery associated with the duality between free-

dom and restriction often presented in American literature through the opposition between East and West.[4]

Frontier mythology refers to a cluster of images, values, and archetypes
that grew out of the confrontation between the uncivilized and the civilized
world—what Frederick Jackson Turner called the "meeting point between
savagery and civilization."[5] Civilization is associated with the past and with
Europe, which early American thinkers found withering and moribund, the
dead hand of the past. Civilization, then, is identified with society—its institutions, laws, and restrictions, its demands for compromise, its cultural
refinement and emphasis on manners, its industrial development, and its
class distinctions. The wilderness that civilization confronts suggests many
opposing ideas. Rather than the restrictive demands of society, the wilderness offers the possibility of individual freedom, where individuals can test
themselves against nature without demands for social responsibility and
compromises of being part of a community. Cultural refinement and emphasis on manners give way to pragmatic empiricism. Agrarianism, rather
than industrialism, is the major force. Class distinctions disappear. In the
wilderness breathes the all-enfolding spirit, a deity worshipped by Indians,
transcendentalists, and naturalists alike. These positive images are associated with the pastoral frontier, made familiar through the works of Cooper
and Thoreau. But another image cluster grew out of the gothic frontier, this
one offering violence, captivity, and metamorphosis. These are the product
of the Puritans' confrontation with the dark forces represented to them by
the Indians, and which Ellison acknowledges African Americans have often
symbolized in American literature. Both pastoral and gothic frontier imagery are important to Ellison.

The literary importance of these image clusters appears in many works
through recognizable archetypal patterns.[6] Repeatedly American literature
emphasizes innocent Americans in conflict with the oppositions suggested
by the East/West, civilization/wilderness grid. These archetypal American
figures, attempting to free themselves from civilization's constrictions,
move into the wilderness where, as R. W. B. Lewis demonstrated, they become new Adams in the Garden. The process, though, according to Richard
Slotkin, often requires a ritualistic hunt in which these American hunters
regenerate themselves through violence and return to familial bonds of civilization with a renewed awareness of their own individuality. The transformation, Leslie Fiedler and D. H. Lawrence have pointed out, often involves
coming to terms with the nonrational forces that the native American or African American has come to represent.

Ellison's work marks an advance over those who have dichotomized the oppositions of frontier mythology, for Ellison works to intertwine ideas from both sides of the dualities. It is not simply a question of substituting another more positive value (freedom, for example) for a negative one (restriction). Rather, Ellison attempts to synthesize conflicting ideas into an operating whole that can account for the variety of American life. For Ellison, the frontier represents amalgamation: "The movement toward the frontier—the movement from the East to the West and the Southwest—was not simply a geographical movement. . . . It was also a movement toward a more vernacular American character. When I say vernacular, . . . I mean the intermixing of traditional styles and perspectives, in response to the experience of extending the nation geographically" (quoted in Anderson, "Territory," 102, 104). As a result of these attitudes, Ellison favors the tripartite dialectic of thesis/antithesis=synthesis. Dualities in continual opposition produce a gestalt that is larger than the two forces by themselves.[7] For this reason dualities are central to his method as he raises such oppositions as Adam/Christ, freedom/restriction, black/white, positive/negative, good/evil, love/hate, life/death, one/many, self/mask, visible/invisible, illusion/disillusion, ideal/real, father/son, summer/winter, Christmas/Fourth of July, Brer Bear/Brer Rabbit, comedy/tragedy, shadow/act, order/chaos, past/present, and sex/violence, among others in his work. "In the beginning was not only the word," Ellison writes in his 1956 essay "Society, Morality, and the Novel," "but the contradiction of the word" (*GT,* 243). In other words, initially Americans declared human equality but lived the contradiction of slavery. This struggle produced the ambivalent American experience. Metaphorically, the frontier, the boundary between civilization and savagery, synthesizes such opposing forces.

The results of this dialectic are oxymoronic and paradoxical, similar to *Invisible Man*'s purpose of making darkness visible. Ellison seeks images that tie together apparent opposites. The image of moving without moving, central to the Trueblood episode in *Invisible Man,* is one such oxymoron. In some ways electricity provides another paradigm for Ellison's thought, since it is a phenomenon that depends on opposites; without both positive and negative, no power flows. Jazz's emphasis on restricted freedom provides another such metaphor, for "true Jazz is an art of individual assertion within and against the group. Each true jazz moment (as distinct from the uninspired commercial performance) springs from a contest in which each artist challenges all the rest; each solo flight, or improvisation, represents (like the successive canvases of a painter) a definition of his identity: as individual, as member of the collectivity and as a link in the chain of tradition" (*SA,* 234).

Individual talent/tradition, freedom/restriction, chaos/order—these seeming oppositions find mediation on the frontier or the border. Another aspect of the frontier mythology important to *Invisible Man* is Ellison's transformation of the innocent figure identified by R. W. B. Lewis as the American Adam. In the nineteenth century, when the pastoral vision of the wilderness predominated over the Puritan one of evil, the figure that often personified the new American was the New Adam—innocent, full of possibility and potential. Ellison and other contemporary American novelists do not use Adamic figures as realistically possible heroic characters, but Ellison does present an innocent Adam in dramatic tension with Adam's counterpointing figure in religious typology: Christ. The conflict between an innocent Adam and an aware Christ is a sustaining part of the narrative pattern in *Invisible Man,* as well as in other post–World War II novels.

In these works the main characters begin as American Adams, believing some illusions spawned by the frontier vision of the American wilderness as Eden and the American as innocent (characterized by self-centered individuality, denial of the past, desire for simplicity and harmony, recoil from death, materialism, anarchic freedom, and self-righteousness). The characters are established as Adamic through grappling with these problems; often, too, clusters of images are associated with the American as Adam (nakedness, blindness or sleep, garden, tree, snake, open air). Events challenge their illusions and force them toward knowledge. Usually the main characters must face death; either their own lives are threatened, or they witness the death of another character, as Ellison's narrator witnesses Tod Clifton's death. The resulting awareness dawns slowly in most cases, suggesting a gap between seeing and understanding and the difficulty in overcoming illusions.

When the main characters finally achieve knowledge, they attempt to become conscious Messiahs who see clearly that their purpose is to transform the world into one of hope, community, and love or at least one in which it is easier to live. The characters usually understand the illusory nature of their world and know that for destructive illusions to be overthrown, they must be clearly articulated. Contemporary writers emphasize that language both creates illusions and strips away inhumane beliefs to create humane ones. Usually when the characters become Christ-like, they also become writers (*logos*), as Ellison's narrator does. Besides an understanding of language, the Christ-like traits are an awareness of discord, complexity, human limitation, the problems of the past, and the need for community and love.

The metamorphosis from Adam to Christ owes much to the Puritan emphasis on biblical typology, where "characters and events of the Old Testament are prefigurations and prophecies of future events, mainly of Christ and His works."[8] What gives the transformation its particular connection with elements of frontier mythology and Ralph Ellison, whose frontier background connected him to native American culture, is the corresponding movement in Indian culture. Joseph Campbell in *The Masks of God* points out the significance of two opposing figures: the "hunter" or "warrior" and the "shaman."[9] Transformation, metamorphosis, and process—significant elements of Ellison's southwestern worldview—become part of the underpinning structure of *Invisible Man* as well. Ultimately Ellison synthesizes elements of warrior and shaman, Adam and Christ, in a composite hero who merges values, and so it is not surprising to learn that the narrator in *Invisible Man* offers up his story from a "border area" (5). It is the voice of the frontier.

In his acceptance speech for the National Book Award of 1952, Ellison asserted that *Invisible Man*'s chief significance is its "experimental attitude, and its attempt to return to the mood of personal moral responsibility for democracy which typified the best of our nineteenth-century fiction" (*SA*, 102). Not only was Ellison influenced by traditional American ideals in literature, but his boyhood in Oklahoma acted out some of the positive aspects of the American frontier belief in a free and open frontier:

Like Huck we observed, we judged, we imitated and evaded as we could the dullness, corruption and blindness of "civilization." We were undoubtedly comic because, as the saying goes, we weren't supposed to know what it was all about. But to ourselves we were "boys," members of a wild, free outlaw tribe which transcended the category of race. Rather we were Americans born into the forty-sixth state, and thus, into the context of Negro-American post-Civil War history, "frontiersmen." And isn't one of the implicit functions of the American Frontier to encourage the individual to a kind of dreamy wakefulness, a state in which he makes—in all ignorance of the accepted limitations of the possible—rash efforts, quixotic gestures, hopeful testings of the complexity of the known and the given? (*SA*, xv)

Thus Ellison, raised in Oklahoma when it was still the territory ahead, sensed the power of a frontier world of possibility. He soon encountered a world where the frontier ethos did not obtain, at least for an African American adult. *Invisible Man* dramatizes this revelation: it is an American bildungsroman in which the narrator moves from a frontier belief in freedom, simplicity, possibility, and harmony to a confrontation with the reality of restriction. The awareness that results emphasizes the "personal moral responsibility for democracy," which Ellison states is the significance of the fiction.

Prologue

The Prologue, set at the end of the action, introduces most of the major themes and images. There the nameless writer-narrator, called variously by critics (Invisible Man, Invisible, IM, Jack-the-Bear, Jack, "P," and "N"), explains the title as a reference to poor sight, a recurring metaphor in contemporary American fiction for innocence and ignorance: "That invisibility to which I refer occurs because of a peculiar disposition of the eyes of those with whom I come in contact. A matter of the construction of their *inner* eyes, those eyes with which they look through their physical eyes upon reality" (*IM,* 3). Living in an underground basement, "in the great American tradition of tinkers," the narrator has rigged it so that he has 1,369 lights[10] powered by electricity drained illegally from "Monopolated Light & Power," thus introducing the light/darkness duality, as well as the image of electricity, that recurs throughout the novel.[11] But he is also a "thinker-tinker" who writes and shapes the story of his experience. It is a narrative answering Louis Armstrong's question, "What Did I Do to Be so Black and Blue?" (10). As he listens to Armstrong and prepares to tell his tale, the narrator eats vanilla ice cream with sloe gin poured over it, adding black to the traditional American colors of red, white, and blue. Both the story and Armstrong's pun are concerned with innocent suffering to which both respond in the tragicomic language of the blues.

In the Prologue, Ellison employs magical realism to enhance the novel's emphasis on dreams[12] after the narrator smokes a marijuana cigarette and has a dream in which he hears "not only in time, but in space as well." The spatial metaphor is an underground one, for in the dream the narrator penetrates three lower layers. At the first he hears an old woman singing a spiritual. At the second level is, ironically, "*a beautiful girl the color of ivory pleading in a voice like my mother's as she stood before a group of slaveowners who bid for her naked body*" (7). On the third and lowest level is a preacher who echoes the sermon about the "blackness of darkness" that Ishmael stumbles on in a black church in New Bedford in the "Carpet-bag" chapter of *Moby Dick.* Ellison's dream preacher's text is the "Blackness of Blackness," and his call-and-response sermon suggests Ellison's awareness of contraries and ambiguity:

"Black will git you . . ."
"Yes, it will . . ."
". . . an' black won't . . ."
"Naw, it won't"
"It do . . ."
"It do, Lawd . . ."
". . . an' it don't." (8)

Ambivalence and duality appear on the first level as well. There the singer of spirituals says she loved and hated her master who was also father of her sons (to which the narrator echoing Robert Frost replies, *"I too have become acquainted with ambivalence"*). She explains that she loved her master but that she loved freedom more. When the narrator asks what freedom is, she answers: *"It's all mixed up. First I think it's one thing, then I think it's another. It gits my head to spinning. I guess now it ain't nothing but knowing how to say what I got up in my head"* (9).

Chapters 1–7: Battle Royal, College, and Jim Trueblood

In chapter 1 the narrator returns to the beginning of his story. This chapter functions as what Kenneth Burke called a "representative anecdote," or "an episode in which the entire novel is implicit."[13] Many of the events, character types, themes, and images that recur in this boomeranging work appear here: blacks fighting blacks in a scene of chaotic violence; oratory; a nude woman; sight, color, clown, animal, electricity, running, and dancing imagery; and dualities of innocence/experience, black/white, appearance/reality, order/chaos, and others. One important theme, the search for identity, is explicit.

Ellison emphasizes the narrator's innocent belief in the outer world of appearance. His first hint that something exists beneath the surface comes when he overhears his dying grandfather, "a quiet old man who never made any trouble" (14), tell his father: " 'Son, after I'm gone I want you to keep up the good fight. I never told you, but our life is a war and I have been a traitor all my born days, a spy in the enemy's country ever since I give up my gun back in the Reconstruction. Live with your head in the lion's mouth. I want you to overcome 'em with yeses, undermine 'em with grins, agree 'em to death and destruction, let 'em swoller you till they vomit or bust wide open' " (13–14). His grandfather's words confront him with the enigma of contradiction between appearance and reality, mask and identity.

Although he is puzzled by his grandfather's statement (there will be a long gap between hearing and understanding),[14] he ultimately achieves the complex sense of identity that mediates between appearance and reality. Ellison emphasizes the narrator's innocence (his home town is named "Greenwood") by having him participate in a "battle royal" before the city's most prominent white citizens—"bankers, lawyers, judges, doctors, fire chiefs, teachers, merchants . . . even one of the more fashionable pastors" (15). The narrator attends the occasion innocently believing that he is supposed to deliver his valedictory speech, stressing his belief that "humility was the . . . very essence of progress." However, he again finds disparity between appearance and reality, for the meeting he expects to be a sedate, stately gathering turns out to be a drunken stag party. These "great men" force him to fight several other black boys, all blindfolded (reinforcing the sight imagery), before he can give his speech. But before they fight, they are further humiliated by being forced to watch a naked blonde with a small American flag tattooed on her belly dance. Just as American Adamic ideals of freedom, equality, and opportunity have been held out before but denied many black people, the girl stands before the boys as an object of desire; the men, however, would never allow them to possess her. The white woman, whatever her individual status, represents power in black/white relations. She must be both desired and forbidden to fulfill her function.

After the fight the boys are told to get their reward—coins, a few crumpled bills, and gold pieces scattered about a small rug. To their horror they discover that the rug is electrified and see one boy "literally dance upon his back, his elbows beating a frenzied tattoo upon the floor, his muscles twitching like the flesh of a horse stung by many flies" (22). The narrator, foreshadowing his ability to use humor and to assimilate varied forces, reacts differently: "Ignoring the shock by laughing, as I brushed the coins off quickly, I discovered that I could contain the electricity—a contradiction, but it works" (22). The gold pieces, they discover in another pointed image, are counterfeit.

Finally allowed to give his speech, he delivers it, visualizing himself as a "potential Booker T. Washington," and makes it through with only one crucial slip: he mistakenly says "social equality" instead of "social responsibility" and is forced to correct himself.[15] Nonetheless, his frontier faith in progress is restored by receiving from these "dignitaries" a briefcase with a scholarship to a Negro college inside. That night in a dream his grandfather appears and tells him to open his briefcase. Inside he finds envelope within envelope with the last one having an official seal and a message that reads, " 'To Whom It May Concern. . . . Keep This Nigger-Boy Running' " (26).

In chapter 2 Ellison associates the narrator with the American Adam by having him recall his college. The narrator's memories flow with a flood of nostalgia for what he later refers to as "this Eden" (86) with its harmonious garden imagery. Overwhelmed by his own sense of purpose as a student, he fails to see that this garden contains mockingbirds and a rumbling black powerhouse, an image that suggests the black college president, Dr. Bledsoe, for whom power is the goal. In his Adamic innocence, the narrator bungles the responsibility of keeping the white school trustee Mr. Norton from seeing the squalid nearby environment: the incestuous sharecropper Trueblood and the apocalyptic, Blakean world of chaos, the Golden Day, a whorehouse-tavern visited by black inmates of an insane asylum for veterans.

The Trueblood episode is one of the most important in the novel, for Trueblood, a character who combines the abilities of blues singers from African American culture with humor and tale telling from southwestern culture, offers the narrator a model for overcoming his own invisibility. Assigned to drive Mr. Norton around, the narrator unconsciously takes him to the out-of-the-way area where Jim Trueblood's log cabin is located. Norton has already suggested (in language that recalls Poe) that he had an unnatural attraction to a dead daughter: " 'She was a being more rare, more beautiful, purer, more perfect and more delicate than the wildest dream of a poet' " (p. 33). It is no surprise that when Norton learns from the narrator that Jim Trueblood has impregnated both his wife and his daughter, he is fascinated (" 'You have looked upon chaos and are not destroyed!' " [40]) and forces the narrator to stop so he can hear Trueblood's story.

As Trueblood begins, the narrator recognizes that Trueblood is an accomplished storyteller: "He cleared his throat, his eyes gleaming and his voice taking on a deep, incantatory quality, as though he had told the story many, many times" (42). Trueblood tells how because of economic circumstances and no heat for his home, his daughter, Matty Lou, who "looks just like the old lady did when she was young" (42), had to sleep between him and his wife to stay warm. With a wink to folklore, Trueblood says that the night was black "as the middle of a bucket of tar" (42). He fell asleep and began to dream that he had gone to the home of a white man, Mr. Broadnax, to get some "fat meat." Breaking taboo, he had entered by the front door and walked around until he came to the bedroom. Suddenly a white woman in a silky nightgown stepped out of the grandfather clock and pulled him down onto the bed. Freeing himself, he ran for the clock door, which "had some kinda crinkly stuff like steel wool on the facing" (45), and entered a long dark tunnel.

Suddenly he awoke to discover that Matty Lou was beating her fists against him and crying, and he realized that he was having intercourse with his daughter: " 'I can't move 'cause I figgers if I moved it would be a sin. And I figgers too, that if I don't move it maybe ain't no sin, 'cause it happened when I was asleep.' " Then he decided that he actually needed was to " 'move without movin' " (46), but he was unable to achieve that goal when Matty Lou began to move. At that point, his wife, Kate, awoke and tried to kill him with an ax. He went away to ponder his sin, tried to pray but could not, and then, " 'I starts singin'. . . . I sings me some blues that night ain't never been sang before, and while I'm singin' them blues I makes up my mind that I ain't nobody but myself and ain't nothin' I can do but let whatever is gonna happen, happen' " (51).

Houston A. Baker, Jr., describes the blues as "a synthesis. . . . Combining work songs, group seculars, field hollers, sacred harmonies, proverbial wisdom, folk philosophy, political commentary, ribald humor, elegiac lament, and much more, they constitute an amalgam that seems always to have been in motion in America—always becoming, shaping, transforming, displacing the peculiar experiences of Africans in the New World."[16] The blues are a mediating force, a "matrix" that brings together conflicting forces and "avoids simple dualities" (Baker 1984, 9). Ellison makes it clear in *Shadow and Act* that the blues are an integrative force: "The blues speak to us simultaneously of the tragic and the comic aspects of the human condition and they express a profound sense of life shared by many Negro Americans precisely because their lives have combined these modes" (250). When Trueblood sings the blues, he comes to terms with his identity and experience through an integrative artistic performance.

As Baker points out in perhaps the most brilliant essay on *Invisible Man,* Trueblood's tale combines parodic Freudianism, anthropology, and ideology.[17] Most important is Trueblood's continuing performance as a trickster who realizes that by becoming the white community's stereotypical black ("They just nigguhs, leave 'em do it" [45]), he fulfills their expectations and becomes a "true blood," or pure stereotype. In this way Trueblood, after learning the redemptive power of singing the blues, yesses 'em to death by giving whites the story they want, and in return, as Baker notes, he receives barter: "Food, drink, tobacco, and audience time are commodities the sharecropper receives in barter for the commodity he delivers—his story. The narrative of incest, after its first telling, accrues an ever-spiraling exchange value" (Baker 1984, 192).

After Norton hears the story, he gives Trueblood a hundred dollar bill, but Norton, overwhelmed by the story, needs whiskey to revive. The narra-

tor, still acting innocently, takes him to the Golden Day, whose name perhaps subtly satirizes Lewis Mumford's book of that title, which minimizes
the importance of slavery to American life.[18] There the narrator meets people who try to enlighten him about his invisibility as an African American,
but again the narrator's ignorant innocence and single-minded self-interest
keep him from seeing clearly.

Before arriving at the tavern, they must cross to the other side of the
road to pass a group of veterans from the nearby veterans' hospital. Ellison
introduces a recurring image when the narrator thinks that the vets
"looked like a chain gang" (55) as they block the road; actually they are
the mental casualties of the war the narrator's grandfather waged without
his gun. These veterans represent education toward a profession, the end
product of the path the narrator has set out on: "Many of the men had
been doctors, lawyers, teachers, Civil Service workers. . . . They were supposed to be members of the professions toward which at various times I
vaguely aspired myself" (57).

One of the vets, a fat one who had been a doctor, becomes especially important, serving as a kind of oracle. His credibility is established when he
quickly diagnoses the condition that had stumped Norton's physicians. The
vet is in the hospital, he explains, because he had learned "that my work
could bring me no dignity" (71) after "ten men in masks drove me out from
the city at midnight and beat me with whips for saving a human life. And I
was forced to the utmost degradation because I possessed skilled hands and
the belief that my knowledge could bring me dignity" (72). The vet, seeing
that the narrator does not understand, exclaims, "He registers with his
senses but short-circuits his brain. Nothing has meaning. He takes it in but
he doesn't digest it. . . . Already he's learned to repress not only his emotions but his humanity. He's invisible, a walking personification of the
Negative, the most perfect achievement of your dreams, sir! The mechanical
man!" (72)

Meanwhile the Golden Day, in an apocalyptic scene mirroring the battle
royal fight, the paint factory explosion, and the Harlem riot, explodes in
frenzy when the crazy vets knock unconscious their attendant Supercargo
(Superego) who is responsible for keeping them quiet ("I feel he's inside my
head," one says [65]).[19] With the fat vet's help, the narrator revives Norton
and returns to the school. Although Trueblood learns to sing the blues in response to his experiences and the vet offers strategic advice, it will take a
long time before the narrator learns these lessons. He must first have his
own tragicomic experiences resulting from his visit to the sharecropper and

the Golden Day. On the return to the campus, Dr. Bledsoe is infuriated that a white supporter penetrated into the heart of darkness.

Ellison makes it clear that another one of the narrator's problems is his automatic acceptance that the world is as it is supposed to be; he believes in the myth of the "black rite of Horatio Alger" (87), which leads him to think that young men who do their jobs will gain harmony, success, and dignity. The myth of the American as Adam emphasized the new American hero's ability to gain materially in this Eden of opportunity. In a *Paris Review* interview, Ellison commented on this aspect of the narrator's character: "The major flaw in the hero's character is his unquestioning willingness to do what is required of him by others as a way to success, and this was the specific form of his 'innocence' " (*SA*, 177). Homer A. Barbee, a black orator (both literally and figuratively blind), articulates this myth as it was supposedly embodied by the Founder and then reembodied by Dr. Bledsoe. Believing the myth, the narrator cannot see the world as it really is—one in which Bledsoe manipulates both whites and blacks in order to hold on to his power. Because Dr. Bledsoe is afraid the narrator will innocently destroy more of his connections, he devises a scheme to get rid of the narrator forever, making it appear that he will only be expelled for a while. Bledsoe gives him sealed envelopes that he says will help him get a job in New York but that will actually keep him from doing so.

The narrator feels that he has been cast out of Eden; as he leaves, he looks back to see the peaceful beauty of the place, but he also sees a snake: "A flash of movement drew my eye to the side of the highway now, and I saw a moccasin wiggle swiftly along the gray concrete, vanishing into a length of iron pipe that lay beside the road" (119–20). Unlike Adam, the narrator has neither lost his innocence nor acquired knowledge; if he had, he would know that the college was no Eden and Bledsoe no benevolent god. The episode, with the snake, is a parody of the Genesis story, just as the first chapter was a parody of a high school commencement.

Dr. Bledsoe's power is far-reaching, for he both expels the narrator and has the vet, the former surgeon who talked to Mr. Norton at the Golden Day, transferred, and he too is on the bus. The vet again gives the narrator advice, telling him clearly that he must strike through the mask of the world of appearance: "For God's sake, learn to look beneath the surface. . . . Come out of the fog, young man. And remember you don't have to be a complete fool in order to succeed" (118). In another statement that recalls Oedipal themes and foreshadows Rinehart, the old vet tells him: "Be your own father, young man. And remember, the world is possibility if only you'll discover it" (120). Believing as he does in the world of possibility, the narrator is too concerned with his sense of loss to attend to the vet's advice. The frontier ethos to which he subscribes whispers that by hard, honest work he will achieve all his goals. Cast out of the college, he still retains his innocence; he will require more experiences to gain understanding, first involving the seven letters of introduction he carries on his journey north.

Chapters 8–13: Up North and the Paint Factory

After the narrator arrives in New York, Ellison again uses minor characters to demonstrate the narrator's innocence and to emphasize the importance of African American folklore and culture. Expecting the letters to bring success, the narrator delivers all but one. Along the way he gets advice from another fool-trickster mentor, this time a jiver ("My name is Peter Wheatstraw, I'm the Devil's only son-in-law" [134]) who has a wheelbarrow loaded with discarded blueprints—symbolic plans. " 'Folks is always making plans and changing 'em,' " says the jiver. The narrator, still believing in the myth of progress, replies: " 'Yes, that's right . . . but that's a mistake. You have to stick to the plan.' " To which the jiver replies: " 'You kinda young, daddy-o' " (133).

Peter Wheatstraw, whose name comes from an African American folksong about a blues singer, sings lyrics from Count Basie's and Jimmy Rushing's "Boogie Woogie Blues" (O'Meally 1980, 87).[20] Thus he embodies African American culture and tradition. The Adamic narrator, trying to create himself anew and forget the past, acts as though he does not understand, to which Wheatstraw replies: " 'Now I know you from down home, how come you trying to act like you never heard that before! Hell, ain't nobody out here this morning but us colored—Why you trying to deny me?' " (132). Wheatstraw recognizes the narrator's attempts to deny his past and his heritage, and he introduces folk references to Brer Bear and Brer Rabbit that will return throughout the novel.[21] In folk culture Brer Rabbit and Brer Bear are usually opposing figures, with the slight, witty rabbit trickster overcoming the slow-witted bear. Ultimately the narrator, emphasizing amalgamation, combines elements of both Jack-the-Rabbit and Jack-the-Bear.

Some awareness of his own ignorance comes when the narrator delivers his final letter to the significantly named Mr. Emerson. He learns of Bledsoe's duplicity because Mr. Emerson's son, a young white liberal (" 'Some of the finest people I know are Neg—' ") homosexual (his club, Calamus, is an insider reference to Walt Whitman's homosexual poems), shows him Bledsoe's letter, which echoes *The Great Gatsby*'s emphasis on constantly grasping for an ever-disappearing dream: "I beg of you, sir, to help him continue in the direction of that promise which, like the horizon, recedes ever brightly and distantly beyond the hopeful traveler" (145).

Defeated and confused, the narrator walks out into the street and suddenly recalls words to an old song about picking "poor Robin clean" (147). "Robin," like "Jonathan," was a common name for the American innocent in nineteenth-century American fiction,[22] and the narrator then paraphrases Bledsoe's letter to apply to himself, an innocent American Robin: " 'The Robin bearing this letter is a former student. Please hope him to death, and keep him running' " (147).

Before he can give up his commitment to the self-centered myth of progress, the narrator must gain firsthand experience of American capitalism (traditionally the way to individual success), which he does by taking a job at Liberty Paints. Its motto, "If It's Optic White, It's the Right White," suggests both "white is right" and visual illusion. For his first assignment he again experiences the disparity between simple appearance and complex reality. Having noted on his way to work the advertisement, "Keep American Pure With Liberty Paints" (149), he is first put to work for Kimbro (a "slave driver") mixing ten black drops of "dope" into every can of white paint. Although the narrator can detect a "gray tinge . . . through the whiteness," Kimbro sees it as "the purest white that can be found" (153), uniting the sight, invisibility, appearance, and amalgamation themes.

By having the narrator go down deep into the bowels of Liberty Paints (where he is transferred after innocently mistaking the "dope" for concentrated paint remover), Ellison foreshadows the end of the novel when the narrator will descend to his underground hole and then arise with Christlike knowledge. In charge of this underworld is Lucius Brockway, who paranoically believes that the narrator is part of a conspiracy to take his job. Brockway starts a fight, allowing the pressure to rise in a boiler so that it explodes. This explosion ends the parodic descent into the underworld and prepares for a parodic rebirth out of the factory hospital machine where factory doctors use the narrator as a human guinea pig.

The machine scene recalls images of castration and being forced to dance. When the narrator awakens in the machine, he is connected to an electrical current that supposedly simulates "a prefrontal lobotomy without the negative effects of the knife" (180). That this is a symbolic castration is reinforced when one of the attendants suggests literally, " 'Why not a castration, doctor?' " The pulsing current causes him to dance "between the nodes" (180).

The most obvious theme in this episode is the narrator's search for identity. While he is inside the machine, one of the doctors writes on a card and asks, "WHO ... ARE ... YOU?" The narrator thinks: "I could no more escape than I could think of my identity. Perhaps, I thought, the two things are involved with each other. When I discover who I am, I'll be free" (184–85). Even so, it is clear that he retains elements from his African American past, almost despite himself. Although he cannot remember his name, he recalls folk rhymes and stories from his past, as well as how to play the dozens, a black verbal street game of insults, usually about someone's mother. When the doctor asks on the card, "WHO WAS BUCKEYE THE RABBIT," the narrator feels "giddy with the delight of self-discovery," and recalls:

> *Buckeye the Rabbit*
> *Shake it, shake it*
> *Buckeye the Rabbit*
> *Break it, break it* ... (184)

Then after the next card asking "BOY, WHO WAS BRER RABBIT?" the narrator thinks mockingly and plays the dozens, "He was your mother's back-door man. . . . Anyone knew that they were one and the same: 'Buckeye' when you were very young and hid yourself behind wide innocent eyes; 'Brer,' when you were older" (184). Thus, folk experience provides a basis for establishing his identity and connects him with the past.

Although this descent into and ascent out of the underworld provide no final knowledge, the journey gives the narrator some direction. As he leaves on the subway, he sees "a young platinum blonde [who] nibbled at a red Delicious apple" (190), suggesting the narrator has gained some knowledge and is leaving the naive state represented by the college and its myth of individual material progress. Returning to Men's House, he has grown into some awareness about the myth of business success and realizes "that I could live there no longer, that phase of my life was past" (194).

Thus ends the first half of the novel: the Adamic, capitalistic section in which the narrator has tried to define himself through the traditional American institutions of education and business. The second half of the novel pulses from the one to the many, and the narrator must reconcile self, the "Brotherhood," and true brotherhood as he moves from frontier simplicity to an awareness of complexity.

This movement first comes through the woman who befriends him, Mary Rambo, whose name implies Christian community. She mothers him when he leaves the hospital, and she constantly reminds him that whatever he does should be "a credit to the race" (194). He sees her as "a force, a stable, familiar force like something out of my past which kept me from whirl-

ing off into some unknown which I dared not face" (196). One of the negative aspects of the frontier myth, as *The Great Gatsby* shows, suggests that
the hope and promise of the future negate the events of the past, but the
Christian heritage of Mary begins to connect the narrator with his Negro
past. Earlier he had tried to deny his heritage. When offered the standard
southern black meal of pork chops, grits, and eggs in a restaurant, he had
bristled and ordered orange juice and toast instead (135). But after meeting
Mary, he becomes aware that his African American, Christian background
contradicts the past-denying nature of the myth. Walking out into the
streets, the narrator stumbles upon an old, black "Car'lina" man selling hot
yams. He buys and eats one, affirming his connection to the past and the
verbal freedom that he finds in it by declaring, "They're my birthmark. . . .
I yam what I am!" (201). (This is a small example of creative language, one
of the attributes of the figure toward which the narrator is moving; his story
will be the major example of using language to create the world.) Then
Ellison reinforces his amalgamation theme by having the narrator buy another yam, one with both positive and negative aspects since one end is
frostbitten.

Walking on, he is overwhelmed by the images of African American
history—the pile of things belonging to an old couple being evicted ("dis-
possessed"), items such as straightening combs and free papers from African
American history. Confused and angered, he begins to speak without any
conscious plan to incite, bewildered by all that has happened. He simply responds to the heritage he sees in images before him. The result, however, is
that a riot begins. By appearing to have started it willfully, he impresses
Brother Jack, the local leader of the Brotherhood (which suggests the Communist party and other left-wing groups). The narrator's path toward understanding will again be short-circuited.

Chapters 14–22: The Brotherhood and Tod Clifton

Ironically the Brotherhood's emphasis is also on history, but it is a denial of the individual's connection with his historical past. The Brotherhood's history is in the future; history is moving in an obvious direction.
Brother Jack tells the narrator he must deny that his past is part of the dis-
possessed old couple's, saying that the "old agrarian self" is "dead and you
will throw it off completely and emerge something new. *History* had been
born in your brain" (221). Finding the frontier myth of the denial of the
past in a new form, the narrator begins to believe that the Brotherhood
points to a new Eden: "So that was the way it was. And no complaints, I

thought, looking at the map; you started looking for red men and you found them—even though of a different tribe and in a bright new world. The world was strange if you stopped to think about it; still it was a world that could be controlled by science, and the Brotherhood had both science and history under control" (288). These references to Columbus's mistaken discovery of America and to Miranda's "O brave new world" in Shakespeare's *The Tempest* suggest the Edenic mythic context of this statement.[23] There is a similar irony in the narrator's labeling the Brotherhood a "bright new world" and Miranda's exclaiming "brave new world" when she sees the representatives of the Old World, for the narrator will discover eventually that the Brotherhood can no more easily provide harmonious self-identity than the college or the business world and that it can neither control history nor deny the past.

From the beginning of his association with the Brotherhood, the narrator has difficulty getting rid of the past. The morning he leaves Mary's to take the Brotherhood apartment, he smashes a bank shaped like a grinning black man with "FEED ME" across its chest while trying to quiet people banging on the pipes. Symbol of past exploitation of black people, the bank is part of his own past, and, although he breaks it and tries to throw it away several times, he cannot. The pieces remain in his briefcase. As he moves from innocence to awareness, the narrator must come to terms with all of these symbols of his past.

Other reminders of the narrator's heritage come from Brother Tarp, who first gives him a picture of Frederick Douglass. Later, after telling the narrator that he limps because he spent 19 years on a chain gang for saying "no" to a man, Tarp gives the narrator a link of chain, "a thick dark, oily piece of filed steel that had been twisted open and forced partly back in place" (293). Tarp's gift serves as an icon of the suffering of the past. Tarp explains: " 'I'd like to pass it on to you, son. There,' he said, handing it to me. 'Funny thing to give somebody, but I think it's got a heap of signifying wrapped up in it and it might help you remember what we're really fighting against. I don't think of it in terms of but two words, *yes* and *no;* but it signifies a heap more. . . .' " (293, Ellison's ellipses).

Even with these reminders of his heritage, the narrator gets lost in the Brotherhood's sense of history. Before he can gain any real understanding of the past and true brotherhood, he will be influenced by two people: Tod Clifton and Rinehart. Both provide alternative courses of action for innocence to follow. Clifton's way is to become an innocent martyr; Rinehart's is to learn how to manipulate selfishly the chaos underlying the world.

When Tod Clifton, whose first name means "dead" in German, learns how much the Brotherhood has exploited his innocent belief in it, he chooses to become a martyr, "to plunge outside history" (285). The narrator finds him in the street hawking Sambo dolls, each one "a grinning doll of orange-and-black tissue paper with thin flat cardboard disks forming its head and feet and which some mysterious mechanism was causing to move up and down in a loose-jointed, shoulder-shaking, infuriatingly sensuous motion, a dance that was completely detached from the black, mask-like face" (326). The doll, with smiling faces on both sides, controlled by invisible black strings, symbolizes for Clifton the Brotherhood's manipulation of black people. While the narrator watches, Clifton deliberately gets into a fight with a policeman who helps him "plunge outside of history" (331) by shooting him. Watching Clifton die, the narrator realizes he can no longer deny his sense of individual responsibility as the Brotherhood has demanded.

But he is not ready to understand, as Tod Clifton did, that the Brotherhood had no real interest in Harlem except as an object of manipulation. When the narrator meets with the Central Committee and urges the Brotherhood to organize the energy flowing in Harlem because of Clifton's death, Brother Jack reprimands him for taking "personal responsibility" and for giving " 'a traitorous merchant of vile instruments of anti-Negro, anti-minority racist bigotry . . . the funeral of a hero' " (352). The narrator, testing his new-found commitment to life over death, then asks: " 'But hell, isn't the shooting of an unarmed man of more importance politically than the fact that he sold obscene dolls?' " (353). Brother Jack makes it clear that he is committed to ideology first and reveals that he, like the Reverend Barbee, is both literally and figuratively blind when he pops out his glass eye in a fit of anger.

Chapter 23: Rinehart

The Brotherhood decides to "sacrifice" Harlem to keep from upsetting "the larger plan" (378). Into the vacuum created by the Brotherhood's decision to leave Harlem alone steps Ras the Exhorter/Destroyer, who believes the narrator is a traitor to black people and the black nationalism he represents. Avoiding Ras's goons, the narrator discovers the second major alternative for innocence to follow: Rinehart. Disguising himself with sunglasses and a hat, the narrator is mistaken for Rinehart, thereby learning the various roles Rinehart plays: "Rine the runner and Rine the gambler and Rine the briber and Rine the lover and Rinehart the Reverend" (326). In his 1958 essay Ellison identified Rinehart's name as "Bliss Proteus Rinehart" and explained the character's purpose: "Rinehart's role in the formal structure of the narrative is to suggest to the hero a mode of escape from Ras, and a means of applying in yet another form, his grandfather's cryptic advice to his own situation" (*SA*, 56–57).

But if Rinehart suggests a mode of escape to the narrator, Ellison made it clear in his National Book Award acceptance speech that Rinehart as Proteus represents both the negative as well as the positive aspects of American experience:

For the novelist, Proteus stands for both America and the inheritance of illusion through which all men must fight to achieve reality; the offended god stands for our sins against those principles we all hold sacred. The way home we seek is that condition of man's being at home in the world, which is called love, and which we term democracy. Our task then is always to challenge the apparent forms of reality—that is, the fixed manners and values of the few, and to struggle with it until it reveals its mad, vari-implicated chaos, its false faces, and on until it surrenders its insight, its truth. (*SA*, 105–6)

Thus, Rinehart transforms from classical myth the figure of Proteus into the modern world through a vision of America as the new Edenic world of opportunity and freedom that symbolizes the extreme consequences of a belief in the possibilities of self. He is the isolated, manipulative self produced by frontier mythology: "His world was possibility and he knew it. He was years ahead of me and I was a fool. I must have been crazy and blind. The world in which we lived was without boundaries. A vast seething, hot world of fluidity, and Rine the rascal was at home" (376). As the narrator struggles to understand Rinehart, he suddenly recognizes that the rigidity of the institutions through which he has tried to define himself (education, business, the Brotherhood) is counterpointed by Rinehart's freedom, which leads to chaotic formlessness: "All boundaries down, freedom was not only the recognition of necessity, it was the recognition of possibility. And sitting there trembling I caught a brief glimpse of the possibilities posed by Rinehart's multiple personalities and turned away. It was too vast and confusing to contemplate" (377).

The narrator's dilemma is a familiar American one, positing the open frontier against the restricted civilized world, the isolated Adam versus the communal Christ: "Our fate is to become one, and yet many" (435). How does the one realize self without jeopardizing the allegiance to the many? How does one find the freedom of Rinehart without falling into shapeless anarchy? How does one become committed to brotherhood without deny-

ing individuality (as Brother Jack does)? Ellison's oxymoronic answer is that
these goals are achieved through organized chaos, unified diversity, and restricted freedom.

Chapters 24–25: The Harlem Riot and the Coal Hole

By recognizing Rinehart's reality, the narrator is ready to discover freedom in artistic creation, a restricted freedom that combines tradition and
the individual talent. Before rebirth, however, comes a symbolic death, a
second descent into the underworld. The descent and rebirth take place in
various stages. First, by understanding Rinehart, the narrator grasps that he
has been accepting as true subjective versions of reality formulated in words
and imposed on him by others, "each attempting to force his picture of reality upon me and neither giving a hoot in hell for how things looked to me"
(384). He now sees that models of reality that deny the past are not accepta-
ble: "I began to accept my past and, as I accepted it, I felt memories welling
up within me" (383).

The literal underworld lies beneath a manhole into which the narrator
falls while running through the streets: "It's a kind of death without hang-
ing, I thought, a death alive" (428). To light his way and to prepare the
way for his own imaginative version of reality, he burns all of the paper
definitions of his life: his diploma, the paper with his Brotherhood name,
the anonymous letter denouncing him (on which he recognizes Brother
Jack's handwriting), Clifton's doll. Collapsing on the floor, he dreams
that he is castrated[24] by people who have attempted to straitjacket him in
the past, "*Jack and old Emerson and Bledsoe and Norton and Ras and the
school superintendent and a number of others whom I failed to recognize*"
(429). Awakening, "in spite of the dream, I was whole" (431). And in his
wholeness he becomes the writer of his story, the creator of his version of
reality. But he now knows that his is just one version of reality, a blueprint
that may easily be scrapped and collected by Peter Wheatstraw: "The
mind that has conceived a plan of living must never lose sight of the chaos
against which that pattern was conceived. That goes for societies as well as
for individuals" (438).

Epilogue

The narrator is now ready for rebirth from his underground hole, a struc-
tural pattern Ellison acknowledges: "I certainly structured it on patterns of
rebirth. That is a pattern that is implicit in tragedy, in the blues, and in

Christian mythology" (O'Brien, 73). Like Christ, the narrator recognizes a connection with the larger community: "There's a possibility that even an invisible man has a socially responsible role to play" (439). More than merely understanding he is part of a whole, he emphasizes that "in spite of all I find that I love" (437).

As the narrator prepares for his rebirth, he affirms again part of the Adamic myth of America, thereby becoming an integrative figure, one who contains or consolidates opposing forces. Recalling his grandfather's cryptic emphasis on "yes," he decides that "yes" is an affirmation of the "principle on which the country was built" (433). Part of that principle is a frontier belief in the individual's unlimited freedom to make what he wishes of his life. He recognizes that he has gone full circle:

Like almost everyone else in our country, I started out with my share of optimism. I believed in hard work and progress and action, but now, after first being "for" society and then "against" it, I assign myself no rank or any limit, and such attitude is very much against the trend of the times. But my world has become one of infinite possibilities. . . . Until some gang succeeds in putting the world in a strait jacket, its definition is possibility. Step outside the narrow borders of what men call reality and you step into chaos—ask Rinehart, he's a master of it—or imagination. (435)

Imagination allows infinite possibilities but avoids chaos for the narrator, who combines a frontier belief in opportunity and simplicity with a mature awareness of complexity, suffering, and brotherhood. At the same time that imagination provides freedom, it creates patterns and gives form to chaos so that one can find that border area between shapelessness and rigidity that in many ways is the real Eden for American writers.[25] In a 1955 *Paris Review* interview, Ellison stated that his writing attempts to achieve a similar goal: "I feel that with my decision to devote myself to the novel I took on one of the responsibilities inherited by those who practice the craft in the United States: that of describing for all that fragment of the huge diverse American experience which I know best, and which offers me the possibility of contributing not only to the growth of the literature but to the shaping of the culture as I should like it to be. The American novel is in this sense a conquest of the frontier; as it describes our experience, it creates it" (*SA*, 183). Similarly, Ellison's narrator, like the American Adam on his way West, is able to conquer the frontier but only after reaching his Christ-like awareness of discord, complexity, community, and love. Then he describes and creates

his version of reality in an affirmative act of writing that connects him with
other heroic figures who make defeat positive:

> Oedipus is defeated and Christ is defeated; they're both defeated in one sense, and
> yet they live. Raskolnikov is defeated; he's found out and sent to Siberia. But
> there's a promise of redemption. . . . You've got an ambiguous movement from de-
> feat to transcendence in those works. Ahab is defeated but Ishmael isn't. Ishmael
> brings back the story and the lesson; he's gone to the underworld and has returned.
> Gatsby ends up dead but the narrator does not; he give us the account. . . . You
> have those ambiguous defeats and survivals which constitute the pattern of all liter-
> ature. (O'Brien, 67)

Theme

Invisible Man exemplifies well the frontier myth. Ellison has said that
"it's a novel about innocence and human error, a struggle through illusion to
reality" (*SA,* 177). Resembling a bildungsroman, the novel first shows the
narrator's blinded innocent belief in a harmonious world of opportunity
(the college, the paint factory, the Brotherhood). Ellison associates the narrator with an American Adam by portraying his naiveté, his desire for
peaceful existence, his belief in material progress and opportunity, his denial
of the past, and by various specific references to Eden. After a series of experiences that challenge the narrator's view of reality (especially his witnessing
Tod Clifton's death and learning about Rinehart's fluidity), the narrator
makes a final underworld journey to knowledge and is then reborn in a
manner that suggests his Christ-like awareness. Throughout the novel,
Ellison hints that the narrator is becoming a Messianic figure—through
Mary and especially through verses of songs that the narrator recalls at important times. At the end of the novel, he is associated with these Christ-like
traits: acceptance of the past, awareness of complexity, commitment to love
and human community. But, finally, he is a composite figure, an amalgamation, for he believes in the individual's existing within a larger community. Through creative use of language, he expresses his individuality and at
the same time plays his "socially responsible role." Retaining individuality,
he reaches out to this larger community through art so that the one and the
many pulsate in creative tension. His final question demonstrates that his
freedom is not solipsistic: "Who knows but that, on the lower frequencies, I
speak for you?" (439).

Other important themes besides the innocence/experience, rebirth,
transformation, and regeneration ones emphasized in the movement from

the innocent Adam toward the composite Adam/Christ are the themes of the concomitant searches for identity, father, mother, and home; social themes relating to the struggle between African Americans and whites; the power of language and humor; the recognition of mutability; and the value of accepting one's past and culture, among others.

Character

One criticism of *Invisible Man* is that Ellison relies on stereotyped or flat characters indicated by tag names—Wrestrum (Restroom), Tobit (Two Bits), Tod (German for "dead"), Hambro (brother to Ham, ancestral tribe of black people), Jack (money, masturbation), Bledsoe (bled so, seeming sacrifice), Trueblood, Ras (race, raze), Mary Rambo (mother), Sybil (sought as oracle), and Rinehart (rind and heart, surface and interior). Some feminists find Ellison's female characters stereotyped, pointing to the nude dancing girl; Jack's girlfriend, Emma; Sybil; and even Mary Rambo as being less fully realized as human beings than male characters like Jim Trueblood and Ras. Carolyn W. Sylvander, for example, charges, "While Ellison uses the artist's skill to depict and explore and evaluate the humanity of Black Men, to thereby confute the effects of stereotyping, he remains blind to the humanity of his women characters."[26] Claudia Tate, on the other hand, believes the women in Ellison's novel—the old slave woman in the Prologue, the naked blond dancer, Mary Rambo, Emma, the anonymous white woman, and Sybil—"assist the Invisible Man along his course to freedom" and "force him to recognize their common plight."[27]

Style

In his acceptance speech for the National Book Award Ellison explained the stylistic effects he sought in the novel. By the time he had begun it, he had been writing book reviews and literary analyses for various publications for almost nine years. He had concluded that the "narrow naturalism" of social protest fiction presented a limited vision of human potential and had rejected the confining understatement of most other twentieth-century writers because it failed to articulate the moral emphasis on democracy Ellison felt was necessary in American literature: "I was to dream of a prose which was flexible, and swift as American change is swift, confronting the inequalities and brutalities of our society forthrightly, but yet thrusting forth its images of hope, human fraternity and individual self-realization. It would use the richness of our speech, the idiomatic expression and the rhetorical flourishes from past periods which are still alive among us" (*SA*, 105). The style he sought required an awareness of the "rich diversity" and "almost magical fluidity and freedom" of American life. The result is the amalgamation of naturalism, expressionism, and surrealism, or magical realism, that is now recognizably Ellisonian.

Structure

In his *Paris Review* interview, Ellison identified a three-part structure of the novel: "I began it with a chart of the three-part division. . . . The three parts represent the narrator's movement from, using Kenneth Burke's terms, purpose to passion to perception" (177). Each of the parts, he continued, "begins with a sheet of paper; each piece of paper is exchanged for another and contains a definition of his identity, or the social role he is to play as defined for him by other" (177). There are several other ways of looking at the structure of the novel. Earlier I pointed to a two-part structure, with the first part of the novel concentrating on the individual and the second half, beginning with the Brotherhood sequence, concerned with the individual's relationship to the larger society. Melvin Dixon says that the novel has a boomerang structure since it begins and ends in the same place.[28] Klein also notes the circular nature of the Prologue and Epilogue and delineates the circularity in the rest of the novel: "Moreover, between the Prologue and the Epilogue, the novel moves in a series of circles—concentric planes of meaning, each traveling right back to its beginning, each mode of adventure confirming the circularity of the hero's voyaging. Each adventure is itself a repetition of each of the others and all the hero's experiences come to the same thing, but from a variety of ways of experiencing. His adventures . . . are historical, marking a journey through a history of America since Emancipation which comes out where it entered" (Klein, 112).

Susan L. Blake develops the historical structure, which Klein pointed out, by noting that each major episode of the novel corresponds to a specific era in African American history:

His sojourn in a southern black college modeled on Tuskegee Institute corresponds to Reconstruction; he has entered it on a scholarship presented in a parody of Emancipation, and he leaves it under compulsion, in the company of a disillusioned World War I veteran, in a manner representative of the Great Migration. His first few weeks in New York . . . contain the elements of the hopeful twenties, when industry was god, self-reliance its gospel, and unionism an exciting heresy. . . . His experience in the Brotherhood reflects the Great Depression, when dispossession was the common complaint and communism the intellectual's cure; his disillusionment with the Brotherhood parallels the general post-Depression retreat from communism. And the riot in which he drops out—of sight, of history, of the novel—suggests the Harlem riot of 1943. (Blake, 126–27)

Byerman concludes that the novel's major sequences—"college experience, life in New York, and the Brotherhood"—are built on a pattern of ideological negation, a "negative dialectic." Each section includes an ideological "position" or thesis that "defines the situation of blacks in a certain way, usually for the purpose of manipulation." Then that ideology (for example, the Brotherhood's) is negated by an accidental experience, the antithesis that "is embodied by a disreputable figure" (Ras, Rinehart). Byerman continues, "The narrator is plunged into a violent surrealistic experience that explodes the opposition he has witnessed. Only after this nightmare does a new statement occur. This statement involves an exploration of history related to social action; implicit in each version of it is a new ideology and thus the next dialectical stage" (Byerman, 12).

Symbol and Image

Invisible Man intrigues scholars because of its wealth of recurring images: blacks fighting blacks in scenes of chaotic violence; underground descents and ascents; oratory; nude women; sight, color, clown, animal, electricity, running, and dancing imagery; the obscene broken bank; chain links (Tarp's worn one is contrasted to a smooth, shiny one on Bledsoe's desk); the briefcase; papers (high school diploma, letters from Bledsoe, new name from Jack, threatening anonymous letter, and ultimately the narrator's autobiography set down in black and white); Brer Rabbit and Brer Bear; hibernation; and others. For Houston Baker, the "black phallus is a dominant symbol in the novel's patterns of behavior," and he defines it "as a symbol of unconstrained force that white men contradictorily envy and seek to destroy" (Baker 1984, 181–82). The fear of the black phallus produces the castration imagery in the battle royal, the Trueblood, and the paint factory hospital machine episodes and the literal castration in the narrator's dream. Moreover, most of the characters bear symbolic value. For example, the narrator, besides suggesting Adam and Christ, resembles Jonah, the prodigal son, Oedipus, Odysseus, Dante, Dostoyevski's underground man, Stephen Dedalus, Ishmael, Huck Finn, Nick Carraway, Lord Raglan's mythic hero, and numerous other literary figures.

Allusion

Ellison's use of literary allusion in *Invisible Man* is so extensive that it receives separate treatment in chapter 4. Allusion allows the integrative power of the imagination to bend tradition to the purposes of the individual talent.

Chapter Four

The Actor's Shadows:
Ellison's Literary Antecedents

In his spirited response to Irving Howe's charge that he had rejected Richard Wright's social protest, Ellison formulated his concept of literary antecedents, saying that "while one can do nothing about choosing one's relatives, one can, as artist, choose one's 'ancestors' " (*SA*, 140). He continued that Richard Wright and Langston Hughes were relatives, while Hemingway, Eliot, Malraux, Dostoyevski, and Faulkner were ancestors, freely chosen as important literary influences. Ellison's synthesizing of varied sources is another aspect of his frontier belief in amalgamation and in his diversity of literary influences, a demonstration of the possibilities of making one out of the many. One of the most fertile areas of Ellison scholarship traces the influence of relatives and ancestors on his work.

Those influences can be broadly grouped into three cultural categories: Western (largely European), mainstream white American, and African American.[1] Ellison's early study of T. S. Eliot led him to the conclusion that literature is the product of previous literature, the tradition, applied by the individual talent. Ellison recognized that as an African American, he was privileged to be able to draw from various traditions. Western culture, especially the Bible, provided a major influence. *Invisible Man* also nods toward Odysseus and Aeneas; to Dante, Shakespeare, and Voltaire; to Dostoyevski, Kierkegaard, Freud, and Joyce. From American literature and culture Ellison has been influenced by Franklin, Cooper, Poe, Emerson, Melville, Twain, Hemingway, Faulkner, and Eliot and by comic books and movies. From African American culture, Ellison has drawn upon folklore, blues, and jazz and the works of Frederick Douglass, Booker T. Washington, W. E. B. Du Bois, James Weldon Johnson, Zora Neale Hurston, and, of course, Richard Wright. But influence points in two directions; a number of later writers have been influenced by Ellison.

Ellison and the European Tradition

Ellison is indebted to the Bible for much of his imagery. Not only does the narrator of *Invisible Man* suggest Adam and Christ, Tod Clifton does as well. The narrator's denial of Peter Wheatstraw, however, suggests Christ's disciple Peter, and his underground journey echoes Daniel in the lion's den and Jonah in the belly of the whale. Douglas Robinson in *American Apocalypses: The Image of the End of the World in American Literature* uses Jonah as the central image in his book and in his analysis of *Invisible Man,* noting that "the novel is plotted around a series of symbolic descents and returns, deaths and rebirths," and the character's ethical growth mirrors Jonah's.[2]

The underworld journey is reminiscent of other classical figures, such as Odysseus and Aeneas, as well. Archie D. Sanders compares *The Odyssey* and *Invisible Man,* pointing out the similar use of the journey structure and the elements in the plot: "The protagonist . . . is an orator and politician, as was Odysseus; he tells his own tale. . . . Odysseus' crafty nature is paralleled by Jack's [the narrator's] ingeniousness. And like Odysseus, who began his journey homeward to Ithaca after the Battle of Troy, Jack begins his trek after the 'battle royal.' "[3] Sanders calls young Emerson a "kind of Circe" who tries to seduce the narrator, the machine sequence "Jack's descent into Hades," and Brother Jack "Cyclopean."

Another specific allusion points to a different masterpiece of classical literature, Virgil's *The Aeneid.* The reference is the character of Sybil, the wife of a prominent Brotherhood official. Because the narrator deliberately seeks out Sybil to provide him information about the Brotherhood's activities in Harlem, she represents for him a kind of oracle, similar to the Cumaean Sybil in the *Aeneid.* The narrator's Sybil, however, can provide no prophecy; rather, she reaffirms his invisibility by seeing him only as a stereotype: the black phallus. Ellison's scene with Sybil, Charles W. Scruggs demonstrates, parodies Virgil:

Aeneas, too, comes to the Sybil for information, for he has been told that he will discover his destiny when she guides him through the Underworld. In the Elysian Fields his father, Anchises, reveals to him that he will be the ancestor of Romulus, the founder of Rome. In his typically outrageous way, Ellison makes a punning allusion to this situation. As Sybil drinks her way into oblivion. . . , the narrator exclaim[s]: "What's happening here . . . a new birth of a nation" (394)? The joke is twofold: not only does Ellison allude to Griffith's famous film about the Reconstruction in which all the racial stereotypes are given a rebirth, but he is also obliquely alluding to the new nation that the Cumaean Sybil makes possible for Aeneas's descendants.[4]

Scruggs also notes Ellison's and Virgil's similar themes of the search for home and desire for reunification of a shattered people. Odysseus and Aeneas contribute to the underworld metaphor, as does Dante. Ellison alludes explicitly to Dante in the Prologue during the narrator's reefer-induced dream when he "descended, like Dante, into its depths" (7). Ronald J. Butler examines the relationship between Ellison and Dante and concludes that Dante provided the elaborate circular structure that Ellison uses: "In fact, the book is made up of an overture, the Battle Royal . . . and nine major episodes, which then serve as variations. This narrative design, therefore, is strikingly similar to that found in the *Inferno*. Each work takes the form of massive inverted cones, then concentric circles arranged in an exact progression to dramatize its central themes."[5] Butler finds similarities between the specific scenes in the two works; the Trueblood episode, for example, "bears close resemblance to Circle Two, where Dante depicts the carnal" (64).

Shakespearean allusions enter in the scene of Tod Clifton's funeral. The narrator's funeral speech draws from Mark Antony's oration at the death of Caesar in *Julius Caesar*. The narrator takes a similar paradoxical approach to Antony's professed purpose of not praising Caesar when his real purpose is the opposite. The narrator suggests to the audience that his speech is purposeless—" 'What are you waiting for me to tell you? . . . What good will it do?' " (343)—when his real purpose is to arouse their indignation. Leonard Deutsch points out that "both orators use a standard device of oratory; the rhetorical refrain, Antony's phrase 'and Brutus is an honorable man,' has its parallel in the invisible man's repeated assertion, 'his name was Clifton (and they shot him).' . . . And both gradually shift to a more emotional appeal; Antony cries: 'My heart is in the coffin there with Caesar' . . . which is perfectly paralleled by the invisible man's lament: 'He's in the box and we're in there with him' " (Deutsch 1989, 99).

Another specific allusion leads to a different European literary influence. When the narrator refers to the college as the "best of all possible worlds," he takes the line from Voltaire's *Candide*. Marcia R. Lieberman notes that both Voltaire's hero and the narrator in Ellison's novel are youthful innocents who undertake picaresque adventures after being "expelled early in life from a paradisaical [*sic*] environment" and who come to similar moral stances: "Like Candide, he [Ellison's narrator] matures into skepticism, avoiding cynicism."[6]

One writer from the Western tradition to whom Ellison has often pointed as an important ancestor is Dostoyevski. He told John Hersey that Dostoyevski made him aware of "what is possible in depicting a society in which class lines either are fluid or have broken down without the cultural style and values on either extreme of society being dissipated" (Hersey 1987, 297). Through Dostoyevski, according to Joseph Frank, Ellison recognized that the tension between the aristocracy and peasants in nineteenth-century Russia corresponded to the relationship between American whites and blacks.[7] That interest led Ellison to Dostoyevski's *Notes from Underground,* which provided not only the underground metaphor, but, as Robert Bone indicates, some fundamental attitudes about theme: "In exploring the lower depths of human personality, Dostoyevski poses questions about the nature of reality, the meaning of social responsibility, and the limit of human possibility, all of which are pursued with lively interest in *Invisible Man.* Both authors, moreover, share a central concern with individuality, with that which enables man to insist upon himself in the face of all rational systems."[8] Dostoyevski's underground man articulated a view of the world labeled absurd by twentieth-century existential philosophers, and *Invisible Man* confronts absurdity and suggests existential themes as well.[9] But the narrator's allusion to Soren Kierkegaard in the Prologue points to Ellison's optimism: "All sickness is not unto death, neither is invisibility" (11).

Ellison's own brand of existentialism came more directly from André Malraux. On his second day in New York, he learned of Malraux when Langston Hughes asked him to return two borrowed Malraux novels, and Ellison heard Malraux appeal for aid to the Spanish loyalists "at the same party where I first heard the folk singer Leadbelly perform" (*SA,* 163). He came to Malraux when Marxism beckoned, and Malraux was supposedly a Marxist writer, but he found, as he noted in the *Paris Review* interview, something else: "I was intrigued by Malraux, who at that time was being claimed by the Communists. I noticed, however, that whenever the heroes of *Man's Fate* regarded their condition during moments of heightened self-consciousness, their thinking was something other than Marxist" (*SA,* 168–69). Impressed by *Man's Fate,* he had his Modern Library edition bound in leather (*GT,* 294).

Ultimately Malraux lead him beyond politics: "When Malraux drew upon revolution as the settings for his novel, he drew for his real themes upon much deeper levels of his characters' consciousness than their concern with Marxism; and it is to these deeper concerns, to the realm of tragedy, that they turned when facing death" (*GT,* 297). Malraux's interest in "the individual caught up consciously in a historical situation, a revolutionary situation" helped him to assess his own fictional material. "From him," he continued, "I learned that the condition of that type of individual is essentially the same, regardless of his culture or the political climate in which he finds his existence" (Hersey 1987, 297). Deutsch notes that both writers "explore the conflict between destiny and free will, fate and individual volition. Both speculate about values in an absurd universe and about achieving meaning and dignity in life" (Deutsch 1989, 100).

Finally, and perhaps most significant, from Malraux Ellison learned the power of art to give shape to chaos. In "Richard Wright's Blues" Ellison quotes Malraux: "The organized significance of art is stronger than all the multiplicity of the world; . . . that significance alone enables man to conquer chaos and to master destiny" (*SA,* 83). In fact, according to Rudolf Dietze, Ellison's emphasis on the primacy of art was shaped by Ellison's early reading of Malraux's *The Psychology of Art.* Dietze concludes that Ellison "quotes, echoes, and paraphrases Malraux in almost everything that he writes."[10]

Another important literary ancestor is James Joyce. Ellison has called his novel "a portrait of the artist as rabble-rouser" (*SA,* 197). In his *Paris Review* interview he said that he began to learn how to use myth and ritual from reading "Eliot, Joyce and Hemingway": "When I started writing, I knew that in both *The Waste Land* and *Ulysses* ancient myth and ritual were used to give form and significance to the material; but it took me a few years to realize that the myths and rites which we find functioning in our everyday lives could be used in the same way" (*SA,* 174). Ellison mentions (and puns on) Joyce explicitly in the novel, as the narrator recalls having studied Joyce and Yeats with Professor Woodridge at the college and the professor's revision of Joyce: " 'Stephen's problem, like ours, was not actually one of creating the uncreated conscience of his race, but of creating the *uncreated features of his face*' " (268).

Robert N. List believes that Joyce's influence was so pervasive in Ellison's work that List devoted a book to the subject: *Dedalus in Harlem: The Joyce-Ellison Connection.*[11] List finds numerous Joycean connections of imagery, language, and theme. The birdlike girl whom Stephen sees on the beach in *A Portrait of the Artist as a Young Man,* for example, seems to have influenced Ellison's imagery. The nude dancing girl in the battle royal scene is described as being "like a fair bird-girl girdled in veils calling to me from the angry surface of some gray and threatening sea" (*IM,* 16). List also attributes to Joyce Ellison's sight imagery, Odysseus references, and "Joycean words such as 'confused,' 'confess,' 'apologize,' 'betrayal,' 'wake,' and 'hesitate,' words that all reinforce the invisibility theme" (List, 65). In fact, in List's rather overstated view, almost all of the major themes—invisibility, the mechanization of modern life, and the search for the father—come from Joyce's influence.

In addition to the fact that Ellison read Joyce, one reason for similarity between Joyce and Ellison results from the two writers' working with similar influences, such as classical myth and Freud. Ellison read Freud as a student at Tuskegee and again as an aide to psychologist Harry Stack Sullivan shortly after his arrival in New York. Freud appears directly in *Invisible Man:* when the narrator enters young Mr. Emerson's office, he sees an "open book, something called *Totem and Taboo*" (137), on the table. Freud's *Totem and Taboo,* written in 1912 and 1913, contains many of the Freudian ideas that appear in *Invisible Man:* the search for the father, the Oedipus complex, societal rituals, and taboos (against incest, for example). A pun on Freud's id-ego-superego triumvirate gives the name to the vets' keeper, Supercargo. Perhaps Ellison was drawn to Freud's concept of the ego's mediating between the opposing forces of id and superego as he formulated his own approach to duality and oppositions.

Anther significant influence that Ellison has acknowledged is Lord Raglan, noting that he was "reading *The Hero* by Lord Raglan and speculating on the nature of Negro leadership in the United States" (*SA,* 177) when he wrote the first paragraph of *Invisible Man.* In *The Hero* Lord Raglan analyzes various heroic figures and develops a 22-point pattern of heroic characteristics and then grades such heroes as Oedipus, Romulus, Perseus, Dionysus, Apollo, Moses, King Arthur, and Robin Hood on how fully they fit the pattern.[12] Lawrence J. Clipper applies Lord Raglan's pattern to Ellison. While he finds little correspondence between the first six and last five items in Raglan's list of 22 items common to mythic heroes, Clipper finds many other parallels. John S. Wright calls Ellison's narrator a "thoroughgoing mock-heroic counterpart to Lord Raglan's hero of tradition."[13] Wright suggests that Ellison was drawn to a minor figure in Raglan's array of characters: the Spielman, "a figure half-trickster, half-devil, who, like the Norse God Loki, is the sacred plotter and wily father of artifice who sets the conflict in motion and drags the demons and giants toward their ultimate defeat" (Wright 1988, 163). The Prologue's singer of spirituals, Peter Wheatstraw (a "demonic spielman"), Trueblood, the old vet, and Tod Clifton lead the narrator to legitimate heroes, Frederick Douglass and especially Louis Armstrong.

American Culture

Ellison draws from numerous mainstream American writers, from comic books, and from film in a variety of ways from brief suggestions to extensive and direct allusions. His allusions to writers in the American canon are so comprehensive that two books concentrate on Ellison and the American tradition: Valerie Bonita Gray's *Invisible Man's Literary Heritage: Benito Cereno and Moby-Dick*[14] and Alan Nadel's *Invisible Criticism: Ralph Ellison and the American Canon.* While Gray's is a rather superficial comparison of Ellison and Melville, Nadel provides a general analysis of the effect of allusion in a literary work. Drawing from and taking issue with Northrop Frye, Harold Bloom, Jacques Derrida, George Steiner, and others, Nadel attempts to establish his point that writers such as Ellison alter the meaning of allusions when they become part of the fabric of their work.

Brief allusions to Benjamin Franklin's *Autobiography* appear in *Invisible Man.* As he experiments with electricity, the narrator describes himself as being in the "great American tradition of tinkers. That makes me kin to Ford, Edison and Franklin. Call me, since I have a theory and a concept, a 'thinker-tinker' " (6). Franklin's autobiography is a model of the first-person story of a young person's movement from innocence to experience, and Franklin established the fundamentals of the American dream of success toward which Ellison's young narrator initially works. Franklin's emphasis on appearance over reality no doubt interested Ellison as well. Shortly before his expulsion from college, the narrator recalls walking past a bakery stuffing "rolls dripping with yellow butter" (105) into his pocket, an image that suggests young Ben Franklin's arrival in Philadelphia. Later in New York, the young narrator decides that the only way he can succeed is to reject "c.p. (colored people's) time": "I would have to get a watch. I would do everything to schedule" (125). Franklin's schedule, of course, led to Fitzgerald's subtle parody in *The Great Gatsby,* where the young Jay Gatz wrote his schedule (which included studying electricity) on the inside back cover of *Hopalong Cassidy.*

Another brief allusion may recall Ellison's reading of James Fenimore Cooper, a major creator of the American frontier myth. Ellison acknowledged reading *The Last of the Mohicans* ten times. As Phyllis R. Klotman suggests, Ellison's emphasis on the power of names—and namelessness—may draw from Cooper. Although Cooper's hero had the unglamorous name of Natty Bumppo, throughout his long literary career Bumppo, following Indian tradition, achieved several different names, each one indicating a new identity: Deerslayer, Hawkeye, Leatherstocking, the old Trapper, *la long Carbine* (Klotman, 280).

A direct punning reference to Edgar Allan Poe appears in the novel's opening lines. After the narrator asserts that he is an invisible man, he says that he is "not a spook like those who haunted Edgar Allan Poe" (3). The pun is on *spook,* a derogatory name for an African American, as well as a reference to ghosts and spirits. But as Mary F. Sisney notes, the narrator is also asserting that he is not like the black people who haunted Poe: "[Ellison's narrator] is not, for instance, like the jet black, wooly-haired savages found on that all-black island in *The Narrative of Arthur Gordon Pym.* To Pym, these blacks 'appeared to be the most wicked, hypocritical, vindictive, bloodthirsty, and altogether fiendish race of men upon the face of the globe.' "[15] Sisney also concludes that when the narrator sees Mr. Norton as that "formless white death" (*IM,* 66), Ellison alludes to Poe who had depicted a white death in *Arthur Gordon Pym,* and Mr. Norton's unnatural attraction for his dead daughter recalls Poe, who asserted in "The Philosophy of Composition" that the death of a beautiful woman is the most poetical of subjects.

The nineteenth-century American writer with whom Ellison has the most ambivalent relationship is Ralph Waldo Emerson. Part of the ambivalence results from the fact that Ellison's father had named Ellison for Emerson, a circumstance that made him "uncomfortable" and caused him "much puzzlement" (*SA,* 150–51). Yet ultimately Ellison realized that "I cannot escape the obligation of attempting to achieve some of the things which he asked of the American writer" (*SA,* 166). Another reason for the ambivalence derives from Ellison's awareness of the difference between Emerson's interpreters and Emerson himself. In a letter to Alan Nadel, Ellison made the distinction clear: "Rather than go after Emerson's oracular stance, I went after some of the bombast that has been made of his pronouncements. . . . It might help if you pointed up the distinction you make between my trustee 'Emerson' and ole Waldo; who strikes me, incidentally, as being as difficult to pin down as the narrator's grandfather" (Nadel, 159). A similar ambivalence emerges in the novel as Emerson, who appears directly and indirectly, receives negative and positive treatment.

The direct reference to Emerson comes from Mr. Norton who associates himself with Emerson when he tells the narrator: " 'I am a New Englander, like Emerson. You must learn about him, for he was important to your people. He had a hand in your destiny' " (32). Because Norton is portrayed negatively, Emerson's name in this context is also unfavorable; the negative associations are reinforced by the characters named Emerson. Although Mr.

Emerson, Sr., never appears, he represents the twentieth-century capitalist version of Emersonian individualism, and his son is a debased version of Emersonian idealism. Nadel concludes that the negative allusions to Emerson force "us to see Emerson's inability to recognize evil, his blindness to the complicated form it takes in the actual world. One consequence of that failing in his philosophy is that it is easily adapted by intentionally manipulative people" (Nadel, 116).

Another negative association with Emerson comes from Brother Jack's single eye, which suggests a connection between the Brotherhood and Emerson. Jack's one-eyed vision recalls Emerson's famous "transparent eyeball" statement in "Nature": "Standing on the bare ground,—my head bathed by the blithe air, and uplifted into infinite space,—all mean egotism vanishes. I become a transparent eyeball; I am nothing; I see all."[16] Brother Jack, like Emerson, believes history is progressing toward a utopian future; the individual must get in touch with the power moving history onward. (For Emerson the power was the "divine necessity"; for Jack, the Brotherhood.) Both men's idealism results in an unwillingness to act on behalf of suffering humanity. For example, Emerson, in "Ode Inscribed to W. E. Channing," refuses to work for political reform, especially abolition:

> I cannot leave
> My honied thought
> For the priest's cant,
> Or statesman's rant.

And Ellison characterizes Emerson's attitude toward the fugitive slave law as intellectual evasion (*SA*, 36).

Despite these negative characterizations, Ellison ultimately embraces some Emersonian ideas. Deutsch finds that the "Emersonian realization of the Emersonian potential within the protagonist himself is one of the novel's major thematic concerns."[17] Deutsch concludes that Ellison adopted his Adam and Christ imagery from Emerson, for whom "Christ is not literally God, but a symbol of the greatness in man," and the narrator must learn that he "can only find 'Jesus' or 'God' when he looks inside of himself" (Deutsch 1972, 162). David Vanderworken also believes that Ellison upholds Emerson and sees the novel's Epilogue as "Ellison's reaffirmation of Emersonian self-reliance."[18]

While Ellison demonstrates ambivalence toward Emerson, he embraces Melville as a literary ancestor with an epigraph from *Benito Cereno*: " 'You are saved,' cried Captain Delano, more and more astonished and pained;

'you are saved: what has cast such a shadow upon you?' " Although Ellison
leaves out the answer—"the Negro"—he seems to have selected the epigraph to suggest the complex relationship between whites and blacks resulting from slavery and to indicate his debt to Melville. In his essays
Ellison has often praised Melville as one of the nineteenth-century American writers who "took a moral responsibility for democracy" and who represented African Americans in the broadest possible way—"as a symbol of
Man" (SA, 32).

Besides the epigraph, other allusions to *Benito Cereno* appear. The
Golden Day episode, Nadel notes, offers several comparisons: "Like 'Benito
Cereno,' the Golden Day chapter contains an uprising of enslaved blacks, in
which they overthrow their oppressors and take part in a few moments of
ultimately futile chaos. Their overseer, furthermore, bears the name
'Supercargo,' which is the title for the financial overseer on a ship" (Nadel,
105). Additionally, the enervated Norton, who "represents the old order,"
compares with Melville's weakened Spanish captain, the vets with the
slaves, and Melville's innocent American Captain Amaso Delano with
Ellison's innocent narrator. Both books therefore criticize "American blindness masked as American optimism" (Nadel, 105).

Direct allusions to *Moby Dick* also appear, beginning with the preacher's
subject of the "blackness of blackness" in the narrator's reefer-induced
dream. In fact, Ellison's novel is frequently compared with *Moby Dick* to
suggest its profundity and impact. O'Meally notes: "Like *Moby Dick, Invisible Man* is a capacious novel, one that tries many things: Both are rhetorical
tours de force containing letters, sermons, fights, songs, political speeches,
dreams, and descriptions of private homes, meeting halls, offices, brothels,
bars, and churches" (O'Meally 1988, 2). Ellison echoes Melville's famous
first line with his now almost equally famous, "I am an invisible man" and
later with "Call me Jack-the-Bear."

Gray finds four major themes that connect *Moby Dick* and *Invisible
Man:* democracy, individuality, alienation, and ambiguity. Additionally,
Gray notes that both use white and black color imagery, with Ellison revers-
ing Melville (Gray, 58). Elizabeth A. Schultz takes her comparisons to a
deeper level and finds fundamental similarities: "It may be postulated that
Melville in *Moby Dick* saw reality as broadly complex for three fundamental
reasons—its multiplicity, its mutability, and its ambiguity—and that conditions of American life exacerbated this complexity; in *Invisible Man*
Ellison confirms Melville's perception of reality. As reflected in *Moby Dick*
and again in *Invisible Man,* American democracy intensifies these conditions of reality by establishing possibilities for diversity, by promoting

change, and by failing to rectify the discrepancy between the actuality of life in America and its central ideals."[19] Schultz notes more similarities: both novels have a youthful narrator "who leaves an idyllic, limited, known place to journey into a dangerous, complex and unknown universe," and both use catalogs, sight imagery, diversity of rhetorical forms, oxymoronic language, and ascent and descent imagery.

In an interview Ellison explained his view of Ahab as a tragic hero who moved "beyond the concern with simply slaughtering whales for their food and oil value" and began to pursue the whale as "the inscrutable nature of existence, of man's relationship to the total scheme." In his pursuit Ahab "discovers his true relationship to nature" and that "he could not impose his will upon nature." But "Ahab as a tragic hero is sure to be destroyed because he has gone beyond the point where the individual can impose his will upon the chaos of the world" (Geller, 161). Ellison's narrator in *Invisible Man* ultimately understands the delicate balance of possibility, chaos, individual will, and societal responsibility; these are "moral" conclusions that prepare him to reenter society.

Another nineteenth-century American romantic writer whose presence is felt in *Invisible Man,* particularly the college section, is Walt Whitman. When the narrator first recalls the campus, the repetitive language echoes Whitman: "Oh long green stretch of campus, Oh, quiet songs at dusk, Oh, moon that kissed the steeple and flooded the perfumed nights, Oh, bugle that called in the morning, Oh, drum that marched us militarily at noon" (28–29). Whitmanian language appears again in Homer Barbee's encomium to the college founder, specifically allusions to Whitman's "When Lilacs Last in the Dooryard Bloom'd." The major symbols from Whitman's poem—lilacs, the star, a solitary singer, the funeral train—reappear in Barbee's speech.[20] On his way to the speech, the narrator recalls that he "moved slow through the dusk so restless with scents of lilac" (85). During his speech Barbee recalls the founder's final "slow, sorrowful" train ride while the "looming great North Star" shimmers (99). His death recalls "the dark night of slavery" and "their majestic sun snatched behind a cloud" (101). The solitary singer is not a thrush but a "thin brown girl" whose "voice seemed to become a disembodied force that sought to enter her" (90). By recalling Whitman's elegy to Lincoln, whose death meant that Reconstruction would prove a farce, Ellison reinforces the historical allegory about reconstruction that underpins the college section.

The nineteenth-century writer who dramatized Reconstruction's failure as it happened was Mark Twain, and it is no surprise to find Twain is a strong influence. Part of Ellison's interest in Twain comes from similar frontier connections. Ellison's second essay collection title, *Going to the Territory*, recalls Huck's decision to "light out for the Territory ahead." By looking to the frontier, Twain, according to Ellison, extended his style: "Twain, seeking for what Melville called 'the common continent of man,' drew upon the rich folklore of the frontier (not omitting the Negro's) in order to 'Americanize' his idiom, thus broadening his stylistic appeal" (*SA*, 35).

In fact, in a 1946 essay written when Ellison was at work on *Invisible Man*, he finds frontier mythology at the heart of *The Adventures of Huckleberry Finn*. Huck's decision to tear up his letter and steal Jim out of slavery is "a key point of the novel and, by an ironic reversal, of American fiction" because it presents "the basic moral issue centering around Negroes and the white American's democratic ethics. It dramatizes as well the highest point of tension generated by the clash between the direct, human relationships of the frontier and the abstract, inhuman, market-dominated relationships fostered by the rising middle-class—which in Twain's day was already compromising dangerously with the most inhuman aspects of the defeated slave system" (*SA*, 31).

Additionally Ellison finds that *Huck Finn* presents the frontier dialectic in ambiguous conflict because Huck "embodies the two major conflicting drives operating in nineteenth-century America. And if humanism is man's basic attitude toward a social order which he accepts, and individualism his basic attitude toward one he rejects, one might say that Twain, by allowing these two attitudes to argue dialectically in his work of art, was as highly moral an artist as he was a believer in democracy, and vice versa" (*SA*, 33–34).

Direct allusion to Twain comes in the scene between young Mr. Emerson and the narrator, although, as Nadel suggests, the references to Huck Finn in this scene may allude more to Leslie Fiedler's infamous essay, "Come Back to the Raft Ag'in, Huck Honey!" than to Twain's novel. A decade later Ellison commented on Fiedler's suggestion of a homoerotic relationship between Huck and Jim: "I believe him [Fiedler] so profoundly disturbed by the manner in which the deep dichotomies symbolized by blackness and whiteness are resolved that, forgetting to look at the specific form of the novel, he leaped squarely into the middle of that tangle of symbolism which he is dedicated to unsnarling, and yelled out his most terrifying name for chaos. Other things being equal, he might have called it 'rape,' 'incest,' 'parricide' or 'miscegenation' " (*SA*, 51). Ellison's awareness of Fiedler's thesis is indicated by his making young Mr. Emerson a homosexual who "moves with a long hip-swinging stride" (137) and attempts to seduce the narrator by saying that he wants to be "Huckleberry" to the narrator's Jim. The narrator's rejection of young Mr. Emerson's job offer to become his valet suggests Ellison's rejection of Fiedler's thesis; for Ellison Twain's novel is too complex to be reduced to Fiedler's terms.

Other specific allusions to *The Adventures of Huckleberry Finn* appear in *Invisible Man*. Nadel points to similarities between the paint factory episode and the fog scene in Twain's novel. As the narrator approaches the paint factory, he comments three times on the fog he has to pass through to get there. Both scenes suggest an ending: Huck and Jim pass Cairo and the Ohio River in the fog and lose Jim's dream of freedom in the North; the paint factory means the end of the narrator's attempts to achieve the traditional American dream. Nadel also notes similarities between the violent conclusions of the two scenes: the sinking of the raft and the explosion in the paint factory.[21] These specific allusions indicate how Ellison aligned himself with those nineteenth-century writers who, Ellison believed, made the novel a moral force for democratic values.

In contrast, Ellison has often attacked the lack of moral commitment among twentieth-century American writers. He is particularly ambivalent about Ernest Hemingway. In fact, Ellison's attitude toward Hemingway seems to have gone through three distinct periods. In his early work, he emulated Hemingway's style; then he rejected Hemingway's understatement and apparent denial of democratic principles; and finally he concluded that Hemingway was a writer who affirmed the ideals of liberty and democracy.

Ellison was first drawn to Hemingway's style by reading his stories "in the Negro barbershops, and the pages of *Esquire* magazine" back in Oklahoma City.[22] Enthralled, he "read him to learn his sentence structure and how to organize a story" (*SA,* 168), and, as Franklin did with Addison and Steele's essays, Ellison copied Hemingway's stories in longhand "in an effort to study their rhythms, so as not just to know them but to possess them."[23] As Ellison formulated his style, he questioned Hemingway's understatement, particularly for African American literature. In a 1940 review of Langston Hughes's autobiography *The Big Sea,* Ellison praised Hughes for emphasizing the "crystallized folk experience of the blues, spirituals, and folk tales" but criticized him for understatement and urged Hughes to "tell us more of how he felt and thought." Ellison continued, "To be effective the Negro writer must be explicit; thus realistic; thus dramatic."[24]

By the time he wrote "Twentieth Century Fiction and the Black Mask of Humanity" in 1946, Ellison had revised his opinion and concluded that Hemingway, by ignoring black characters and by depending on understatement, was, like Emerson, guilty of "intellectual evasion." By elevating style over democratic values, Hemingway demonstrated "a gross insensitivity to fraternal values" (*SA*, 35) and along with other twentieth-century "hard-boiled" writers retreated into "technical perfection rather than moral insight. . . . Instead of recreating and extending the national myth as he did this, the writer now restricted himself to elaborating his personal myth" (*SA*, 38).

By 1957, Ellison had again revised his opinion of Hemingway. In "Society, Morality, and the Novel" Ellison restated his general opinion that American writers of the 1920s were guilty of "moral irresponsibility" through the "revolution of the word" (*GT*, 254) and that they romanticized the "brave lonely man, broken by war and betrayed by politicians—who had lost faith in everything except the basic processes of existence and his own physical strength" (*GT*, 255). In Hemingway, though, Ellison discovered a paradox and found that Hemingway "affirms the old American values by the eloquence of his denial; makes his moral point by stating explicitly that he does not believe in morality; achieves his eloquence through denying eloquence; and is most moral when he denies the validity of a national morality which the nation has not bothered to live up to since the Civil War" (*GT*, 255–56). The fault lay not in Hemingway, according to Ellison, but in his readers who failed to feel the despair at the loss of American democratic ideals beneath the surface of his understated words.

By 1963 Ellison's admiration for Hemingway had returned full force; he explained to Irving Howe that Hemingway was an ancestor and Wright merely a relative because Hemingway's work was "imbued with a spirit beyond the tragic with which I could feel at home, for it was very close to the feeling of the blues, which are, perhaps, as close as Americans can come to expressing the spirit of tragedy." Most important, "Hemingway was a greater artist than Wright, who although a Negro like myself, and perhaps a great man, understood little if anything of these, at least to me, important things. Because Hemingway loved the American language and the joy of writing, making the flight of birds, the loping of lions across an African plain, the mysteries of drink and moonlight, the unique styles of diverse peoples and individuals come alive on the page. Because he was in many ways the true father-as-artist of so many of us who came to writing during the late thirties" (*SA*, 141).

The relationship between Hemingway's view of life and the blues is apparent in *The Sun Also Rises*, in which, Ellison said, Jake Barnes becomes a blues singer comparable to Trueblood by telling the story of his experiences: "Ball-less, humiliated, malicious, even masochistic, he still has a steady eye upon it all and has the most eloquent ability to convey the texture of the experience" (O'Brien, 68). For Ellison, Hemingway's work recalls both blues and jazz, especially jazz as an amalgamated, assimilative art: "You hear references to opera, to church music, to anything, in something by Louis Armstrong or any other jazzman of the thirties, forties, and fifties. So this acquaintance with jazz made me quite aware that allusions to ideas and to other works of art were always turning up in Hemingway" (Garrett, 224).

Although *Invisible Man* was written when Ellison questioned Hemingway's moral commitment, Hemingway allusions such as the bullfight painting on the wall of the bar where the narrator and Brother Jack discuss the Brotherhood and other Hemingway echoes appear in the novel. O'Meally suggests that the narrator, as well as the main characters of Ellison's short stories, is "an intelligent and sensitive youngster, a brown-skinned cousin of Nick Adams, straining toward manhood in a world full of the blues." O'Meally also notes that some of *Invisible Man*'s metaphors correspond to Hemingway's work, "notably the metaphors of life as a war, a game or a fight (or a prizefight, or even a bullfight)—life as an encounter between the individual and the forces set against him." Ultimately Ellison's narrator, like Hemingway's initiates, "learns at last to confront his experience directly, and he earns the perspective that it takes to do what Jake Barnes can do—to tell his troubling tale with the force and eloquence of an artist" (O'Meally 1987, 255–56).

Gerald Gordon notes similarities between Ellison's rhetorical techniques in the Tod Clifton death and funeral scenes and Hemingway's approach in *The Sun Also Rises,* particularly the language concerning the death of Vicente Girones during the running of the bulls. Both use "a dispassionate, reportorial style that conveys a heightened emotion without tricks; a solemn, dirge-like tone throughout; an overloading of run-on sentences connected mainly by 'and' to approximate the uninterrupted flow of time and experience; and a heavy reliance on nouns which suggest 'things' in the phenomenal world."[25]

While Ellison eventually resolved his ambivalence toward Hemingway, throughout his career he has maintained a mixed attitude toward William Faulkner. On one hand, he found that Faulkner too often created stereotyped African Americans characters, blacks who fulfilled southern cardboard images: "Taking his cue from the Southern mentality in which the Negro is often dissociated into a malignant stereotype (the bad nigger) on the one hand and a benign stereotype (the good nigger) on the other, most often Faulkner presents characters embodying both." The purpose of this "dissociation," Ellison continues, "seems to be that of avoiding moral pain and thus to justify the South's racial code" (*SA,* 42). But Ellison recognizes that the "sensitive Southerner, the artist, is apt to feel its effects acutely" and to realize that the "social order harms whites no less than blacks." Despite Faulkner's reliance on stereotypes, Ellison credits him with being one of the few twentieth-century writers who continue the nineteenth-century emphasis on morally responsible literature: "Faulkner fights out the moral problem which was repressed after the nineteenth century. . . . Thus we must turn to him for that continuity of moral purpose which made for the greatness of our classics" (*SA*, 43).

Faulkner's greatness is especially apparent, Ellison wrote in 1946, in "The Bear," published in *Go Down, Moses. Go Down, Moses* depends on frontier mythology more than any other Faulkner work, except perhaps *Absalom, Absalom!* and with Sam Fathers Faulkner dramatized the similarity between the African American and native American experience, for Fathers is part black and part Indian. In the story Faulkner "brings us as close to the moral implication of the Negro as Twain or Melville. In the 'difficult' fourth section . . . we find an argument in progress in which one voice (that of a Southern abolitionist) seeks to define Negro humanity against the other's enumeration of those stereotypes which many Southerners believe to be the Negro's basic traits. Significantly, the mentor of the young hero of this story, a man of great moral stature, is socially a Negro" (*SA*, 43).

A decade later, in "Society, Morality, and the Novel," Ellison reaffirmed his high regard for "The Bear," calling it "one of the most sublime stories in the language" (*GT*, 261). In *Go Down, Moses*, Ellison concludes, "Faulkner comes most passionately to grips with the moral implications of slavery, the American land, progress and materialism, tradition and moral identity—all major themes of the American novel." With Ike McCaslin, who represents "a form of Christian humanism," Faulkner "demonstrates one way in which the individual American can assert his freedom from the bonds of history, tradition, and things, and thus achieve moral identity" (*GT*, 270). These comments make it clear that Faulkner's story of a youthful, Adamic innocent who undergoes a transformation in the wilderness after witnessing the death of a shamanistic mentor profoundly affected the broad outline of Ellison's own novel. Faulkner's language of overstatement, in contrast to the enervated understatement of the "narrow naturalists," also influenced Ellison. Southern language is "broader" (*GT*, 67) and allows for a fuller range of expression.

Nowhere is Faulkner's influence on Ellison's language more apparent than in chapter 5 during the appearance of Homer Barbee, who recalls Faulkner's Reverend Shegog in *The Sound and the Fury*, whose "voice consumed him, until he was nothing."[26] In the chapel the narrator looks at the millionaires "come down to portray themselves, not merely acting out the myth of their goodness, and wealth and success and power and benevolence and authority in cardboard masks, but themselves, these virtues concretely!" And he thinks of the others—"those who had set me here in this Eden, whom we knew though we didn't know, who were unfamiliar in their familiarity, who trailed their words to us through blood and violence and ridicule and condescension with drawling smiles, and who exhorted and threatened, intimidated with innocent words as they described to us the limitations of our lives and the vast boldness of our aspirations" (87). The rhetorical devices—repetition, parallelism, and antithesis—owe much to Faulkner, and, as Michael Allen concludes, Faulkner provided Ellison with models of characters whose interior language allowed them to achieve a level of consciousness necessary to confront profound moral questions.[27]

Of all of the canonical writers who influenced Ellison, perhaps the most important is T. S. Eliot.[28] "The Waste Land," as Ellison has said repeatedly, seized his imagination and set him off to the Tuskegee library, where he trailed Eliot's allusions to their sources. Eliot, like Twain, a midwesterner close to the "strong brown god" of the Mississippi River, led Ellison to understand the relationship between the individual artist and the tradition. In his essay "Tradition and the Individual Talent," Eliot emphasizes that artists do not slavishly follow previous writers but bend them to their purposes: "Yet if the only form of tradition, of handing down, consisted in following the ways of the immediate generation before us in a blind or timid adherence to its successes, 'tradition' should positively be discouraged." What is required, Eliot continues, is to develop "the historical sense," which "compels a man to write not merely with his own generation in his bones, but with a feeling that the whole of the literature of Europe" and which "is a sense of the timeless as well as of the temporal and of the timeless and of the temporal together. . . ."[29]

Ellison's historical analysis of American literature corresponds with one aspect of Eliot's analysis of British literary history as well. When Eliot examined British poetry in "The Metaphysical Poets," he decided that a historical discontinuity, a "dissociation of sensibility," began in the seventeenth century and that later poetry suffered a loss of coherence between thought and feeling. Similarly, Ellison finds a comparable historical discontinuity in early twentieth-century American writers, whose works are "dissociated" from the moral purpose that characterized nineteenth-century American tradition. Ellison's purpose therefore was to reestablish the tradition, to fuse the timeless and the temporal.

To achieve his goal, Eliot wove literary allusions into the fabric of his work. Ellison adopted this strategy but reconceived allusion in his own cultural terms. When Steve Cannon asked him about a reference to Frederick Douglass in *Invisible Man,* Ellison responded: "That's *allusion,* that's riffing. When you put a detail in its proper place in an action, it gathers up associations and meaning and starts speaking to the reader's sense of significance. Just as it spoke to *you* as you struggled to give order to your material. Placed in the right context, and at the optimum stage of an action, it vibrates and becomes symbolically eloquent. That's poetry, I mean, in the larger sense of the term."[30] (Riffing is a jazz technique where an artist improvises upon another artist's musical leitmotif until it takes new shapes and creates new sounds. In this way the artist achieves the presentness of the past.)

Speaking with West Point graduates in 1969, Ellison explained the connection between Eliot and jazz:

Now, the jazz musician, the jazz soloist, is anything if not eclectic. He knows his rhythms; he knows the tradition of his form, so to speak; and he can draw upon an endless pattern of sounds which he recombines on the spur of the moment into a meaningful musical experience, if he's successful. And I had a sense that all of these references of Eliot's, all of this snatching of phrases from the German, from the French, from the Sanskrit, and so on, were attuned to that type of American cultural expressiveness which one got in jazz and which one still gets in good jazz. (*GT,* 40)

Through Eliot, Ellison developed literary riffing as a broad concept and as a specific practice, and Ellison riffs on Eliot in a variety of ways in *Invisible Man.* He makes his debt to Eliot clear with an epigraph that emphasizes the invisibility theme and sight imagery by quoting Harry from Eliot's *Family Reunion:*

> I tell you, it is not me you are looking at,
> Not me you are grinning at, not me your confidential looks
> Incriminate, but that other person, if person
> You thought I was: let your necrophily
> Feed upon that carcase [*sic*].

In the Prologue, when the narrator says that "the end is in the beginning and lies far ahead" (5), he restates Eliot's opening line, "In my beginning is my end" from "East Coker" of the *Four Quartets.* Allusions to "The Waste Land" are especially apparent. The college has "no fountain but one that was broken, corroded and dry"; "no rain" falls on "the hard dry crust of the still so recent past"; and no "odor or seed burst[s] in springtime, only the yellow contents of the cistern spread over the lawn's dead grass" in the school's "flower-studded wasteland" (29). Eliot's famous line "O O O O that Shakespeherian Rag" reappears as "oh, oh, oh, those multimillionaires!"

Dietze finds comparisons between Ellison's narrator and Eliot's statements about Tiresias as the main character of "The Waste Land": "For Tiresias, the message is give, sympathize, control; in *Invisible Man,* the hero comes to the insight that 'Life is to be lived, not controlled' " (Dietze, *Genesis,* 109). Mary Ellen Williams Walsh finds several other parallels, pointing out the similarities between the Founder's impotence and the Fisher King, the one-eyed Brother Jack and Eliot's one-eyed Smyrna merchant, symbolic deaths by water, and similar conclusions: "Just as *The Waste Land* closes with the ancient answers for the restoration of the Fisher King's domain, the Epilogue to *Invisible Man* contains the answers the protagonist finds for the revitalization of America and the restoration of humanity to black people."[31] The figure needed to restore Eliot's waste land is a Christ-like hero; Ellison's narrator becomes one.

Ellison draws widely from various American culture sources besides literature, music, and folklore—including comic book and movie references. The narrator's pun, "I yam what I am," not only recalls the biblical passage from Exodus (3:14) in which God tells Moses, "I am that I am," but it also echoes Popeye the Sailor. At Tod Clifton's funeral, the narrator says, " 'The blood ran like blood in a comic-book killing, on a comic-book street in a comic-book town on a comic-book day in a comic-book world' " (345). Movie references appear early after the narrator gets to New York, as he plans to be "*charming.* Like Ronald Colman" [*sic*] (125). Peter Wheatstraw, the significant clown, has "Charlie Chaplin pants" (132). The factory machine sequence visually recalls various *Frankenstein* movies with the wires attached to the narrator's body: "It was as though I were acting out a scene from some crazy movie" (189), and what he hears sounds "like a soundtrack reversed at high speed" (187).[32] When the narrator goes to the woman's home after lecturing on "the woman question," he walks past a mirror that mirrors him in another mirror that "now like a surge of the sea tossed our images back and forth, back and forth, furiously multiplying the time and the place and the circumstances" (314). This scene visually recalls a famous scene in Orson Welles's *Citizen Kane* (1941), where Kane walks in front of a large mirror that duplicates his image and suggests his fragmentation. In the scene with Sybil, the narrator's question, " 'What's happening

here . . . a new birth of a nation?' " echoes both D. W. Griffith's famous
racist film and the Cumaean Sybil's prophecy that Aeneas will be the ancestor of Romulus, the founder of Rome. Ras in costume looks like both
"them African guys . . . in the moving pictures" and cowboys (425).
Another film reference occurs shortly after the narrator arrives in New
York and summarizes the frontier themes implicit in *Invisible Man:* "In the
evening I went out to a movie, a picture of frontier life with heroic Indian
fighting and struggles against flood, storm and forest fire, with the out-
numbered settlers winning each engagement; an epic of wagon trains rolling
ever westward. I forgot myself (although there was no one like me taking
part in the adventures) and left the dark room in a lighter mood" (130).
The narrator at this point embraces the frontier myth of simplicity and
achievement and progress, a myth given life in western movies.[33] (Ellison's
favorite director is John Ford, whose films he watches again and again
[Anderson, 100].)

African American Culture

Although literary scholarship concerned with African American literature has been written steadily throughout the twentieth century, the 1970s
and 1980s witnessed an explosion of sophisticated literary scholarship pre-
dominantly by African Americans trained in literary theory who emphasized that the continuity of black literature could be analyzed through
thematic prisms drawn from African American culture and from literary
theories involving Freudianism, Marxism, structuralism, poststructuralism,
and new historicism. Most of these critics stress Ellison's central role in African American literature and *Invisible Man* as a seminal document in African
American literature.

The first major book on Ellison, O'Meally's *The Craft of Ralph Ellison*
(1980), also concentrated on Ellison's connection with African American
culture. O'Meally emphasized that black folklore, defined as "a dynamic,
current process of speaking and singing in certain circumstances" such as
"sermons, tales, games, jokes, boasts, toasts, dozens, blues, spirituals," provides "the key to Ellison's fictional world" (O'Meally 1980, 2). O'Meally's
book, which examined Ellison's work throughout his career, remains the
most significant work on Ellison.

While Ellison alludes to blues, folklore, jazz, and other elements of black
culture throughout his work, African American writers and historic figures
also appear. One of the most predominant is Frederick Douglass, whose
Narrative, like *Invisible Man,* follows the frontier paradigm, as young

Douglass undergoes a transformation in a symbolic wilderness after a violent confrontation with the slave breaker, Covey. Although Douglass points toward escape as his ultimate goal, he withholds his exact means of gaining freedom on the grounds that the knowledge might endanger other slaves who attempt to use a similar method. Thus, although physical escape dominates the narrative, it is muted and turns the emphasis to Douglass's mental escape, which he achieves by resisting Covey. By making personal internal struggle the focus of his narrative, Douglass makes the inward, personal battle the primary one. As Donald B. Gibson concludes, the "true climax of the autobiography is the private, psychological one, explicitly revealing the formation on Douglass' part of a new consciousness, a different awareness and sense of self, and a firm resolve for the future."[34] Valerie Smith points to Douglass's *Narrative* as a paradigmatic work in African American literature and a source for Ellison and other black writers. Her thesis is that "slave narrators and protagonist-narrators of certain twentieth-century novels by Afro-American writers affirm and legitimize their psychological autonomy by telling the stories of their own lives."[35]

Ellison alludes to Douglass in the Brotherhood section when Brother Tarp puts Douglass's portrait on the narrator's office wall. Contemplating Douglass's picture, the narrator points to the themes of oratory, naming, identity, and transformation as he thinks "how magical it was that he had talked his way from slavery to a government ministry": "Perhaps, I thought, something of the kind is happening to me. Douglass came north to escape and find work in the shipyards; a big fellow in a sailor's suit who, like me, had taken another name. What had his true name been? Whatever it was, it was as *Douglass* that he became himself, defined himself. And not as a boatwright as he'd expected, but as an orator. Perhaps the sense of magic lay in the unexpected transformations. 'You start Saul, and end up Paul,' my grandfather had often said" (288).

Another figure from black history appearing directly in the novel is Booker T. Washington, who serves as a model for both the founder and Bledsoe. The narrator alludes to Washington's famous Atlanta Exposition address in his battle royal address. Later Brother Jack asks the narrator if he would like to be "the new Booker T. Washington" (231). However, *Invisible Man,* which began as Ellison contemplated the failure of Negro leadership in America, becomes, as Kostelanetz puts it, an attack on "The Politics of Ellison's Booker."[36]

Washington had long come under attack by black intellectuals, most notably by W. E. B. Du Bois in *The Souls of Black Folk* (1903), in which Du Bois presented his concept of double-consciousness. The following quo-

tation, probably Du Bois's most famous passage, serves as the source for
several Ellison allusions:

> The Negro is a sort of seventh son, born with a veil, and gifted with second-sight in
> this American world,—a world which yields him no true self-consciousness, but
> only lets him see himself through the revelation of the other world. It is a peculiar
> sensation, this double-consciousness, this sense of always looking at one's self by the
> tape of a world that looks on in amused contempt and pity. One ever feels his
> twoness,—an American, a Negro; two souls, two thoughts, two unreconciled striv-
> ings; two warring ideals in one dark body, whose dogged strength alone keeps it
> from being torn asunder.[37]

Ellison alludes to this passage indirectly by emphasizing sight imagery and
consciousness. Du Bois's veil and his criticism of Washington return specifically in the statue of the college founder, "the cold Father symbol," with his
hands outstretched to lift a veil from the face of a kneeling slave. Du Bois's
presence is felt because the narrator is puzzled, "unable to decide whether
the veil is really being lifted, or lowered more firmly in place; whether I am
witnessing a revelation or a more efficient blinding" (28). A subtle allusion
to Du Bois's "talented tenth," the top 10 percent of African American society, the professionals on whom he pinned his hopes for the future, comes
from the fact that the white power figures in the battle royal scene invite ten
black boys to participate.

Another early twentieth-century African American author to whom
Ellison alludes directly is James Weldon Johnson. Bledsoe's gleeful explanation about how he maintains his power—" 'Your arms are too short to
box with me, son' " (111)—alludes to the opening lines of Johnson's poem,
"Prodigal Son": "Young man, young man / Yo' arms too short / To box
with God."[38] The allusion suggests the theme of Bledsoe's godlike power.
Houston Baker calls Johnson's 1912 novel, *The Autobiography of an Ex-
Coloured Man,* a prototype for *Invisible Man.* Both books are concerned
with first-person narrators who tell of their picaresque adventures in both
the South and the North in education, industry, and a seething underworld.
Both narrators learn the value of African American folk history and culture.
The worthless gold coin that Johnson's narrator wears around his neck finds
its analogue in Ellison's narrator's briefcase.[39]

In *From Behind the Veil* Stepto discusses Ellison's relationship with
Johnson, Du Bois, and Washington and identifies Zora Neale Hurston's
Their Eyes Were Watching God (1937) as an important forerunner to *Invisi-
ble Man.* Stepto defines the two major types of black narratives as ascent

and immersion. In the ascent narrative an oppressed figure goes to a free environment and achieves freedom. In the immersion narrative a free protagonist goes South to an oppressed environment and discovers freedom through gaining "tribal literacy." Ellison's achievement, according to Stepto, is that he combines the two traditions. Hurston's novel similarly combines the two traditions and provides a model for Ellison.[40]

None of Ellison's sources is more problematic than Richard Wright. Throughout his career Ellison acknowledged his debt to Wright, explaining how Wright asked him to write his first book review and his first story. Their long literary conversations shortly after both arrived in New York stimulated Ellison's imagination and set him along the road to becoming a writer. He has told of reading *Native Son* wide-eyed as it was written, "as it was, literally ripped off the typewriter" (*GT,* 210). Ellison was Wright's best man when he married Dhimah Rose Meadman in August 1939 (Fabre, *Quest,* 200).

At the time of their close friendship Ellison wrote of Wright's work in glowing terms. In a 1941 *New Masses* article, Ellison praised Wright highly, saying that *Uncle Tom's Children* "represents one of the few instances in which an American Negro writer has successfully delineated the universals embodied in Negro experience" and that the characters possess "an emotional and psychological complexity never before achieved in American Negro writing." And *Native Son,* he continued, "possesses an artistry, penetration of thought, and sheer emotional power that places it into the front rank of American fiction."[41] But their personal correspondence during the early 1940s also demonstrates that while Ellison and Wright approached art and politics with like minds, Ellison was beginning to question Marxist approaches to literature.

When Wright went to Cuernavaca for a delayed honeymoon shortly after *Native Son* was published in 1940, Ellison collected the reviews and wrote to Wright about its reception. Ellison's 22 April 1940 letter to Wright demonstrates his approval of Bigger Thomas from a Marxist perspective:

What was bad in Bigger from the point of view of bourgeois society is good from our point of view. . . . He, Bigger, has what Hegel called "the indignant consciousness" and because of this he is more human than those who sent him to his death, for it was they, not he who fostered the dehumanizing condition which shaped his personality. When the "indignant consciousness" becomes the "theoretical consciousness," indignant man is aware of his historical destiny and fights to achieve it. Would that *all* Negroes were psychologically as free as Bigger and capable of positive action![42]

However, Ellison's concern with Marxist approaches to literature is apparent
in a 14 April 1940 letter:

As I study Max's speech, it seems to me that you were struggling to create a new
terminology, i.e., you were trying to state in terms of human values certain ideas,
concepts, implicit in Marxist philosophy but which, since Marx and later Lenin
were so occupied with economics and politics, have not been stated in humanist
terms of Marxist coloring. This lack I am trying to get at is indicated by the almost
total failure on the part of Marxist-Leninist literature to treat human personality.
Am I shooting up a blind alley in this? (Fabre 1987, 201)

Still, his relationship with Wright was extremely strong. After Wright
published *12 Million Black Voices,* Ellison wrote of their "brotherly" relationship in no uncertain terms in a 3 November 1941 letter:

I have known for a long time that you have suffered many things which I know, and
that the truths which you have learned are Negro truths. . . . Of this, however, I am
now sure more than ever; that you and I are brothers. Back when I first knew you,
remember, I often speculated as to what it was that made the difference between us
and the others who shot up from the same region. . . . I think it is because this past
which filters through your book has always been tender and alive and aching within
us. . . . God! It makes you want to write and write and write, or murder. Like most
of us, I am shy of my naked personal emotions, they are too deep. Yet one gets
strength when he shares his deepest thoughts and emotions with his brother.
(Fabre, "Evolution," 211)

Again, in a 1945 review of *Black Boy* Ellison praised Wright but translated Wright's work into his own terms. Wright's autobiography, Ellison
concluded, drew its strength from its similarity to the blues: "The blues is an
impulse to keep the painful details and episodes of a brutal experience alive
in one's aching consciousness, to finger its jagged grain, and to transcend it,
not by the consolation of philosophy but by squeezing from it a near-tragic,
near-comic lyricism. As a form, the blues is an autobiographical chronicle of
personal catastrophe expressed lyrically" (*SA,* 78–79). He continued that
the blues' "attraction lies in this, that they at once express both the agony of
life and the possibility of conquering it through sheer toughness of spirit."
Ellison concluded (and foreshadowed *Invisible Man*) by saying that in *Black
Boy,* Wright "has converted the American Negro impulse toward self-
annihilation and 'going-under-ground' into a will to confront the world, to
evaluate his experience honestly and throw his findings unashamedly into
the guilty conscience of America" (*SA,* 94).

This powerful relationship began to change. The first reason was personal. Ellison was offended that Wright condescended to him and failed to acknowledge Ellison's education and experience. Ellison told Ishmael Reed, "I don't think that Wright appreciated the background that I brought to his discussion of creative writing because frequently he seemed to assume that I was totally ignorant of the works under discussion. But I didn't argue with him. . . . I listened to him and kept my disagreements to myself" (Reed, 146). Similarly, Ellison told Stepto, "For while I realized that the man [Wright] had much to teach me about art . . . I also realized that he was far from being an intellectual. Not only was he innocent of a serious interest in ideas, but he hadn't *begun* to read the books that I had read, even before entering college" (Stepto, "Study and Experience," 454).

After Ellison gave Wright a story and asked for Wright's comments, their relationship deteriorated. Ellison explained that the story was about a "fight that broke out between a chef and a hallboy in a club, basing it upon a club where I had worked in Oklahoma City." Ellison continued, "I showed this to Dick, and he kept it and kept it and didn't say anything. I let a few weeks go by and then finally said, 'Well, what *about* it? What *about* it?' And he said, 'This is *my* stuff' " (Hersey 1987, 303). According to Constance Webb, Wright continued his accusation: " 'This is my story, my style. You have copied my ideas, my words, my structure! You must find your own symbols—you must tap the content of your own unconscious and use it! You must dig it out of yourself and not duplicate someone else.' "[43] Ellison never showed Wright another story.

The second and more important reason for the changing relationship was that despite similarities in their backgrounds—both came north from relatively poor backgrounds—Ellison sensed some profound differences in their experiences and outlooks. As Wright looked back on growing up in Jackson, Mississippi, through Marxist lenses, he saw limitations, restrictions, and negative experiences. In *Black Boy,* for example, he wrote: "I used to mull over the strange absence of real kindness in Negroes, how unstable was our tenderness, how lacking in genuine passion we were, how void of great hope, how timid our joy, how bare our traditions, how hollow our memories, how lacking we were in those intangible sentiments that bind man to man and how shallow was even our despair. . . . I saw that what had been taken for our emotional strength was our negative confusions, our flights, our fears, our frenzy under pressure." Ellison realized that his experience as a black southwesterner was much more positive and full of hope and possibility.

In his response to Howe, Ellison pointed to this passage as demonstrating the profound difference between his and Wright's "sense of Negro life." Because Wright saw literature as a weapon, he "could not for ideological reasons depict a Negro as intelligent, as creative or as dedicated as himself." In his most succinct and damning comment about Wright, Ellison wrote: "Wright could imagine Bigger, but Bigger could not possibly imagine Richard Wright. Wright saw to that" (*SA*, 114). For these reasons, Ellison asserts that "Wright was no spiritual father of mine, certainly in no sense I recognize" (*SA*, 117), and assigns Wright to the lesser rank of "relative" as distinguished from the "ancestors," Eliot, Hemingway, Dostoyevski, and Malraux.

Although Ellison softened his tone in a 1971 address, "Remembering Richard Wright," it seems clear that he protested Wright's influence too much. In fact, two of Wright's works, *Black Boy* and "The Man Who Lived Underground," are important to Ellison. Joseph Skerrett, Jr., applies Harold Bloom's concept of the anxiety of influence to Ellison's association with Wright and concludes that Ellison, beginning with his review of *Black Boy*, misread Wright. Bloom examines relationships between writers and concludes that younger writers who have strong predecessors feel anxiety, dread, or guilt about the power of the older writer's influence. To counter these feelings, young writers must reject the older writer's influence through what Bloom calls "poetic misprison," a deliberate misreading of the older writer "to clear the imaginative space for himself."[44] Although Bloom applies his theory to poetry, its implication for prose is equally clear: "Poetic Influence—when it involves two strong, authentic poets—always proceeds by a misreading of the prior poet, an act of creative correction that is actually and necessarily a misinterpretation, the history of fruitful poetic influence, which is to say the main tradition of Western poetry since the Renaissance, is a history of anxiety and self-saving caricature, of distortion, of perverse, willful revisionism without which modern poetry as such could not exist" (Bloom, 30). Just such a misreading, Skerrett concludes, produced the split between Wright and Ellison, for when Ellison found the blues in *Black Boy*, he misread his mentor: "By reading Wright's autobiography as a 'blues,' Ellison imputes Wright a dim, uncertain, and inadequate vision of the black American's necessarily complex relationship with his community and culture, and accepts . . . the limitations of Wright's environment as an explanation of his vision. Wright is thus encompassed, encapsulated by his own life-story, which Ellison need not feel representative of his own."[45]

In 1945 Ellison connected Wright with the blues; in 1964 he scorned Wright's understanding of the blues: "And if you think Wright knew anything about the blues, listen to a 'blues' he composed with Paul Robeson singing, a *most* unfortunate collaboration" (*SA,* 140). The difference, Skerrett believes, resulted from the anxiety of influence: " 'Richard Wright's Blues' is an act of definition, a misreading of the father-as-artist that clears the way for antithetical assertion of the ways in which Afro-American experience, Ralph Ellison's experience in particular, functions in the shaping of an artist" (Skerrett, 227).

Ellison did not misread "The Man Who Lived Underground" (1944), but he has maintained throughout his career that he owed much more to Dostoyevski's *Notes from Underground* than to Wright's novella. Nonetheless, it seems clear that "The Man Who Lived Underground" had a profound effect on Ellison. In Wright's story a happily married black man, Fred Daniels, is falsely accused of a murder by three policemen. Under duress, Daniels signs a confession but then escapes from the police station into the street. Seeing water gush from a manhole cover, he hides in the sewer, where he discovers an underground labyrinth, comes to a new understanding of human values, and returns above ground to share his knowledge. But the three policemen return with him to the underground world, shoot him in the chest, and leave him to become "a whirling object rushing alone in the darkness, veering, tossing, lost in the heart of the earth."

The surface similarities between Ellison's novel and Wright's novella are obvious: both are concerned with black men who create underground worlds as they flee the absurdity of the world above. Houston Baker's comments on "The Man Who Lived Underground" also apply to *Invisible Man:* "As a nameless figure in a realm of social timelessness, Wright's protagonist is a quintessentially liminal being. His actions include negation, trespass, parody, burlesque, theft, and mockery. He is the agent of dream-visions that are radically inversive in their symbology. And his ironically imaginative creative acts lead ultimately to a transvaluation of value in which guilt is figured as the founding condition of a new order of existence" (Baker 1984, 159). Besides the underground metaphor, namelessness (Daniels forgets his name), paper definitions of identity (Daniels's signed confession), stolen electric power from above, and dream visions, both works share Christian symbolism. As Baker notes, "Daniels descends into darkness and the cover is placed on his 'tomb' on Friday at dusk. He emerges the following Sunday to the 'spirited singing' of a black congregation" (Baker 1984, 159).

Ultimately, however, the two works' differences, as William Goede and Dietze point out, are more significant than their similarities.[46] Although

Wright's protagonist comes to some profound conclusions about important existential questions, he cannot find an appropriate audience and ends up voiceless in a chaotic void. Ellison's narrator prepares to speak for all and to play a socially responsible role. That wide difference between those two positions is the space that Ellison created for his own distinctly different vision.

Chapter Five
The Jagged Grain: Later Stories, the Second Novel

Invisible Man's success created an intense interest in Ellison's work, and his audience waited for the next novel. Between lecturing abroad and teaching at home, Ellison continued to work and publish enough to keep the interest high. Since *Invisible Man*'s publication in 1952, Ellison has published 11 stories: one section edited out of the novel, a new story about Mary Rambo, a new Buster and Riley story, and eight excerpts from a second novel in progress, titled variously *And Hickman Returns* or *And Hickman Arrives*. Both the edited portion of the novel and the story about Mary develop the positive aspects of her character. The new Buster and Riley story demonstrates how Ellison returned to his southwestern past to fuel his imagination, and the Hickman stories suggest that the long-awaited second novel continues elements that made *Invisible Man* a major work.

The Mary Rambo Stories

"Out of the Hospital and under the Bar" Originally chapter 11 of *Invisible Man*, this 17,500-word chapter was cut because of space limitations and replaced with the 5,600-word hospital machine chapter. When it was first published in 1963, Ellison added a note explaining he wished the novel had included the section because it strengthens Mary's role and would "have made it a better book."[1] He also points out that it fits right after the explosion in the paint factory. The title literally refers to the action as the narrator escapes from the hospital and finds himself underneath a nearby bar, but Ellison may also have been having some fun with his ancestor Hemingway, whose *Across the River and into the Trees* was pilloried as *Across the Street and into the Bar* (Dietze, *Genesis,* 33).

In the story the narrator awakens from the explosion in the machine and sees Mary, wearing a uniform of a cleaning lady, looking in at him and trying to open the machine with her "work-swollen fingers" to release him. She finally gets the lid open and discovers he is memoryless, feeling as if he is in a dream. After Mary gives him a piece of her pork chop sandwich, she tells

him she overheard plans to transfer him to another hospital. Fearful, the
narrator asks her for help, and Mary releases his arm, which he cannot move
even after it is free. When she asks what he did to get put into the machine,
he fabricates a story about running away from an apparently homosexual
white man who tried to give him $20. The narrator says that he finally hit
the man and ran. Mary concludes he killed the man and indicates she will
return later and help him escape.

After she leaves, a dreamy nurse writes in his chart, and doctors look in
on him, but none notices that his arm is loose. When Mary returns with a
round object, she mentions that her 104-year-old mother "knows more
about roots and herbs and midwifery" than anyone, feeds him something
"green, like balled grape leaves that had dried without fading" ("Bar," 261),
and then leaves, telling him he must escape by himself. Climbing out of the
machine and disconnecting the electrodes attached to his navel, the narrator
moves into the darkness and eventually descends in an elevator to the basement. He finds the Engine Room, turns off the switches, and plunges the
hospital into darkness. Running from voices, he realizes he is underneath a
restaurant or a bar with a jukebox. When men come down searching for
him, he hides in a coal bin, and when they return, he climbs a stair and
pushes out through a manhole into the street above. A passerby, thinking he
is a lover escaping a rampaging husband, takes him in and gives him
clothes. The narrator then helps an old blind man who reminds him of his
grandfather cross the street. As the story ends, his memory returns, and he
decides to return to Mary's house.

This story contains many of the themes and images from the novel: invisibility, rebirth, restriction, blindness, running, underground, folkloric references such as Jack-the-Bear and John Henry, and many of the symbols and
allusions associated with the narrator: Adam, Christ, Popeye, Frankenstein,
Frederick Douglass, and Oedipus. In his nakedness ("as ever he was born in
the world") the narrator suggests Adam. The rebirth imagery is reinforced
by the umbilicallike wires and by the fetal position the narrator takes, cling-
ing "with my back pressed against the curved mouth of the hole, my knees
drawn up to my chin like a boy rolling down a hill in an auto tire" ("Bar,"
281) as he hides at the top of the passage leading to the manhole from
which he is forcefully expelled naked.

The comparison to Christ appears shortly after the narrator climbs out of
the machine when he recalls Handel's *Messiah: "He's risen—Smash!"*
("Bar," 266). Mary's assistance at this "big ole rusty baby's" immaculate
birth from the machine reinforces this imagery, but, as Melvin Dixon points
out, Mary's name and function may also suggest Mary Magdalene, as well

as the mother of Jesus: "Mary Rambo, in Ellison's refashioned myth, may be another kind of Mary Magdalene. She redeems herself from the stereotype of black woman as whore, prostitute, or mammy, and acquires the status of one among those women who discover that the stone or lid has been rolled away from the grave (dare I say, machine or incubator?), and who redeem Christ for posterity by announcing his resurrection."[2]

Folklore, Frederick Douglass, and Popeye references combine when Mary ministers to the narrator with the herbal root. Transmitting ancient wisdom into the industrial world, Mary suggests Sandy Jenkins who supplied Frederick Douglass with a special conjure root (O'Meally 1980, 109; Dixon, "Mary," 103). Like Popeye who gains strength from spinach, the narrator's strength is restored by a green, leafy substance. Ellison's hero is eclectic, drawing power from high and low.

Allusions to Oedipus receive particular emphasis here. After the narrator returns above ground, he reaches "the forking of three streets" ("Bar," 285) and bumps into a blind man who seems strikingly familiar. When the old man asks for assistance at this "dangerous crossing," the narrator leads him out in front of a car and then pulls him back, thinking, "It was as though I had deliberately tried to guide this stranger, whom I'd barely seen, into the path of a car." When he apologizes for being too intent on knowing "something definite about myself," the old man says, "Well, a young fellow has to keep moving" ("Bar," 287). This comment, reminiscent of the narrator's grandfather's dream comment about keeping "this nigger boy running," suddenly causes the narrator to realize the similarity between the blind man and his grandfather, and the various Oedipal references coalesce.

Perhaps Ellison decided to excise this chapter rather than another section so as to mute the unmistakable connections with Wright's "The Man Who Lived Underground." Like Fred Daniels in Wright's story, Ellison's narrator sloshes his way through an underground labyrinth where he hears music above him, hides like a "nigger in the coal pile," compares himself to a scurrying rat in a sewer, and confronts a corpse. Whatever the reasons, the decision to replace this chapter with the rewritten, shorter one, according to Kerry McSweeney, strengthens the book: "For all its bizarre incidents, the episode quite lacks the exhilarating one-damn-thing-after-another-sheer-happening comic quality of the Golden Day chapter. Moreover, the symbolic incidents are much too heavy-handed and much too univocal in meaning—they thud rather than ping."[3] O'Meally agrees, calling the story "snarled, in places, with minute descriptions and conventional symbols conventionally rendered." Still, O'Meally finds the dialogue "spirited, the prose rhythms often captivating," and the story "a fascinating piece for study" (O'Meally 1980, 106).

More important, as Ellison states in his note and Dixon argues, "Out of the Hospital and under the Bar" strengthens and clarifies Mary Rambo's role as the "technician of the folk, a representative of the cultural syncretism which lies at the root, if you will, of American civilization" (Dixon, "Mary," 103). Ellison commented that "the treatment of Mary as a dominant figure is natural for me. I was raised by my mother, my father died quite early, so she had to be strong, but I never felt that she emasculated me because she always insisted upon my achieving manliness and responsibility" (Carson, 5). Some critics suggest the Mary of the novel is a limiting figure from whom the narrator must escape, such as Bledsoe and Brother Jack, but this excerpt stresses that Mary's vitality and aggressive connection with the folk past provide the narrator with the strength and understanding to liberate himself.

"Did You Ever Dream Lucky?"   Ellison's first story published after *Invisible Man* also broadens the vision of Mary Rambo.[4] Like many of Ellison's other stories, this one is concerned with storytelling, the human response to dashed expectations, initiation, the value of humor, and unrealistic dreams. The title comes from a blues song titled variously "Blues in the Dark" and "Cold in Hand Blues": "Did you ever dream lucky, / Wake up cold in hand?" (O'Meally 1980, 110). As the story begins, Mary Rambo and two of her boarders, Mr. Portwood, a Red Cap (Ellison has a bit of fun with this porter's name), and Mrs. Garfield, a retired cook, are just finishing a Thanksgiving meal and thinking about the young roomers who left quickly to attend a dance where they have the chance to win a car. Playing with color imagery, Mr. Portwood accuses them of lacking proper respect: " 'They black and trying to get to heaven in a Cadillac' " and " 'Too green to be polite.' " Mary begins to signify on the phrase *green:* " 'What *green?*' She said, singing full-throatedly now, her voice suddenly folk-toned and deep with echoes of sermons and blue trombones, 'Lawd, *I* was green.' " Ellison's description of Mary's full, folk-toned singing voice connects her with his storytellers like Trueblood, Tarp, and Jefferson, and she has now established the theme of the story she is about to tell based on the theme of innocence, or greenness. Her listeners get the after-dinner wine and, with another phrase that suggests the blues singer, wait "for Mary's old contralto to resume its flight, its tragic-comic ascendence" ("Lucky," 135–36).

The story she tells, or the "lie" as she and Portwood call it six times, concerns the time two cars wrecked on the street below the apartment she and her daughter Lucy shared. Something had been flung out of one of the cars "like a cannon ball" and landed near the curb. Mary and Lucy rushed below and found a bag that "clinked" loudly with a "sweet metal-like sound" when they kicked it. Mary then sat down on the bag like it was some "kinda egg" on which she was "nesting." Wrapping the bag in an apron, Mary and Lucy sneaked it into the apartment and hid it in the toilet flush box, where its presence worked "like a dose of salts" as they found themselves going often to the bathroom to flush the toilet and hear the clinking. Frightened that they would be discovered, they waited to open it, spending their money in their dreams. Finally, one day when Lucy had gone to the dentist, Mary pulled up the bag, now "green with canker" and *"coold"* like the lines from the song, cut it open, looked at the contents, and immediately took to bed. When Lucy returned, Mary told her that she thought they ought to buy a car. When Lucy protested and asked why, Mary answered, " 'Cause how else we gon' use two sets of auto chains?' " ("Lucky," 145).

The repeated references to this story as a lie suggest one of Ellison's continuing concerns: the individual's ability to achieve freedom in restriction through storytelling. Although Mary's story concerns restriction—by poverty, ignorance, and law—she achieves freedom by formulating the story the way she wants it, and its major effect comes from the method of telling it: from Mary's folk-toned voice, her vivid description ("You can hear them clapping their hands and shouting and the tambourines is a-shaking and a-beating, and that ole levee camp trombone they has is going *Wah-wah, Wah-wah, Wah-wah-wah!*" ["Lucky," 137]), her gestures (she uses two table knives to demonstrate the collision), and, most of all, her O'Henry-like structuring to save the most important bit of information until the end. Similarly, Mary structured her telling Lucy her discovery in such a way that she could rely on humor to lessen the "tragedy" of learning of their dashed hopes.

Other Ellison concerns, images, and techniques are apparent. This is another story, as its emphasis on greenness indicates, about initiation. Ellison again creates the image of something that appears to be valuable that turns out to be worthless, comparable to the gold coins in the battle royal scene. And Ellison also uses allusions in the story. The biblical ones are literal as Mary recollects reading the passage, "Store ye up riches in heaven." At one point Mrs. Garfield alludes to Shakespeare: " 'Mr. Garfield often said that the possession of great wealth brought with it the slings and arrows of outrageous responsibility.' "

Stories of lost treasure flourish in black folklore, as O'Meally demonstrates, especially "comic folktales in which high hopes are deflated"

(O'Meally 1980, 112). As J. Frank Dobie's *Coronado's Children* and *Apache Gold and Yaqui Silver* attest, western and southwestern folklore also abounds with stories of lost treasure, since the West often represented the place where all possibility, particularly material success, existed. The Thanksgiving setting suggests that the story's emphasis on achieving dreams connects with the larger American dream. As the story ends, Mary hopes the young people win the car, and Mrs. Garfield says it would be a "comfort" just to know that "they *can* win one." As O'Meally states, this story acknowledges that the "starry-eyed Afro-American . . . may . . . *dream* lucky, but will probably wake up cold in hand" (O'Meally 1980, 113). Nonetheless, the American dream of promise continues to beckon for the black, white, and the green of all colors.

Buster and Riley Redux: "A Coupla Scalped Indians"

Twenty-three years after Ellison left Oklahoma and 12 years after the last Buster and Riley story, he returned to an Oklahoma setting and an adolescent duo. The title puns on the two boy's recent circumcisions. The first-person 11-year-old narrator, although never identified as Riley, is Buster's friend and companion, and if not identical to at least comparable to the Riley of the previous stories. These two characters are closer to Huck Finn and Tom Sawyer than the earlier Buster and Riley, who had parents, since the narrator here is an orphan taken care of by Miss Janey. This story reinforces Ellison's frontier emphasis on freedom within restriction; initiation; amalgamation; transformation; magical realism; similarities between African Americans and native Americans; and the power of jazz, the imagination, and storytelling.

As the story begins, Buster and the narrator are returning from a day practicing Boy Scout tests in the woods when they are lured toward a "far-away and sparklike sound" of a carnival with "the notes of horns bursting like bright metallic bubbles against the sky."[5] No scoutmaster or organized scout troop is available to these black boys, so they follow a Boy Scout's handbook Buster had found. But these boys are eclectic: they practice Boy Scout tests carrying army surplus mess kits and canteens, but they want to be Indians so they wear cloth headbands with turkey feathers. As the narrator says, "We were more interested in being *Indian* scouts than simply *boy* scouts" ("Scalped," 227). *Boy* suggests lack of maturity, and this story, as the title indicates, is one of sexual maturity and initiation. The doctor who had "scalped" them told them "it would make us men" (to which Buster replied he was a man already and wanted to be an Indian). They have gone out shortly after their operations even though their penises are bandaged and painful because Buster believes "a real stud Indian could take the tests even right after the doctor had just finished sewing on him" (227).

As Buster and the narrator discuss the sounds of the horns coming from the carnival, Ellison reemphasizes the theme of eclectic amalgamation as the boys apply sacred and profane comparisons. Buster says, " 'Those fools is starting to shout amazing grace on those horns,' " and the trumpet is saying, " 'Well pat your feet and clap your hands / 'Cause I'm going to play 'em to the promised land.' " Along with religious sounds, the horns are "playing the dozens with the whole wide world" talking about undergarments ("draw's"): " 'Ya'lls' mamas don't wear 'em. Is strictly without 'em.' " The narrator, seemingly more concerned with restriction and difference, cautions Buster to be careful " 'cussing and playing the dozens if we're going to be boy scouts. Those white boys don't play that mess.' " Buster, apostle of freedom and amalgamation, replies: " 'You doggone right they don't,' he said, the turkey feather vibrating about his ear. 'Those guys can't take it, man. Besides, who wants to be just like them? Me, *I'm* gon' be a scout and play the twelves, too!' "

To get to the carnival, the boys must pass Aunt Mackie's house, which is protected by her vicious dog. Aunt Mackie, *"talker-with spirits, prophetess-of-disaster, odd-dweller-alone in a riverside shack surrounded by sunflowers, morning-glories, and strange magical weeds,"* strikes terror in their hearts (228). Trying to sneak past Aunt Mackie's, the narrator is separated from Buster, who is engaged with the dog, and finds himself beneath the window of her shack. Gazing through the window frame, a Hitchcockian voyeur, the narrator sees a "brown naked woman" with "a young, girlish body, with slender, well-rounded hips" dancing sensuously and drinking wine. As she turns around, "above the smooth shoulders of the girlish form I saw the wrinkled face of old Aunt Mackie" (231). Still, the girlish body arouses the "scalped" Indian, and he begins to get an erection despite his bandage; this initiation into sex is truly an intertwining of pain and pleasure as he "feels a warm pain grow beneath my bandage" (234). Suddenly Aunt Mackie discovers him peeping in the window and sentences him to kiss her wrinkled face "with long hairs on the chin." As he does, he tries to think that *"it's just like kissing some sweaty woman at church,"* (234) but his hand finds its way to her breast at the same time. Guilty and in pain, he begins crying and notices that Aunt Mackie's hair is not sleek and black as he first thought but is "mixed here and there with gray" (234).

When she asks why he cries, he explains his operation, and she makes him show her his bandaged penis, at which, suggesting castration, she says,

" 'Boy, you have been pruned.' " Asked about emasculating women by David Carson, Ellison replied: "I'd say that you would be closer to the truth if you saw the early women in my fiction from the perspective of Mark Twain; in terms of the symbolism of woman standing for established values rather than as, in Freudian terms, castrators. I would say that they were 'circumcisers' " (Carson, 5). The narrator protests Aunt Mackie's suggestion that he's "pruned," or powerless, and thinks, *"Just the same I am a man!"* combining the fear of castration and initiation themes. Looking at her again, he realizes that just as her hair is not as he first thought, neither is her body, for "across the curvature of her stomach I saw a long, puckered, crescent-shaped scar" (235) Aunt Mackie is another eclectic figure, combining youth and age, beauty and ugliness, pleasure and pain.

Finished with her examination and now interested in this youth's age, Aunt Mackie is surprised and seemingly disappointed he is only 11 and, wrapping her robe around her, sends him home. Moving out into the moonlight night, hearing the plop of a "moon-mad" fish, and smelling the scent of "moonflowers," the narrator questions the reality of his memory but concludes, "All was real." The crescent of her scar is mirrored by the crescent of the moon, traditional symbol of imagination. The conclusion of "A Coupla Scalped Indians," a moment of magical realism, demonstrates the story's emphasis on the power of the imagination and storytelling. The narrator recalls, like the narrator in *Invisible Man,* an experience from the chaos of memory and shapes it through imagination and language into art.

The Hickman Stories

Ellison has been working on his second novel, *And Hickman Arrives,* since 1958, shortly after he and Fanny returned from two years in Italy. With Saul Bellow's urging, Ellison planned to teach at Bard College, and since Bellow was spending the year in Minnesota, Bellow offered the Ellisons his house. There Ellison began seriously writing the novel originally conceived in 1955. Additionally Bellow asked Ellison for a contribution to the *Noble Savage,* and Ellison sent the first excerpt, "And Hickman Arrives" (1960). Political assassinations and a fire that destroyed some manuscript pages, among other reasons, slowed his progress, but between 1960 and 1977 Ellison published seven more stories, usually with a line stating "Excerpt from a novel in progress."

The novel takes place "roughly from 1954 to 1956 or 1957" and is set primarily in Washington, D.C., but it goes back "to some of the childhood experiences of Hickman, who is an elderly man in time present" (Hersey

1987, 307). The setting for the time past is various southern states as the traveling evangelist Hickman moves throughout the South—from Georgia to Alabama to Oklahoma—as he takes his show on the road. In readings around the country, Ellison has identified Oklahoma as the setting for some of the stories set in the past. The main characters are the Rev. Alonzo Zuber Hickman and the orphan Bliss, a light-skinned boy of indeterminate race raised by Hickman as a traveling evangelist. During sermons, the boy hides in a white coffin until Hickman begins preaching of Christ's agony on the cross, and Bliss rises up from the coffin. Bliss eventually disappears into the white community and later reappears as the racist Senator Sunraider from an unidentified New England state (probably Massachusetts), who is later shot by another character, a young man from Oklahoma named Severen. In an interview Ellison said of the characters: "One man learns how to operate in society to the extent that he loses a great part of his capacity for, shall we say, poetry or for really dealing with life. And another man who seems caught at a very humble stage of society seems to have achieved quite a high level of humanity" (Geller, 160).

A second story line is derived from the senator's activities. He makes a blatantly offensive speech in which he suggests that so many blacks are driving Cadillacs that the cars have lost their appeal to whites. In protest, a black jazz musician burns his Cadillac on the senator's lawn. The speech inspires a racist southerner to write the senator a letter about some obscure sexual practice among blacks. The lawn burning also leads a group of journalists to discuss political acts of black people.

Throughout the years since the publication of *Invisible Man*, Ellison has alternated between talking freely and reluctantly about his second novel, realizing that the audience expectantly awaited its publication. In an interview in Montreal on 25 October 1963, a month before President Kennedy's assassination, Ellison talked easily about the novel and identified its major themes as they were developing then. He noted that as in *Invisible Man*, he continued his interest in the search for identity along with "the theme of memory or the suppression of memory in the United States": "One of the techniques which seems to have worked out for taking advantage of the high mobility which is possible in the States is forgetting what the past was, in the larger historical sense, but also in terms of the individual's immediate background. . . . You have this, what I call 'passing for white,' which refers to a form of rejecting one's own background in order to become that of some prestige group or to try to imitate the group which has prestige at a particular moment."[6] Almost 20 years later, Ellison again pointed to the theme of past and present: "It's just a matter of the past being active in the present—or of the characters becoming aware of the manner in which the past operates on their present lives" (Hersey 1987, 307). Commenting on the style, Ellison told McPherson in 1970 that the book would be "realism extended beyond realism" (McPherson, 27), and McPherson concluded that the book would deal with the complexity of "the Negro church and its ritual."

Rather than discussing the stories as they were published chronologically, I will examine them as they fit into the apparent structure of the novel. Still, given the history of *Invisible Man* where the first chapter published, the battle royal scene, then became the first chapter of the novel, it appears that the first story published, "And Hickman Arrives," will also be the first chapter of the second novel.

"And Hickman Arrives"   Like many of the other stories from the second novel, "And Hickman Arrives" has two distinct time periods. In the present, a group of 44 southern blacks led by the Reverend A. Z. Hickman arrive in Washington, D.C., on a chartered plane and head straight for the office of Senator Sunraider, a notorious racist who represents an unnamed New England state. Sunraider's secretary, a young white Mississippian, tries to shoo them away, saying they are mistaken in thinking that he knows them: " 'I've heard Senator Sunraider state that the only colored he knows is the boy who shines shoes at his golf club.' "[7] She refuses to believe they have an urgent message to deliver.

Turned away from the senator's office and his hotel, the group the next day goes to the Lincoln Memorial to pray and then to the Senate's visitors' gallery where Senator Sunraider speaks about foreign aid. As they watch his delivery, one member of the group, Sister Neal, makes it clear that there is a connection between these southern black people and the racist senator when she recognizes that Sunraider patterns his delivery after Hickman and exclaims, " 'Yeah—why, Reveren', that's *you!* He's still doing you! Oh, my Lord . . . still doing you after all these years and yet he can say all those mean things he says" ("Hickman," 697).

As they watch, they realize in horror that a young man has pulled a gun and is shooting at the senator. At this point, the omniscient narrator enters Hickman's consciousness as Hickman concludes this man "is the one," obviously the assassin about whom Hickman has come to warn Sunraider. Hickman then realizes that Sunraider, whom he calls "Bliss," has been shot and stands cruciform, "his arms lower now, but still outspread, with a stain blooming on the front of his jacket." Sunraider reverts to "the old idiomatic cry" and, to reinforce the Christ imagery, yells, "Lord, LAWD, WHY HAST

THOU . . . ?" (698). Hickman, calling the assassin "Severen," tries to get him to stop, but, in a visual and ironic echo of the Lincoln assassination, Severen jumps over the rail.

When Sunraider, seriously wounded but still alive, calls for Hickman from his hospital bed, the point of view shifts to the senator's. As he hears Hickman's voice calling him "Bliss," he "seemed to dream, to remember, to recall to himself an uneasy dream" (699). At this point the story maintains Bliss-Sunraider's point of view but flashes back to when the six-year-old Bliss served as Hickman's assistant evangelist as they traveled through the South around 1920. Bliss recollects how Hickman had used him as a living prop during his sermons by being "resurrected so that the sinners can find life ever-lasting" (699). Hickman had dressed Bliss in a white suit, hid him in a small silk-lined coffin behind Hickman on the stage, and taught him how to rise out of the coffin just at the right moment of the sermon and say, "LORD, LORD, WHY HAST THOU FORSAKEN ME?" Ellison reinforces the biblical overtones by having Bliss breathe through a plastic tube in the lid of the coffin, recalling Moses' breathing through a reed while hiding in what Huck Finn called the "Bulrushers," and by having Bliss hold his "Easter bunny" to keep him company in the coffin. Besides the obvious religious overtones of Easter, the rabbit imagery echoes the trickster rabbit imagery from *Invisible Man.* Bliss then recollects one night when he performed his resurrection act and a "tall redheaded woman in a purple dress" came screaming into the service, calling out, "He's mine, MINE! That's Cudworth, my child. My baby. You gipsy niggers stole him, my baby. You robbed him of his birthright" ("Hickman," 708).

The story returns to Hickman's voice as he tells the wounded senator what happened after the red-haired woman arrived. In a tug of war Hickman likens to the dispute Solomon judged, the red-haired woman and Sister Bearmasher, a "six-foot city woman from Birmingham" (710), pulled and tugged on Bliss. All of them ended up in the white woman's "rubber-tired buggy" with two white horses, and they raced off into the countryside, which blazed with the burning of a country barn. As the story ends, Hickman recalls how he and Sister Bearmasher were taken to jail and suggests that Bliss was taken from him. He remembers how he prayed but left something out of the prayer: " 'I should have been praying for you, back there all torn up inside by those women's hands. . . . I prayed the wrong prayer. I left you out Bliss, and I guess right then and there you started to wander' " ("Hickman," 712).

Just as the battle royal chapter prefigured the rest of *Invisible Man,* so "And Hickman Arrives" presents most of the themes, images, and tech-

niques of the developing second novel: past versus present; identity; resurrection; transformation; the power of the word; ascent, descent, and fire imagery; Moses, Christ, and other biblical and literary references; and shifting
point of view. The characters' names are also suggestive. *Hickman* implies
the lower status of the evangelist, "caught at a very humble stage of society,"
in Ellison's words. But it also, as Blake notes, recalls Eugene O'Neill's main
character in *The Ice Man Cometh,*

> another mythic rendition of the American experience. Each of them, Theodore
> Hickman ("Hickey") the salesman and A. Z. Hickman, the preacher, is both
> preacher and salesman. Each comes to his potential converts—for Hickey, as
> Iceman, "cometh" to Harry Hope's saloon, Hickman "arrives" in Washington—
> with a gospel of self-recognition. Each preaches birth into a new life through death
> to a false one. Each establishes a sense of identity between himself and his subject.
> Though Hickey's gospel is ultimately ironic and Daddy Hickman's straight, Ellison
> uses the mythic character of the consummate salesman to touch the themes of illu-
> sion and identity and to tie his conception of the American experience to what
> American society already accepts as an American myth. (Blake, 133)

Senator Sunraider, the son who raids the people who raised and sustained
him, raider of the sun or reality, is also named Bliss, recalling the name
Ellison identified as Rinehart's first name in "Change the Joke and Slip the
Yoke." Like Rinehart, Bliss becomes a shape changer, a trickster who is the
master of chaos because he lacks a moral center to sustain him. Discon-
nected from a meaningful past, "passing for white," Bliss loses his identity
and his soul and achieves a kind of death. His death requires a rebirth, an
ascension, and certainly there are numerous images of death and rebirth,
with the central visual image of Bliss's rising out of the coffin. The Christ
imagery associated with Bliss—his cruciform position at the moment of his
shooting, his repeating of Christ's words on Golgotha, and his Easter
bunny—reinforce this imagery.

Bliss-Sunraider suggests other biblical and literary figures. Like Moses he
breathes beneath water and arises; like Jonah he descends and ascends. The
ironic Christ imagery, indeterminate race, and identity crisis suggest
Faulkner's Joe Christmas. In his renaming and recreating himself, he is reminiscent of F. Scott Fitzgerald's Gatsby, who also created himself anew.
Hickman thinks of Bliss: "Even his name's not his own name. Made himself
from the ground up you might say" ("Hickman," 698).

While these overtones are subtle, other literary allusions are direct.
Hickman's nickname, "God's Trombone," comes from the title of James

Weldon Johnson's *God's Trombones: Seven Negro Sermons in Verse* (1927) and suggests the importance of African American churches, as well as acknowledging Ellison's connection with Johnson's *The Autobiography of an Ex-Coloured Man,* another book about passing for white. Another direct allusion is to Emerson, whom Hickman describes as a "philosopher" who "knew that every tub has to sit on its own bottom" ("Hickman," 701).

The literary and biblical allusions demonstrate that in the Hickman stories, Ellison continues the theme of the amalgamation of eclectic cultural forces with the same cautions as before made more emphatic now. Just as Rinehart's eclecticism tried to combine so many contradictory roles that it crossed over the border into chaos, so Bliss's protean shape changing yields disorder. The frontier allowed and required possibility, but as Ellison made clear in *Invisible Man,* the American frontier emphasis on ignoring the lessons of the past was one of the negative aspects of the frontier myth. Perhaps the predominant theme of the Hickman stories is the necessity of applying to the present the moral judgments validated by history. Characters who extend frontier possibility for individualistic reasons are irresponsibly opportunistic.

"The Roof, the Steeple, and the People"   The second story published also follows chronologically, since it takes place when Bliss was a young boy growing up in an unidentified southern or southwestern town. The title refers to a popular child's rhyme and hand game. As the child intertwines the fingers of both hands so that the fingers are inside the double fist, the child says, "Here is the roof." Then the index fingers are raised into an upside-down V shape, and the child says, "And here is the steeple." Finally, the child, usually wiggling the fingers at the same time, rolls the fist over so that the intertwined fingers point up and says: "Open the church and here are the people." It is an image of transformation, verbal games, and hand and finger imagery recalling Washington's emphasis on segregation in the Atlanta Exposition Address ("separate as the fingers, yet one as the hand").

As the story begins, "Daddy" Hickman tells Bliss that he will take him to "one of the Devil's hangouts" where he can watch "the marvelous happenings in the dark," obviously in reference to a movie theater because Hickman believes that Bliss must learn to "preach goodness out of badness . . . hope out of hopelessness" and that he should "get some idea of what you will have to fight against, because I don't believe you can really lead folks if you never have to face up to any of the temptations they face." After all, "Christ had to put on the flesh."[8] But Hickman is concerned about peo-

ple who get "mixed up with those shadows spread out against the wall" because they "lose touch with who they're supposed to be." Consequently Bliss
will get to go only once. It is the preacher's "main job . . . to help folks find
themselves and to keep reminding them to remember who they are"
("Roof," 116).

The time then shifts to a few days earlier when Bliss learns about the existence of movies from his friend, Body, who talks about a Jewish friend,
Sammy Leaderman, who has "a machine with people in it." Bliss tries to understand, calling it first a kodak, then wondering if it is a nickelodeon he
had heard about "when we were out there preaching in Denver," and then a
magic lantern. As they talk about this mysterious new thing, they also talk
about Jews, since Sammy is a Jew: "He a Jew; but he looks white" (118).
When Bliss says that Sammy calls him a "rabbi," Body misunderstands and
wonders why Sammy calls him a "rabbit," returning to the rabbit, trickster
imagery associated with Bliss. Bliss also recalls how when he and Hickman
were in Tulsa needing money to return home, a black porter who could
"talk some Jewish" went into a store run by Jews and raised $50 for their re-
turn. This conversation about mixing and amalgamation, as O'Meally says,
leads Bliss to "the inescapability of the world of contradictions: sometimes
black is white, white is Jewish, black is Jewish, sacred is profane" (O'Meally
1980, 130).

Returning to the subject of the machine with people in it, Body tells Bliss
that in the box are life-sized people, trains, horses, Indians who get killed,
and cowboys who chase the train but no colored. Bliss responds, "Then
that's got to be magic. . . . Because that's the only way they can get rid of
the colored" ("Roof," 125).

The story returns to the beginning time period as Bliss and Hickman
head to the movie theater. Bliss thinks that perhaps he would rather not see
movies directly but simply "see the flickery scenes unreeling inside my eye
just as Daddy Hickman could make people relive the action of the Word."
Actually he realizes that Hickman is too late, for "already the landscape of
my mind had been trampled by the great droves of galloping horses and
charging redskins and the yelling charges of cowboys and cavalrymen, and I
had reeled before exploding faces that imprinted themselves upon one's
eyeball with the impact of a water-soaked snowball. . . . And I had . . . seen
. . . meanness transcendent, yawning in one overwhelming face; and heroic
goodness expressed in actions as cleanly violent as a cyclone seen from a
distance" ("Roof," 126–27). His imagination has taken over, spurred by
Body's and the other kids' reenactments of the movies they have seen. He
would rather not see it just once and then have to long for what he could not

see. But even as he thinks that he would rather not just see it once, he "ascended, climbed, holding reluctantly Daddy Hickman's huge hand" (128) as they climb up toward the roof, since the "colored" section of the segregated theater is upstairs.

The hand imagery that holds this story together points in several directions. The allusion to Washington suggests the story's underlying emphasis on segregation and racism. The youthful Bliss's holding "Daddy" Hickman's hand indicates this is another story of initiation. Hand imagery also appears in the discussion with Body, whom Bliss calls his "right hand." Intertwined, Body and Bliss are like body and soul, perhaps, foreshadowing Bliss's transformation and loss of soul.

"The Roof, the Steeple, and the People" also emphasizes the responsibility of the artist. O'Meally points out that Ellison connects the preacher's craft and duty with that of the artist who, in Ellison's view, also must accept moral responsibility and lead his or her audience to know who they are (O'Meally 1980, 127). Art that glorifies heroic violence or makes "meanness transcendent" evades responsibility.

"Juneteenth"   The title of this story refers to the date slaves in Texas were freed. African Americans in Texas celebrate 19 June 1865 as Emancipation Day because on that day Major General Gordon Granger of the Union Army entered Galveston and declared: "In accordance with a proclamation from the executive of the United States, all slaves are free." When Lincoln had issued his Emancipation Proclamation on 1 January 1863, Texas paid allegiance to Jefferson Davis as president of the Confederacy and ignored Lincoln's order. Now widely celebrated in the Southwest, the day was less well known except to black people during Ellison's formative years. In the story it becomes the occasion for Daddy Hickman to deliver a sermon about whites' mistreatment of blacks. In this dialogue Daddy Hickman uses Reverend Bliss as a kind of chorus so that Bliss's "piccolo voice" counterpoints Hickman's "baritone" trombone.

The story, which again emphasizes amalgamation and cultural assimilation, is presented from Sunraider-Bliss's point of view as he remembers "a bunch of old-fashioned Negroes celebrating an illusion of emancipation, and getting it mixed up with the Resurrection, minstrel shows and vaudeville routines."[9] Lying wounded in a hospital bed, Bliss thinks, "Lord, it hurts. Lordless and without loyalty, it hurts. Wordless, it hurts." But then he begins to remember "after all the roving years and flickering scenes." The language and imagery point back to Brer Bear and Brer Rabbit in *Invisible Man* and to the hands of "The Roof, the Steeple, and the People," when

Bliss asks himself if he must return to the times when Hickman, "like a great, kindly, daddy bear along the streets" walked with him, "my hand lost in his huge paw" ("Juneteenth," 262).

Bliss recalls how he knew his role, to represent the "part of the younger generation." Daddy Hickman consciously amalgamates by drawing from Passover rituals, which raise story to mythic levels: "The Hebrew children have their Passover so that they can keep their history alive in their memories—so let us take one more page from their book and, on this great day of deliverance, on this day of emancipation, let's us tell ourselves our story" (263). Thus, Daddy Hickman tells how black people were brought out of Africa to suffer under slavery, becoming "eyeless, tongueless, drumless, danceless, songless, hornless, soundless, sightless, dayless, nightless, wrongless, rightless, motherless, fatherless—scattered" (269).

As Hickman spins his story, Ellison merges classical, biblical, and literary allusions. The major classical reference is to the myth of Cadmus's sowing of dragon's teeth, which were then reborn as armed men who fought among themselves until only five survived. Cadmus used the survivors to found and build the city of Thebes and introduced the alphabet to the Greeks. This one allusion suggests fragmentation, rebirth, and language. In Ellison's story, Africans brought in chains were fragmented, "chopped . . . up into little bitty pieces like a farmer when he cuts up a potato" (267). Hickman likens the African American diaspora to the sowing of the dragon's teeth: "They scattered us just like a dope-fiend farmer planting a field with dragon teeth!" (268).

Then Hickman turns to his primary biblical text for his next metaphor, the book of Ezekiel from the Old Testament, as he compares the sowing of the bones of black people into the earth "like the valley of Dry Bones in Ezekiel's dream." He continues: "Son of man . . . under the ground" (271). With the imagery from Ezekiel, Ellison also points to one of his most important sources, Eliot's "The Waste Land," for Ezekiel's valley of ashes and dry bones was one of Eliot's major sources. Eliot emphasized the need for a powerful, sustaining myth; Daddy Hickman attempts to create such a myth.

The burial of the fragmented people prefaces their rebirth as African Americans, an amalgamated people: "Ah, but though divided and scattered, ground down and battered into the earth like a spike being pounded by a ten pound sledge, we were on the ground and in the earth and the earth was red and black like the earth of Africa. And as we moldered underground we were mixed with this land. We liked it. It fitted us fine. It was in us and we were in it. And then—praise God—deep in the ground, deep in the womb of this land, we began to stir!" ("Juneteenth," 270). In the dialogue this rebirth is emphasized when Bliss asks, "These dry bones live?" and Daddy Hickman replies, "Amen! And we heard and rose up" (272) He states that they were "rebirthed dancing, were rebirthed crying affirmation of the Word, quickening our transcended flesh" (272).

Ellison commented on this story's emphasis on fragmentation and reassimilation in his interview with Stepto and Harper, who asked about students who were upset because Hickman calls Africans who came to America in chains "heathen." Ellison replied,

Oh, for God's sake! I didn't make that statement, *Hickman* did. He was preaching about transcendence; about the recovery from fragmentation; about the slave's refusal, with the help of God, to be decimated by slavery. He was speaking as a Christian minister of the role his religion had played in providing a sense of unity and hope to a people that had been deliberately deprived of a functional continuity with their religions and traditions. Hickman didn't attend college but, hell, he knew that all of our African ancestors didn't belong to the same tribe, speak the same tongue, or worship the same gods. (Stepto and Harper, 463)

"Juneteenth" returns to Ellison's continuing emphasis on the power of the word through showmanship, amalgamation, and rebirth. Stylistically he uses classical, biblical, and literary allusions and familiar images such as namelessness, facelessness, invisibility, and blindness. Another familiar image, one that possibly reveals Joyce's influence, is the spiral of history. Joyce adopted the concept that history is cyclical from Giambattista Vico, an eighteenth-century philosopher, and structured *Finnegans Wake* so that the first sentence meets the last. As Hickman's sermon ends, he states a similar vision of circular time: "Time will come round when we'll have to be their eyes; time will swim and turn back around. I tell you, time shall swing and spiral back around . . . " [Ellison's ellipsis] ("Juneteenth," 276). In the language of myth, history and time spiral around and are reborn.

"Night-Talk" "Night-Talk," first published in *Quarterly Review of Literature* (1969), is also presented as a recollection that Bliss-Sunraider has after he was wounded. It was published with an author's note that contained a wry parenthetical remark identifying the story as an "excerpt from a novel-in-progress (*very* long in progress)." In the note Ellison also explained that the setting is a Washington, D.C., hospital room "circa 1955, the year the novel was conceived." The note continues:

In [the excerpt] the Senator is passing through alternate periods of lucidity and delirium attending wounds resulting from a gunman's attempt on his life. Hickman, in turn, is weary from the long hours of sleeplessness and emotional strain which have accumulated while he has sought to see the Senator through his ordeal. The men have been separated for many years, and time, conflicts of value, the desire of one to remember nothing and the tendency of the other to remember too much, have rendered communication between them difficult.

Sometimes they actually converse, sometimes the dialogue is illusory and occurs in the isolation of their individual minds, but through it all it is antiphonal in form and an anguished attempt to arrive at the true shape and substance of a sundered past and its meaning.[10]

In the story Hickman and Senator Sunraider talk about the past and remember when the young Bliss "played hooky from services" (317) and caused everyone to search until they finally found him "coming out of a picture house where it was against the law for us to go" (318). Hickman's recollection causes the injured senator to recall in interior monologue (presented in Faulknerian fashion in italics) his own memory of that experience in Atlanta. The story apparently occurs after the action of "And Hickman Arrives" and "The Roof, the Steeple, and the People" because Bliss remembers when his mother disrupted the service, the subject of the former story, and he also seems knowledgeable about movies, which he learned of in the latter story.

Bliss recalls chasing a moving car that had "her" picture on its side. From the rest of the story, the picture is probably an advertisement for a movie starring Mary Pickford, whom Bliss confuses with his mother. After losing the car, Bliss goes to a movie theater. Wary at first that the girl at the ticket window might reject him, he is delighted to get his ticket. Then he is frightened by the ticket taker who questions him about being old enough to see the movie. When the ticket taker is distracted by several young girls (causing him to exclaim, *"Well did Ah evuh wet dream of Jeannie and her cawn sulk hair"* [323]), Bliss tells him that his mother, named "Miz Pickford," is waiting for him in the theater, and Bliss is allowed to enter. Inside, he reflects on the philosophical dimensions of history, shadows, and mirrors until the story ends with a return to Hickman's voice wondering why God had chosen him and Bliss to enter into this complicated relationship.

One of the more complex Hickman stories, "Night-Talk" reveals, besides influences of Joyce, Faulkner, the Bible, Homer, Freud, and numerous other forerunners, the significance of movies on Ellison's vision of life. Joyce is in many ways the predominant force here, particularly the Joyce of *Finnegans Wake*. Just as Joyce playfully created language, so Ellison sprinkles this story with neologisms: "spectacularmythics," "niggonography," "connednation," and "mothermatermammy." Another Joycean reference occurs as Bliss walks into the theater and steps on tiles that depict Daedalus and Icarus: *"Then I was stepping over two blue naked men with widespread wings who were flying on the white tiled lobby floor, only the smaller one was falling into the white tile water."* ("Night," 322).

One prominent theme of this story, as O'Meally accurately notes, concerns the enigma of Bliss's parents. The woman claiming to be his mother at the service had thrown Bliss into a state of intense confusion. Seeking her, he adopts Mary Pickford, perhaps after Hickman had told him that "each man's bedmate is likely to be a mary . . . even though she may be a magdalene" (318). Equally confusing to the young Bliss is the question of his father. Is it Daddy Hickman or is it God the Father? The complexity of these questions leads Bliss to escape into the movie house where he can pass for white and avoid Hickman, for whom in a segregated world it is unlawful to visit the theater.

Especially puzzling is the question of history, to which the wounded senator has been forced to return and to which Ellison returns repeatedly in these stories. As Bliss remembers the day in the movie theater, he wonders, "How the hell do you get love into politics or compassion into history?" ("Night," 325–26). And later, in an allusion to Eliot's "The Hollow Men," he thinks, *"Why couldn't you say, Daddy Hickman: Man is born of woman but then there's history and towns and states and between the passion and the act there are mysteries"* ("Night," 326). Finally in an allusion and pun on both Eliot's "The Love Song of J. Alfred Prufrock" and Andrew Marvell's "To His Coy Mistress," Bliss tries to justify his rebelliousness as he indicates that he has tried to alter history: *"Stretch out their nerves, amplify their voices, extend their grasp until history is rolled into a pall"* (326)

"Cadillac Flambé"   In the first of a sequence of stories concerning the adult Bliss once he becomes Senator Sunraider, a jazz musician, Lee Willie Minifees, upset by some comments that Senator Sunraider made on the floor of the Senate, drives his Cadillac up on the grounds near the senator's Washington residence and sets his car on fire. As it burns, he makes a speech to the onlookers in which he explains his reasons for his actions. As the story ends, the police arrive and straitjacket Minifees.

Although the narrator is unnamed, in an interview Ellison identified one of the narrators as a white newspaperman named McIntyre, "who had had some radical experiences during the thirties and had had an affair, which didn't end well, with a Negro girl" (Hersey 1987, 290, 307). Conceivably

McIntyre is the narrator of both "Cadillac Flambé" and the next story in the sequence, "It Always Breaks Out." In the story the narrator has gone out birdwatching with friends on this spring day. With his binoculars and tape recorder "to record bird songs," he finds himself near the senator's home as the "happening" occurs. Thus Ellison provides a realistic purpose for the narrator's ability to reproduce Minifees's words.

Using the narrator allows Ellison to present a variety of voices. First is the narrator's pompous one that recalls Twain's narrator in "The Celebrated Jumping Frog of Calaveras County." When the narrator first sees Minifees drive his Cadillac on the senator's lawn, he immediately reverts to familiar stereotypes to explain the event:

> At first, in my innocence, I placed the man as a musician, for there was, after all the bull fiddle; then in swift succession I thought him a chauffeur for one of the guests, a driver for a news or fashion magazine or an advertising agency or television. . . . Next I decided that the man had either been sent with equipment to be used in covering the festivities taking place on the terrace, or that he had driven the car over to be photographed against the luxurious background. The waving I interpreted as the expression of simple-minded high spirits aroused by the driver's pleasure in piloting such a luxurious automobile, the simple exuberance of a Negro allowed a role in what he considered an important public spectacle.[11]

In contrast is the brash, sprightly, colloquial language of the jazzman, Minifees, whose visual and verbal performance draws from various sources. Using language from the hymn "Amazing Grace," Minifees introduces the blindness motif familiar to *Invisible Man*: "The *scales* dropped from my eyes. I had been BLIND, but the Senator up there on that hill was making me SEE. He was making me see some things I didn't *want* to see" ("Flambé," 261). As he enters Washington, Minifees emphasizes that the town always causes him to think of the difference between American ideals and reality: "When I'm *here* I never stop thinking about the difference between what it *is* and what it's *supposed* to be. In fact, I have the feeling that somebody put the *Indian* sign on this town a long, long time ago, and I don't want to be here when it takes effect." Visually Minifees recreates the Indian sign, for he chooses the image of the bow and arrow as the device for torching his car. He creates a makeshift arrow out of a tennis ball and a wooden knitting needle, soaks the ball in white gasoline, strings his fiddle bow, lights it, and shoots "his improvised, flame-tipped arrow onto the cloth top of the convertible" ("Flambé," 254).

Several other familiar ideas and images of Ellison's appear. The theme of amalgamation emerges in the narrator's varied brunch of chile con carne, cornbread, and oysters Rockefeller. A character addressing a group of onlookers recalls the numerous speech-making scenes in other Ellison works. Minifees's description of his Cadillac as a cage suggests other Ellison images of restriction. The radio frequency motif from *Invisible Man* reappears as the narrator describes the scene as being like one of those moments, a "brief interruption one sometimes hears while listening to an F.M. broadcast of the musical *Oklahoma!*, say, with the original cast, when the signal fades and a program of quite different wavelength breaks through" (269). Ellison's attraction to nineteenth-century American literature is suggested by Minifees's conclusion—recalling Thoreau and Emerson—that the Cadillac owns him, and he is the tool of his tool, or perhaps the fool of his tool. Creative language is important to Minifees, as it is to other Ellison characters. Minifees yells to the senator that he has unconverted him from his convertible.

Bird imagery is especially predominant in "Cadillac Flambé." O'Meally concludes that the combination of bird and fire imagery recalls the phoenix: "The use of fire and the omnipresence of birds and other images associated with birth, death, and rebirth suggest that the rite is one of fertility and celebration. The flaming Cadillac, like a 'huge fowl being flambéed in cognac,' inevitably summons up the phoenix, dying only to be reborn in fire. Minifees sings as the bird-car groans and dies, with its short-circuited horn 'wailing like some great prehistoric animal heard in the throes of its dying.' But then of course, phoenixlike, the flaming bird gives birth to new life" (O'Meally 1980, 155).

As he stands next to the red flames that engulf his white Cadillac, Minifees wears a white suit, blue tie, and black alligator shoes. Similar to the color imagery that merges red, white, blue, and black as the narrator in *Invisible Man* eats his vanilla ice cream covered with sloe gin listening to Louis Armstrong's "What Did I Do to Be So Black and Blue," "Cadillac Flambé" proclaims black as one with the other traditional American colors.

"It Always Breaks Out"   The "it" of the title is "Nigra politics." The story takes place shortly after the burning of the Cadillac in "Cadillac Flambé." The narrator, a white, liberal newspaperman, probably McIntyre, recounts the details of a gathering of journalists who get together for dinner the evening of the burning. At first the discussion is jovial, as several members of the group comment on the day's events. The narrator reveals his belief that "this fellow today must have been mad. Off his rocker."[12] The tone turns serious when they wonder about the possibility of a "Negro assassin," but another member of the group suggests it is impossible to tell "when those people are doing something politically significant."

At this point a southerner, McGowan, decides to explain "Nigra politics" to the group, saying that "everything the Nigra does is political," foreshadowing the semiologists' examination of meaning in ordinary human activity such as food and dress. McGowan demonstrates his thesis with several examples: " 'If you catch a Nigra in the wrong section of town after dark— he's being political because he knows he's got no business being there. If he brushes against a white man on the street or on a stairway, that's very political' " ("Breaks," 18). He continues with numerous examples from dress to religion to joining the Book-of-the-Month Club to social acts: " 'Let me remark on one of the meanest, lowdownest forms of Nigra politics I have observed, and one which I mention among a bunch of gentlemen only with the greatest reluctance. That's when a sneaky, ornery, smart-alecky Nigra stands up in a crowd of peaceful, well-meaning white folks, who've gathered together in a public place to see Justice done, and that Nigra ups and breaks wind!' " ("Breaks," 23). Although choosing reading material is a political act, McGowan is not concerned about blacks' reading Shakespeare, " 'because no Nigra who ever lived would know how to apply the Bard.' " On the other hand, " 'if you catch you a Nigra reading that lowdown, Nigra-loving Bill Faulkner and *liking* him, there you have you a politically dangerous, integrationist Nigra!' " ("Breaks," 21).

The narrator, who describes himself as a "liberal, ex-radical, northerner," reacts uncomfortably to McGowan's speech, especially when Sam, the black waiter, comes near. Finally, however, the narrator, in language that recalls Melville's "Benito Cereno" and emphasizes Ellison's concern with history, concludes: "For I realized that McGowan was obsessed by history to the point of nightmare. He had the dark man confined in a package and this was the way he carried him everywhere, saw him in everything" ("Breaks," 27).

Nonetheless, the narrator has been forced to question his own liberal approach to racial prejudice. Although he is uncomfortable with McGowan's blatant racism, he acknowledges the other's directness: "For McGowan said things about Negroes with absolute conviction which I dared not even think. Could it be that he was more honest than I, that his free expression of his feelings, his prejudices, made him freer than I? . . . Suddenly I despised his power to make me feel buried fears and possibilities, his power to define so much of the reality in which I lived and which I seldom bother to think about" ("Breaks," 27). Forced to confront his own buried prejudice, the narrator wonders if his "habit of mind, formed during the radical Thirties, prevented" (28) him from understanding Sam. Suddenly he realizes he does not know Sam's last name.

In this story Ellison emphasizes how southerners are seemingly obsessed by black people, cursed in Melville's terms. Black people, the narrator seems to suggest, do not exist for white southerners. Instead they react to the images in their heads: "And was it possible that the main object of McGowan's passion was really an idea, the idea of a non-existent past rather than a living people?" ("Breaks," 27)

As he does throughout these Hickman stories, Ellison refers often to Oklahoma and compares native Americans and African Americans. Commenting on the car burner, one man says, " 'He's as wild as those rich Oklahoma Indians who preferred to travel in hook-and-ladder fire trucks or brand new hearses instead of limousines.' " Later McGowan says that "Nigras" who drink liquor such as Pernod "have jumped the reservation and are out to ruin this nation." And McGowan identifies watching Indians on television as a dangerous political act: " 'What's more, if you allow the Nigra to see Indians killing white folks week after week . . . he's apt to go bad. . . . It doesn't matter that the Indians are always defeated because the Nigra has the feeling deep down that *he* can win' " (20).

"It Always Breaks Out" allows Ellison to explore various speaking voices. In "Cadillac Flambé" the contrast was between the narrator and the vernacular African American language of Minifees. Here it is between the narrator and a southern redneck. Ellison enters Minifees's and McGowan's language with equal vigor and maximum humor, but he makes his serious points too. In this story, first published in the spring of 1963, Ellison could treat the question of assassination with some humor. History would soon make that subject more difficult to discuss with a comic tone.

"Backwacking: A Plea to the Senator" The most recent Hickman story is a relatively light piece that takes the form of a letter to Senator Sunraider from an 80-year-old Alabama redneck who heard the Cadillac speech and was inspired to write to support Sunraider's racism. The author of the letter, Mr. Norm A. Mauler, is particularly upset by a new trend that he has heard of among Negroes, backwacking, a sexual experience between a black man and woman back to back: "HE *and his woman have taken to getting undressed and standing back to back and heel to heel, shoulderblade to shoulderblade, and tale to tale* [sic] *with his against her's and her's against his, and then after they have horsed around and maneuvered like cats in heat and worked as tight together as a tick to a cow's tit,* HE *ups and starts in to* HAVING HER BACKWARDS!"[13] As unlikely as this sounds,

Mauler is sure that it exists, although he has never witnessed it, because he
has heard of it. Moreover, he is convinced that it is another subversive, un-
American activity that black folks have introduced to corrupt the minds of
American youth. Thus, he is writing to urge the senator to do something
about this vile practice.

Ellison primarily is having fun satirizing the southern racists from whom
he attempted to escape when he left Alabama in 1936. His major weapon is
language as he allows his victim to skewer himself. Stereotypes that float in
the white racist's imagination, in this case, the stereotype of the superhu-
man black phallus, have overwhelmed Norm A. Mauler. But as the name
suggests, Ellison is also poking fun in another direction—at Norman
Mailer, author of *The White Negro* (1957), in which Mailer uses stereotypes
of African Americans to discuss the then-popular figure of the hipster.
Mailer claimed that the white hipster had adopted aspects of black rebelliousness, but Mailer resorted to broad stereotypes in the process:

Knowing in the cells of his existence that life was war, nothing but war, the Negro
(all exceptions admitted) could rarely afford the sophisticated inhibitions of civilization, and so he kept for his survival the art of the primitive, he lived in the enormous present, he subsisted for his Saturday night kicks, relinquishing the pleasure
of the mind for the more obligatory pleasure of his body, and in his music he gave
voice to the character and quality of his existence, to his rage and the infinite variations of joy, lust, languor, growl, cramp, pinch, scream and despair of his orgasm.
For jazz is orgasm, it is the music of orgasm, good orgasm, and bad, and so it spoke
across a nation.[14]

Likewise, Ellison's Norm Mauler is concerned about the orgasms produced
by backwacking: "*I am informed that when he and his woman reach the climax of this radical new way of sinning they get blasted by one of the darndest
feelings that has ever been known to hit the likes of Man!*" (446–47). By calling his southern racist a name similar to a northern Jewish intellectual's,
Ellison, as he does in "It Always Breaks Out," points to the similarity of all
forms of racism—raw and enlightened.

"A Song of Innocence"   This title, from William Blake's "Songs
of Innocence" series, refers to the narrator, a seemingly retarded and men-
tally unstable 300-pound man named Cliofus who tells McIntyre about the
time a grade school friend named Severen came to visit him, and he recalled
for Severen events that happened in grade school. Although "A Song of Innocence" in some ways clouds rather than clarifies the details about the

novel,[15] apparently McIntyre, in search of information about Severen, the man who shot Sunraider, has come to interview Cliofus, Severen's childhood friend. Among the recalled items are the teacher, a Miss Mable Kindly, the principal, Dr. Peter Osgood Eliot, and a character who comes to enforce the "law," someone called both "Blue Goose" and "Reverend Samson." Blue Goose takes the boys from the classroom down to the basement to paddle them. After one paddling, a boy named China Jackson had run home, gotten his "daddy's forty-four," and come back shooting. Too influenced by "shoot-em-up cowboy movies," however, he pulls the trigger still holding the barrel at 12 o'clock, and shoots into the ceiling.

Also recalled is a visit to the railroad yards to see a whale "on a long flatcar on planks and canvas painted blue and white to look like ocean waves" and "smelling sick-to-the-stomach sweetish like a whole ocean of embalming fluid." This whale has "two red light bulbs sticking where his eyes were supposed to be." Soon "a little red-headed man smoking a crooked pipe and hobbling on an ole beat-up wooden leg" came out to talk about the whale. When Miss Kindly asks for questions, one of the students named Bernard asks, "If that there whale is an animule, what gives rich milk, where do she carry her tits?"[16]

"A Song of Innocence," more than the other Hickman stories, returns to Ellison's emphasis on the dialectical nature of language and history. (Blake engaged in dialectic by balancing his "Songs of Innocence" with "Songs of Experience.") Other stories focus on Hickman's emphasis on the power of the word to transform; "A Song of Innocence" examines both the positive and negative power of language. Cliofus is full of words, but he views them as having a power unto themselves, saying, "They say that folks misuse words, but I see it the other way around, words misuse people. Usually when you think you're saying what you mean you're really saying what the words want you to say" ("Song," 32). The words pour out of him and others. Bernard's innocent question, for example, is troublesome to the teacher. Nonetheless, through words Cliofus finds stability for both himself and Severen. The words, Cliofus says, are "what makes me *me*." And when Severen asks him, "Do you mean that you always tell the truth?" Cliofus replies, "No, but the truth gets into it" ("Song," 36). Language confuses and obfuscates, but eventually in the dialectical scramble between untruth and truth, the truth will out.

Language also represents freedom for Cliofus and his friends in much the same way as for Buster and Riley. In fact, Cliofus's friends are named Buster, Leroy, and Tommy Dee ("Song," 32). Like the Riley-like narrator of

"A Coupla Scalped Indians," Cliofus is cared for by a Miss Janey (who later writes Hickman and warns him about Severen). References to Indians indicate that Cliofus, like Buster and Riley, is a young black boy growing up in Oklahoma. The Buster of this story resorts to verbal freedom just as the earlier Buster did. When Miss Kindly asks Cliofus a question he cannot answer, Buster "jumped out into the aisle and did a buck dance, singing, "Well, if at first you don't succeed / Well a-keep on a-sucking / Till you do sucka seed" ("Song," 33). Cliofus's answer points to the story's concern with history. Miss Kindly had asked Cliofus who was the father of our country, and when Cliofus in confusion could not answer, she admonished, "You must know history." Cliofus, thinking that she meant a man named "Mister History," responded that he would be pleased to meet him, "But do you think Mr. History would have time to be bothered with somebody like me, mam?" ("Song," 33). History—the past—is obscured and revealed by language. People like Cliofus, whose name is an extension of Clio, the muse of history, are often, like the Zoot-suiters in *Invisible Man,* left out of written history, but art—aware that history is a gambler—acknowledges the boomerang of history. In his diatribe against language, Cliofus says, "No wonder history is a bitch on wheels with wings traveling inside a submarine. Words are behind it all" (32). But words also—in fits and starts—lead us *"into the old calcified night of loneliness toward the unsayable meaning of mankind's outrageous condition in this world"* ("Song," 30). Language that penetrates history rather than obscures it discovers and reveals this truth.

Just as the story returns to recognizable themes, it also demonstrates several familiar influences: a retarded narrator and persistent shadow images recall *The Sound and the Fury;* the *Moby Dick* allusions in the story of the whale and the one-legged man are clear; and school paddlings and Miss Kindly's demand that Cliofus apologize suggest *A Portrait of the Artist as a Young Man.* Ultimately, as O'Meally notes, "A Song of Innocence" is another portrait of the artist as a young man. Despite Cliofus's assault on language—and language's assault on Cliofus—he represents what William Faulkner described in his Nobel Prize acceptance speech: mankind's "puny inexhaustible voice, still talking," enduring, and prevailing.

Intriguing Prospects

Although no story from the new novel has appeared since 1977, Ellison has mentioned some of the other parts of the novel in progress. One section concerns an interview between McIntyre, the journalist, and Minifees, the Cadillac flambéer, in a hospital cell. To get McIntyre there, Ellison had to create a new character: "So for McIntyre to see the man there has to be an intermediary—so suddenly I found myself dealing with a new character, a Negro employed by the hospital, who gets McIntyre past the barriers and to the car-burner" (Hersey 1987, 290). Another section possibly deals with the incident out of which the entire novel evolved after he started thinking about an old man "so outraged by his life that he goes poking around in the cellar to find a forgotten coffin, which he had bought years before to insure against his possible ruin. He discovers that he has lived so long that the coffin is full of termites, and that even the things he had stored in the coffin have fallen apart" (Hersey 1987, 289).

This incident suggests that from the very beginning of the new novel, Ellison has concentrated on history's relationship to the present. The dialectic between past and present, words and actions, ideal and reality, freedom and restriction, innocence and experience—concerns of Ellison throughout his career—continues to permeate his fiction.

Whatever direction Ralph Ellison's second novel takes, its publication will be hailed as one of the major literary events of the twentieth century. Whether it will be another *Finnegans Wake,* a complex novel long in the making and published in parts along the way, will be for Mr. History to decide.

Chapter Six

The Mellow Bugler: Ellison's Nonfiction

To read the nonfiction that Ralph Ellison has published throughout his career is to hear a voice of reason, concern, optimism, and intelligence. From his earliest to his latest essays, Ellison returns repeatedly to those issues that have compelled him as an artist, most of which result from his acute awareness of the unity and diversity of American life: the one and the many, order and chaos, ideal and reality, masks and identity. Among the other themes that appear often in his nonfiction are Ellison's regard for history and the past, abhorrence of racial stereotyping, concern with identity, belief in the power of art to transform, awareness of the richness of African American culture, and emphasis on amalgamation. In most essays, he calls upon his own experience, or at least the created persona, "Ralph Ellison," to support his points.

Ellison's nonfictional works fall into three general groups: uncollected political and literary essays written in the late thirties and forties, primarily for Marxist publications such as *New Masses;* essays, speeches, and interviews from 1942 to 1964 collected in *Shadow and Act;* and essays, speeches, and interviews collected in *Going to the Territory,* most written from 1964 to 1985. Within these groups, Ellison's nonfiction is concerned with three general subjects: literature, music, and African American social and political life.

As a writer, Ellison has been concerned with the purpose of the novel, and he has often stated that American fiction must regain the moral resolve that America's best nineteenth-century writers—Herman Melville, Mark Twain, and Henry James—demonstrated in their best work as they attempted to use the novel to promote democratic principles. These writers understood the significance of slavery on the American experience and portrayed African Americans as representing the most meaningful aspects of democracy. As a former musician and aspiring composer, Ellison returns to his musical background for comparisons of artistic purpose and discipline. Southwestern jazz and blues musicians provide the basis for his understanding of the complex intertwining of tradition and individual talent, the given and the improvised, from which American art, as Ellison perceives it, springs. As an African American, Ellison has been acutely aware of the disparity between American ideals and opportunity and the restrictions forced upon black people, first through slavery, then through jim crow laws, and always through racism. But Ellison refuses to accept sociologists' conclusions that black life is stilted and reduced because of these burdens placed on it. There is, Ellison insists, a flourishing black culture, despite the reality of racism in America, and it is through African American culture—folklore, art, music, dance—that young black men and women discover the intrinsic value of being African American, American, and human.

American reality, Ellison asserts, demonstrates elements of the melting pot. Although it became fashionable in post-1960s America to dismiss the melting pot motif, first eloquently presented by St. John de Crèvecoeur in the *Letters from an American Farmer,* Ellison believes America is a mixture. American language is not English but a transformation of English. American life reveals the diversity of various cultures, all drawing from one another to alter and color the whole. Believing this, Ellison has resisted black nationalist and back-to-Africa movements.

Ellison's varying subjects have led several critics to outline the major ideas in his nonfiction. Berndt Ostendorf in "Ralph Waldo Ellison: Anthropology, Modernism, and Jazz" identifies the three elements of his title as the most important Ellisonian concepts and suggests that they present a thesis, antithesis, and synthesis. By "anthropology," Ostendorf means Ellison's "ritual theory of culture, an interest in transformations, and a concern with the dialogic principle" expressed in language and symbolic action (Ostendorf 1988, 106). Anthropology's open-ended fluidity opposes "stern" modernism's rigidity, which requires an almost reverential attitude toward the liberating yet organizing power of art. Jazz, according to Ostendorf, provides Ellison with a synthesis of fluidity and order, for the jazz artist demonstrates the correlation between tradition and the individual talent.

In his attempt to synthesize Ellison's major ideas, John S. Wright concentrates on four "organizing impulses, four intermingled disciplining strategies for divining order in experience . . . and for converting that experience into potent symbolic action."[1] First the "*syncretic* impulse" emphasizes cultural amalgamation. Second "the *celebratory* impulse" affirms wholeness in African American cultural values. Third, the "*dialectical* impulse" stresses the process through which contrary ideas work toward wholeness. Finally "the *demiurgic* impulse" seeks "cultural power and personal freedom through art."

In their analyses of Ellison's nonfiction, both John Reilly and Valerie Smith suggest that Ellison's persona in his nonfiction is another fictional creation, one based on the details of Ellison's life as an African American growing up on the Oklahoma frontier but nonetheless a construct used to make the same points about living in the world as Ellison's fiction. Ellison's nonfiction, his "generalized autobiography," Reilly concludes, with "its broad frontiersman scheme" is a fiction because "it is like fiction in the selectivity it uses to enforce the compelling significance of a single, unqualified feature of Ellison's life: his certain and intuitive resolve to achieve the birthright of a free citizen of a democracy."[2] Valerie Smith contends that the "character of the artist in Ellison's nonfiction corresponds to the portrait of the protagonist in *Invisible Man*" (Smith, 90). She defines the voice in the nonfiction as an artist and a "figure of rebellion" working "in opposition to the restraints of received literary convention" (Smith, 88).

Ellison presented some of his own generalizations about human development in a 1948 essay, "Harlem Is Nowhere," in which he described the Lafargue Psychiatric Clinic in Harlem. In that essay Ellison identified the "three basic social factors shaping an American Negro's personality" (*SA,* 295). Although he described the way psychiatric patients were evaluated, this statement also defines several of Ellison's larger conclusions about any individual American:

He is viewed as a member of a racial and cultural minority; as an American citizen caught in certain political and economic relationships; and as a modern man living in a revolutionary world. Accordingly, each [person], whether white or black, is approached dynamically as a being possessing a cultural and biological past who seeks to make his way toward the future in a world wherein each discovery about himself must be made in the here and now at the expense of hope, pain and fear—a being who in response to the complex forces of America has become confused. (*SA,* 295)

For Ralph Ellison, living is a dynamic, dialectical process through which people attempt to understand and define themselves and escape confusion. They assert their individuality through tradition, ritual, and language and approach wholeness by drawing from their geographical, biological, cultural, political, artistic, and social histories. With America's pluralism, the result is a cultural diversity, an amalgamation of styles. Although Ellison looks to this ideal, he keeps his sights on reality. While he emphasizes that people can recreate themselves in language, he also understands that language can obscure and confuse and that the ideal may never be reached. But the dynamic process of reaching for the ideal is one of the most important principles of American democracy.

Uncollected Essays

From 1937 to 1964, when *Shadow and Act* was published, Ellison wrote a number of articles he chose not to include in his first collection of essays. Most of these early book reviews and political or social commentaries demonstrate how Ellison looked at the world through leftist lenses. Perhaps the narrow propagandistic focus led him to exclude these pieces from his collection. Indeed, often Ellison is concerned with the class struggle and with other issues that the Marxists had made their own. At the same time, however, these early works reveal his independence as a thinker and artist, for he is often more concerned with style and consciousness than with the depiction of material reality. These early pieces also point to many ideas that recur in Ellison's fiction.

Book reviews constitute more than two-thirds of the uncollected material, and most of the reviews are of books about African American literature. His first review, "Creative and Cultural Lag," was of *These Low Grounds*, Waters Edwin Turpin's novel about four generations of an African American family from the 1860s to the 1930s. The review reveals a Marxist emphasis when Ellison criticizes Turpin for his lack of concern with history, saying that writers must be "alert to social and historical processes" and must "grasp the historical process as a whole, and his group's reaction to it." But Ellison also indicates his interest in characters with highly developed consciousness when he criticizes Turpin for not creating such characters: "Turpin could have given us more than one level of writing. He would have entered into the consciousness of his characters to give us a fuller picture of human beings. . . . A closer examination to [his characters'] consciousness would have thrown into relief more of the social and emotional factors present."[3]

Throughout the reviews, as in the first one, Ellison comments on typical Marxist concerns such as the class struggle, the effect of economic factors, racial strife, and the power of historical forces, as well as his own personal, artistic interest in presenting African Americans with highly developed consciousness. He praises Len Zinberg's *Walk Hard, Talk Loud* for its "Marxist understanding of the economic basis of Negro personality" and "Marxist sense of humanity."[4] Similarly he criticizes Arthur Fauset's biography of Sojourner Truth for failing to allow for "development and change of the individual through dynamic contact with the social and economic factors constituting environment."[5]

As Ellison read and reviewed African American works, he was formulating his own thematic and stylistic considerations. He first articulates his concern for understatement in his 1940 review of Langston Hughes's autobiography *The Big Sea* when he criticizes Hughes for avoiding "analysis and comment" and failing to present "the mind's brooding over experience and transforming it into conscious thought" (Ellison, "Stormy," 20). While Ellison praises Bucklin Moon for avoiding African American stereotypes, he faults Moon's main character for lacking "sufficient urgency of motivation to give the novel organic form."[6] Similarly, in his review of Lonnie Coleman's *Escape the Thunder,* Ellison criticizes Coleman, Moon, and Lillian Smith (in *Strange Fruit*) for failing to create a "positive Negro hero . . . capable of action."[7] In contrast, he praises the "beauty and significance" of Fauset's presentation of Sojourner Truth's "high degree of consciousness and striving under the most unfriendly conditions" (Ellison, "Mystic," 26). The issue of consciousness ultimately led Ellison to break with Wright, as Ellison concluded that Wright's naturalism would not allow him to create a character with as highly developed a consciousness as Wright himself, and these early reviews foreshadow Ellison's concern for conscious African American characters.

In two general surveys of "Recent Negro Fiction," Ellison uses the books he had recently reviewed along with Wright's work to contrast with the "exoticism and narrow Negro middle class ideals" of the New Negro movement of the twenties.[8] Ellison criticizes "Countee Cullen, Claude McKay, Rudolph Fisher, Zora Neil [*sic*] Hurston, Wallace Thurman, and Jessie Fauset" for work that was "timid of theme . . . technically backward . . . confined to the expression of Negro middle class ideals rather than those of the Negro working and agricultural masses." Additionally they "ignored the existence of Negro folklore" and were "unaware of the technical experimentation and direction being taken by American writing as a result of the work . . . of such writers as Joyce, Stein, Anderson, and Hemingway." On the other hand, Wright in *Native Son* and *Uncle Tom's Children* overcomes "the social and cultural isolation of Negro life" through an "artistic sensibility" that moves "into a world of unlimited intellectual and imaginative possibilities" ("Recent," 22). These early uncollected essays on African American literature reveal Ellison's careful study of African American literary tradition. In his collected essays and interviews, Ellison comments infrequently on black writers other than Wright.

In addition to reviewing books about the African American experience,

Ellison drew from his southwestern past and reviewed Frank Goodwyn's *The Magic of Limping John,* a novel set in southwest Texas that uses southwestern folklore. Ellison praises Goodwyn's use of folklore but expresses concern that Goodwyn's material is too "exotic" and "remote," not "weighted with universals."[9] Additionally, Ellison reviewed works by western and southwestern writers Jean Stafford and Conrad Richter.

Most of Ellison's uncollected social and political essays are reports on specific events, such as racial attacks based on neighborhood protection spurred by Father Coughlin's followers ("Judge Lynch in New York"), the establishment of an organization of evicted sharecroppers and farmers ("Camp Lost Colony"), and the spring 1940 Third National Negro Congress in Washington, D.C. ("A Congress Jim Crow Didn't Attend"). These essays provide insight into Ellison's development as a writer, particularly Hemingway's early influence on Ellison's style. In "Judge Lynch in New York," for example, Ellison sets up the events with the following descriptive passage: "It was quiet on the river. People sat on the benches talking softly and enjoying the breeze off the water. There were boats at anchor on the river, riding lazily in the current's flow. Beyond the river was the shore of Jersey, aflame with the brilliant colors of the setting sun. . . . New York was swell."[10] Ellison goes on to describe how three black southern college boys who did not understand the unwritten racial divisions of the North were attacked for being across Amsterdam Avenue and outside the uncharted boundaries to which African Americans were limited. Six years later, Ellison would begin his novel about an innocent black southerner lost on the New York frontier.

Similarly, in "Camp Lost Colony" Ellison describes how a "group of sharecroppers from Texas, Arkansas, and Missouri" had come to New York to present their concerns after attending the National Cotton Congress in Washington, D.C. Ellison explains how the group was led by Owen Whitfield, who the previous summer had established Camp Lost Colony in Missouri for 23 evicted black and white families. This essay demonstrates Ellison's continuing concern with dispossession and also his interest with black leadership in America, another idea of central importance to *Invisible Man.* In fact, Whitfield also appears as a dominant figure in "A Congress Jim Crow Didn't Attend," in which Ellison discusses the participants in the Third National Negro Congress. Called the "hero of the convention," Whitfield, perhaps a model for Jefferson, Trueblood, and Hickman, is described as "the father of twelve children, a farmer for thirty-five years. He speaks with the skill of the Negro folk-preacher, in terms and images the people understand. The people from the farm country shout 'Amen!' and

'It's the truth!' Whitfield is of the earth and his speech is of the earth, and I said 'Amen!' with the farmers."[11]

In contrast is A. Philip Randolph, who speaks with a "deep, resonant voice which helped him to the presidency of the largest Negro union" but also in "unmistakable notes of Red-baiting." As Randolph's voice "droned out abstract phrases," the audience gets restless, and Ellison sits "through the address with a feeling of betrayal. I did not realize it, but I had witnessed a leader in the act of killing his leadership" (Ellison, "Congress," 7). Ellison concludes by recalling Booker T. Washington: "Whitfield and Johnson [Hank Johnson, a Congress of Industrial Organizations organizer from Chicago] and the people behind them are the answer to those who wonder why there is such a scramble to raise the Booker T. Washington symbol anew in Negro life." These real speakers in Washington, D.C., in the spring of 1940 no doubt influenced characters and numerous speaking performances in *Invisible Man*.

Shadow and Act

When Ellison decided to collect his essays, interviews, and speeches written from 1942 to 1964, he turned to one of his favorite ancestors for the title, *Shadow and Act*. T. S. Eliot's "The Hollow Men," perhaps because of the emphasis on a complex dialectical process, provides the allusion:

> Between the idea
> And the reality
> Between the motion
> And the act
> Falls the Shadow.

Ellison's title suggests several meanings. In the introduction Ellison refers to the title and emphasizes the significance of a writer's need to understand both his own personal past and history when he says that the "act of writing requires a constant plunging back into the shadow of the past where time hovers ghostlike" (*SA*, xix). Writing as act requires a constant interaction with the shadow of the past. A second meaning is suggested by the 1949 essay "Shadow and Act," included in the collection, in which Ellison examines three recent films about African Americans, one based on Faulkner's *Intruder in the Dust*. The film, Ellison suggests, is a shadow of the novel, and films in general involve flickering shadowlike images on a two-dimensional plane.

Shadow and Act contains an introduction and three major divisions: "The Seer and the Seen"—interviews, speeches, and essays on literature; "Sound and the Mainstream"—essays about music and musicians; and "Shadow and Act"—"occasional pieces" concerned "with the complex relationship between the Negro American subculture and North American culture as a whole" (*SA*, xviii). Through all three parts Ellison emphasizes the importance of his personal experiences, particularly his Oklahoma past, much quoted in earlier chapters. In fact, some early reviewers labeled the work as autobiography. Both George P. Elliot in the *New York Times Book Review* (25 October 1964) and R. W. B. Lewis in the *New York Review of Books* (28 January 1965) called *Shadow and Act* Ellison's "real autobiography."

In the introduction Ellison stresses what Reilly calls his "fictional" generalized autobiography with its "broad frontiersman scheme." There Ellison describes himself and his friends as "frontiersmen" in a territory that emphasized freedom and possibility, explains how they adopted their Renaissance man ideal, points to the significance of southwestern jazz, and, most important, establishes himself as an initiate who ultimately embraced the significant discipline of writing only after undergoing a variety of experiences. "One might say," Ellison writes, "that with these thin essays for wings I was launched full flight into the dark" (*SA*, xi). And as he searched for his craft, he drew from his frontier experience, especially the emphasis on the possibilities of amalgamation, for "part of our boyish activity expressed a yearning to make any—and everything of quality *Negro American;* to appropriate it, possess it, re-create it in our own group and individual images" (*SA*, xvii).

Related to Ellison's emphasis on autobiography is a second important theme: the fullness and value of African American culture. Ellison scorns "the notion currently projected by certain specialists in the 'Negro Problem,' which characterizes the Negro American as self-hating and defensive" (*SA*, xvii). Like the narrator in *Invisible Man* who learns to reject others' definitions of reality, Ellison learned to repudiate limited definitions of African American life: "I learned that nothing could go unchallenged; especially that feverish industry dedicated to telling Negroes who and what they are, and which can usually be counted upon to deprive both humanity and culture of their complexity" (*SA*, xx).

The issues reappear in the first major section, "The Seer and the Seen," concerned primarily with literature. The section contains interviews with Richard G. Stern titled "That Same Pain, That Same Pleasure" originally published in *December* magazine in 1961, and with Alfred Chester and Vilma Howard titled "The Art of Fiction" published in the *Paris Review* in

1955. In the Stern interview Ellison points to many of the same autobiographical details as he does in the introduction: the importance of the frontier past, the power of the imagination, cultural mixture, ("I learned very early that in the realm of the imagination all people and their ambitions and interests could meet" [*SA*, 12]), and the value of African American culture, the "Negro environment which I found warm and meaningful" (*SA*, 7). In the *Paris Review* interview, Ellison talks specifically about the background, style, structure, and imagery of *Invisible Man*.

The first section also includes two speeches, "Brave Words for a Startling Occasion," Ellison's acceptance speech for the National Book Award in 1953, and "Hidden Name and Complex Fate: A Writer's Experience in the United States," an address to the Library of Congress on 6 January 1964 sponsored by the Gertrude Clarke Whittall Foundation. In his acceptance speech, Ellison stressed the relationship between *Invisible Man* and nineteenth-century American fiction, explained his stylistic purpose, and defined democratic principles: "The way home we seek is that condition of man's being in the world, which is called love, and which we term democracy" (*SA*, 106). The speech at the Library of Congress was explicitly autobiographical, as the title indicates, as Ellison reflected upon having been named for Ralph Waldo Emerson and having become a writer. He mused about the questions of identity that one's name suggests, recalled the humor that revolved around his name, and remembered the powerful literary and oral influences that permeated his boyhood before comparing the best nineteenth-century fiction and its direct confrontation with democratic themes to twentieth-century fiction of understatement.

Ellison includes in section 1 three literary essays written prior to the publication of *Invisible Man*. "Beating that Boy," whose title refers to belabored discussions of "the Negro problem," is a 1945 review of Bucklin Moon's *Primer for White Folks*. "Twentieth Century Fiction and the Black Mask of Humanity" (1946) demonstrates Ellison's concerns about the American literary tradition while he worked on *Invisible Man*, especially his thesis that twentieth-century American novelists had turned away from the social and moral function of literature central to nineteenth-century American writers. "Richard Wright's Blues," a review of Wright's *Black Boy* for the *Antioch Review* in 1945, is important because it demonstrates the complexity of Ellison's relationship with Wright. Written before the split with Wright, Ellison found the blues in Wright's autobiography and praised his relative for breaking from the restrictions of both southern society and the cultural possessiveness of black southern culture.

Two essays in the first section are intellectual bouts with white critics.

"Change the Joke and Slip the Yoke," published in *Partisan Review* in 1958, is a response to a Stanley Edgar Hyman lecture at Brandeis University. Hyman had identified the trickster and the darky entertainer as folk figures important to African American writers. Ellison disagrees with Hyman, saying that the trickster is a much more universal archetype, and the " 'darky' entertainer," Ellison concludes, appealed not to black Americans but to whites for whom blackness had become a metaphor for "the white American's fascination with the symbolism of whiteness and blackness" (*SA*, 47). Ellison points out that the mask of the " 'darky' entertainer" was not limited to black folklore, for the American experience was begun in the masquerade as Indians at the Boston Tea Party. In response to Hyman's comments about the narrator's grandfather in *Invisible Man* as the "smart-man-playing-dumb," Ellison notes that the grandfather's ambiguity rather than his mask indicates his importance.

The second and better-known skirmish was with Irving Howe. "The World and the Jug" combines two separate articles written for Myron Kolatch of the *New Leader*, who asked for Ellison's response to Howe's "Black Boys and Native Sons," published in the August 1963 issue of *Dissent*, in which Howe compared Ellison to Wright and Baldwin and found both younger writers lacking. Ellison's second essay responds to Howe's comments about the first piece and therefore takes on an angrier, more combative tone than many of Ellison's other pieces. Ironically Howe had initially charged Ellison with insufficient anger and called for more protest about racism in his work.

Ellison's argument revolves around the distinction between art and propaganda. Protest writing, Ellison asserts, weakens artistic merit if a writer emphasizes protest rather than craft. Judgments about writing should be based on merit, not on whether it includes "racial suffering, social injustice or ideologies of whatever mammy-made variety." But Ellison contends his novel contains protest: "My goal was not to escape, or hold back, but to work through; to transcend, as the blues transcend the painful conditions with which they deal. The protest is there, not because I was helpless before my racial condition, but because I *put* it there" (*SA*, 137).

The second important part of the argument concerns Ellison's belief in the value of African American experience. Social critics such as Howe, Ellison asserts, refuse to see African Americans as full human beings; rather "when he looks at a Negro he sees not a human being but an abstract embodiment of living hell" (*SA*, 112). This limited view ignores the value of African American culture: "To deny in the interest of revolutionary posture that such possibilities of human richness exist for others, even in Mississippi, is not only to deny us our humanity but to betray the critic's commitment to social reality" (112). Consequently, given his attitude about the merit of African American culture, Ellison believes that the most valuable literature that grows from this experience is celebratory: "I believe that true novels, even when most pessimistic and bitter, arise out of an impulse to celebrate human life and therefore are ritualistic and ceremonial at their core. Thus they would preserve as they destroy, affirm as they reject" (*SA*, 114).

Ellison also stresses the importance of African American culture in part 2, "Sound and the Mainstream," with essays about music over such topics as Minton's Playhouse, Mahalia Jackson, Jimmy Rushing, Charlie Bird, Charlie Christian, and LeRoi Jones's book on the blues, *Blues People*. Throughout these essays, Ellison points to the central importance of jazz and the blues on his own work as he highlights music as one of the richest contributions of African American culture to the American amalgamation.

In "Living with Music," for example, he recalls how as a boy he learned about artistic discipline from early Oklahoma jazzmen. From them he came to understand the dynamics of the dialectic between tradition and the individual talent: "I had learned too that the end of all this discipline and technical mastery was the desire to express an affirmative way of life through its musical tradition and that this tradition insisted that each artist achieve his creativity within its frame. He must learn the best of the past, and add to it his personal vision" (*SA*, 189–90). Similarly Ellison found an interplay between freedom and restriction in Jimmy Rushing's singing. Rushing, like Ellison, was a product of the southwestern frontier, and Ellison believes that Rushing's geographical background was the basis for his individual talent. Ellison's comments on Rushing may just as easily be applied to Ellison himself: "For one of the significant aspects of his art is the imposition of a romantic lyricism upon the blues tradition . . . ; a lyricism which is not of the Deep South, but of the Southwest: a romanticism native to the frontier, imposed upon the violent rawness of a part of the nation which only thirteen years before Rushing's birth was still Indian territory. Thus there is an optimism in it which echoes the spirit of those Negroes who, like Rushing's father, had come to Oklahoma in search of a more human way of life" (*SA*, 245). Rushing therefore communicated the blues as "an art of ambivalence" for they "constantly remind us of our limitations while encouraging us to see how far we can actually go" (*SA*, 246).

Besides dramatizing constant tension between freedom and restriction, jazz presents rituals of initiation and rebirth. In his remembrance of Minton's, "The Golden Age, Time Past," Ellison notes that jam sessions there, like the ones he viewed growing up, demonstrated "apprenticeship, ordeals, initiation ceremonies, . . . rebirth." He continues, "For after the jazzman has learned the fundamentals of jazz . . . , he must then 'find himself,' must be reborn, must find, as it were, his soul" (*SA*, 209). Charlie Parker became just such an example of transformation. His nickname, the "Bird," indicated metamorphosis: "Nicknames are indicative of a change from a given to an achieved identity, whether by rise or fall, and they tell us something of the nicknamed individual's interaction with his fellows" (*SA*, 222). As he remade himself and adopted a mask, Parker moved over the line into chaos and became "a sacrificial figure whose struggles against personal chaos, on stage and off, served as entertainment for a ravenous, sensation-starved, culturally disoriented public" (*SA*, 227). The comments about Parker provide insight into Ellison's conceptions of two of his characters, Rinehart and Senator Sunraider/Bliss, figures who tempt chaos as they don masks.

Another leitmotif in this section, important to Ellison's Hickman stories, is the value of history. In his review of LeRoi Jones's *Blues People*, in which he criticizes Jones for reducing blues to ideology, Ellison strikes out against the American tendency to ignore the past: "Perhaps more than any other people, Americans have been locked in a deadly struggle with time, with history. We've fled the past and trained ourselves to suppress, if not forget, troublesome details of the national memory, and a great part of our optimism, like our progress, has been bought at the cost of ignoring the processes through which we've arrived at any given moment in our national existence" (*SA*, 250).

Ellison's title, of course, also points to the importance of history, and the third section is also titled "Shadow and Act." Something of a grab bag, this section includes a 1958 interview with *Preuves*, the title review of films about African Americans, a Hemingway-influenced piece on a Harlem family during World War II, a description of the Lafargue Psychiatric Clinic written in 1948 but unpublished, and an unpublished 1944 review of Gunnar Myrdal's *An American Dilemma*. As a group, these pieces continue some of the earlier themes, but they are less autobiographical than most of the other selections in *Shadow and Act*.

"The Way It Is," the only early *New Masses* article that Ellison decided to include, demonstrates, as the title indicates, Hemingway's influence and Marxist issues as Ellison describes one Harlem family's response to racial injustice and patriotic demands during World War II. "Harlem Is Nowhere" defines the alienation and discontinuity that Harlem residents, dislocated from cultural roots, felt in the 1940s and serves as an important statement of the concerns from which *Invisible Man* developed. Finally, in his review

of Myrdal's book, Ellison again stresses the value of African American life
by sharply criticizing the European sociologist for accepting the flawed conclusion that African Americans are the product of social pathology rather
than a culture of "great value, of richness" (SA, 316).
When *Shadow and Act* appeared in 1964, American racial disharmony
was high. Riots in Watts, Detroit, Newark, and other American cities
loomed on the horizon. Incendiary comments by Malcolm X, LeRoi Jones,
and James Baldwin made many white Americans uncomfortable. So it is
not surprising that many reviewers found comfort in Ellison's measured
prose. For example, the reviewer for *Choice* (March 1965) called it an "anti-
dote to the more hysterical proclamations coming from the pens of James
Baldwin and LeRoi Jones." Ellison was often called "sane" by reviewers,
mostly white. In fact, few African American reviewers or journals discussed
Shadow and Act.

In his review, R. W. B. Lewis, focusing on autobiographical elements,
identified Ellison's purpose as a definition of identity: "Inquiring into his
experience, his literary and musical education, Ellison has come up with a
number of clues to the fantastic fate of trying to be at the same time a
writer, a Negro, an American, and a human being."[12] Stanley Edgar
Hyman, in a review for the *New Leader* (26 October 1964), emphasized
Ellison's concern with values: "In his insight into the complexity of American experience, Ralph Ellison is the profoundest cultural critic that we
have, and his hard doctrine of freedom, responsibility, and fraternity is a
wisdom rare in our time."[13] Robert Penn Warren, reviewing for *Commentary* (May 1965), found Ellison's concentration on unity from diversity
the most important element of *Shadow and Act*: "*The basic unity of human
experience*—that is what Ellison asserts; and he sets the richness of his own
experience and that of many Negroes he has known, and his own early capacity to absorb the general values of Western culture, over against what
Wright called 'the essential bleakness of black life in America.' "[14]

In *Shadow and Act* Ellison draws from his vivid and specific memory to
recreate a rich and vibrant culture to juxtapose with the dismal one too
often attributed to African American life. Instead Ellison offers "the glori-
ous days of Oklahoma jazz dances, the jam sessions at Halley Richardson's
place on Deep Second, . . . the days when watermelon men with voices like
mellow bugles shouted their wares in time with the rhythm of their horses'
hoofs" (SA, 197). The figure of the young Ralph Ellison coming out of
Oklahoma territory and becoming a famous author is, as Reilly notes, a
"fiction," a shaping of experience by art, and it is an American story most

powerful. His second collection of essays, published 22 years later, offers a new extension of the old persona.

Going to the Territory

This collection takes its title from both Mark Twain and a Bessie Smith song: "Freedom was also to be found in the West of the old Indian Territory. Bessie Smith gave voice to this knowledge when she sang of 'Goin' to the Nation, Going to the Terr'tor',' and it is no accident that much of the symbolism of our folklore is rooted in the imagery of geography" (*GT,* 131). It contains 16 of Ellison's essays, speeches, interviews, and reviews written from 1957 to 1985. A continuation of *Shadow and Act,* it pursues familiar themes: the craft of fiction, the problematic American identity, the complex relationship between black folklore and fiction, Richard Wright's status as a writer, and others. Ellison also returns to figures from his past who have been mentioned before: Hazel Harrison, Ellison's music teacher at Tuskegee, and Inman Page, principal of Ellison's Oklahoma high school. While *Going to the Territory* in some ways is *Shadow and Act* revisited, the tone and mask are decidedly different. Where *Shadow and Act* presents a writer beginning and then reaching the height of his career, *Going to the Territory,* published when Ellison was 72, features the elder statesman, the established mentor figure, late in his career.

Going to the Territory lacks the structure of *Shadow and Act.* Ellison seems to have had a method in mind as he arranged the essays, but he provides no subheads, nor does he include an introduction to set forth the principles of the arrangement. In fact, in a *New York Times Book Review* interview, Ellison discounted any continuity: "These pieces were not conceived of as a collection. They were written as they were called for and they may have some thematic continuity of which I am not aware" (Staples, 15). Yet the essays are grouped around general subjects.

The first six selections, while covering a variety of topics, are connected in their general emphasis on cultural issues: "The Little Man at Chehaw Station" (1978); "On Initiation Rites and Power: Ralph Ellison Speaks at West Point" (1969); a speech questioning the term *culturally deprived,* "What These Children Are Like" (1963); an analysis of Lyndon Johnson, "The Myth of the Flawed White Southerner"; a review of Howard Zinn's *The Southern Mystique;* and a 1970 *Time* article, "What America Would Be Like without Blacks." Next are four essays on elements of Ellison's autobiography: a remembrance of Inman Page; the title essay; an essay about seeing a dramatization of *Tobacco Road* shortly after his arrival in New York,

"An Extravagance of Laughter"; and a 1971 speech, "Remembering Richard Wright." The next two essays are on music, "Homage to Duke Ellington on His Birthday," and art, "The Art of Romare Bearden." The last four selections concentrate on literature: "Society, Morality, and the Novel," the oldest piece, written in 1957; the only interview, "A Very Stern Discipline" (1967); "The Novel as a Function of American Democracy," a lecture at the Philadelphia Free Library (1967); and "Perspective of Literature" (1976), a discussion of literature and the law.

Perhaps Ellison begins with "The Little Man at Chehaw Station" because it covers many of the topics touched upon throughout the collection, and it also establishes the voice of the more mature and established figure rather than the initiate of *Shadow and Act*. It forcefully presents one of Ellison's key issues: his continuing belief in American amalgamation when "ethnic integrity" overshadowed the "melting pot" as a cultural touchstone. To support his thesis that the American amalgamation at its highest achieves unity in diversity through oxymoronic "antagonistic cooperation" (*GT*, 26), Ellison uses three distinct episodes of personal experience. The first refers to the title, Chehaw Station, a railroad stop near Tuskegee, Alabama, and its little man stands for the existence of high critical standards in unexpected places. Ellison learned of the little man from Hazel Harrison, his music teacher at Tuskegee, a highly respected concert pianist, pupil of Ferruccio Busoni, friend of Sergei Prokofiev, Percy Grainger, and Egon Petri. Miss Harrison demanded the highest standards of her students, and she told Ellison that even if he were playing in the waiting room at Chehaw Station, he must play his best "because in this country there'll always be a little man hiding behind the stove." That little man, she went on, will "know the *music*, and the *tradition*, and the standards of *musicianship* required for whatever you set out to perform!" (*GT*, 4). Like the veteran the narrator meets in *Invisible Man*, the little man behind the stove at Chehaw Station will be wise and knowledgeable.

His existence signals Ellison's belief in the possibility of achieving excellence even in the most humble places and also represents the American audience that approaches art with combined cooperation and antagonism: "As representative of the American audience writ small, the little man draws upon the uncodified *Americanness* of his experience . . . as he engages in a silent dialogue with the artist's exposition of forms, offering or rejecting the work of art on the basis of what he feels to be its affirmation or distortion of American experience" (*GT*, 6–7). An undistorted examination of American experience reveals its cultural mixture formerly symbolized by the melting pot whose loss Ellison laments: "Today that metaphor is noisily rejected, vehemently disavowed. In fact, it has come under attack in the name of the newly fashionable code word 'ethnicity' " (*GT,* 21).

To dramatize his point that the melting pot exists, he presents the second episode in which he recalls seeing "a light-skinned, blue-eyed, Afro-American-featured individual" drive up on New York's Riverside Drive in a "shiny new blue Volkswagen Beetle decked out with a gleaming Roll-Royce radiator." As the man got out of the car, Ellison noticed that he wore a dashiki, black riding boots, "fawn-colored riding breeches," and a Homburg hat on his Afro haircut. Carrying a riding crop and a Japanese camera, the man got out of the car, set the timer on the camera, and took "a series of self portraits." Recalling Lee Willie Minifees, Ellison's Cadillac flambéer, the Volks-Rolls driver symbolizes the melting pot and "an American compulsion to improvise upon the given": "His garments were, literally and figuratively, of many colors and cultures, his racial identity interwoven of many strands. . . . Whatever the identity he presumed to project, he was exercising an American freedom and was a product of the melting pot and the conscious or unconscious comedy it brews" (*GT,* 24).

Like the little man at the station, the driver represents the audience with whom the American artist must communicate, and Ellison concludes with a third example that combines high standards in unexpected places with the melting pot theme. He recalls hearing a sophisticated argument "over which of two celebrated Metropolitan Opera divas was the superior soprano" (*GT,* 34) as he walked through a tenement building in San Juan Hill doing research for the Federal Writers' Project during the depression. The voices spoke "a Southern idiomatic vernacular such as was spoken by formally uneducated Afro-American working men" (*GT,* 33). Entering the room, he discovered that the four workingmen arguing opera were coal heavers who doubled as extras at the Met, and they, like the other examples in this essay, demonstrate the cultural pluralism common to audiences in a democratic society.

Ellison presents related issues in "On Initiation Rites and Power," a 1969 speech at West Point. Again he uses his autobiography to point to the importance of initiation rites and other rituals as organizing principles in both society and literature. Writers who grasp the power of rites and rituals in a pluralistic society can perceive how art fulfills a unifying function. Without this awareness lies chaos: "So that our failure to grasp the mysterious possibilities generated by our unity within diversity and our freedom within unfreedom can lead to great confusion" (*GT,* 52). A novelist, "through the agency of mere words," can reduce society "to manageable proportions; to proportions which will reflect *one* man's vision, *one* man's sense of the

human condition, and in such volatile and eloquent ways that each rhythm
. . . becomes expressive of *his* sense of life and, by extension, that of the
reader" (*GT,* 54).

Both rituals and language can have negative effects, as demonstrated by
the battle royal scene that defined racial distinctions in *Invisible Man.* But at
West Point Ellison emphasized another key point: democratic principles derived from our national ideals, articulated in documents of state—the Declaration of Independence, the Constitution, and the Bill of Rights—and
restated in our best literature provide stability: "In this process our traditions
and national ideals move and function like a firm ground bass, like the deep
tones of your marvelous organ there in the chapel, repeating themselves con-
tinually while new melodies and obbligatos sound high above" (*GT,* 55).

In the speeches such as this one at West Point, Ellison's new persona is especially apparent. Invited to speak before a group of students who had
studied his novel, he came as an established novelist. Two of the speeches in
the group of autobiographical pieces, "Portrait of Inman Page" and "Going
to the Territory," were presented at the 1979 Ralph Ellison Festival at
Brown University, in ceremonies to honor a celebrated writer. In his introduction to the title speech, Ellison acknowledged the circumstances:

Once again I must wonder at the sheer unexpectedness of life in these United
States. Even the most celebrated of writers would find this scene exhilarating, but
for me—well, it is simply overwhelming. It's as though I am being rebuked—even
if ever so gently—for every instance in which I doubted the possibility of communi-
cating my peculiar vision to my fellow Americans. Now I realize how fortunate I
am to have held on to literature as a medium for transcending the divisions of our
society, for your presence affirms that faith most generously. (*GT,* 120)

Ellison continues to stress the southwestern initiate in these autobiographical speeches and essays, but, as the elder spokesman, the position
from which he remembers the details is much further removed than in
Shadow and Act. In the essay written for this collection, "An Extravagance of
Laughter," Ellison returns to the youthful figure trying to understand the
world as he concentrates on a singular incident in New York in 1936, but it
is from the perspective of a 70-year-old man rather than a middle-aged one.
In fact, "An Extravagance of Laughter" emphasizes the masks or personas
we adopt, as well the power of laughter. Although some masks are necessary
parts of life, others obscure rather than define identity. Art that punctures
limiting masks serves an important function.

The specific incident on which he focuses is the night he and Langston

Hughes went to a dramatization of Erskine Caldwell's *Tobacco Road*. As he watched actors represent the rednecks from whom he had recently escaped, he suddenly was gripped by laughter so overwhelming that the audience and cast began to look at him. To explain, he recalls how upon arriving in New York he had discovered that New York had racial divisions rather than the freedom he expected but that the rules of conduct were not defined as they were in the South. Because of the uncertainty caused by the conflict "between the dream in my head and the murky, seek-and-find-it shiftings of the New York scene" (*GT,* 157), he had developed the mask of "a sophisticated New Yorker" (*GT,* 180) to cover his uneasiness. As he watched the play that took him back to the South, he suddenly became aware of his mask, and his laughter was at himself:

> For me the shock of Caldwell's art began when Ellie May and Lov were swept up by a forbidden sexual attraction so strong that, uttering sounds of animal passion, they went floundering and skittering back-to back across the stage. . . . I was reduced to such helpless laughter that I distracted the entire balcony and embarrassed both myself and my host. . . .
>
> Then it was as though I had been stripped naked, kicked out of a low-flying plane onto an Alabama road, and ordered to laugh for my life. I laughed and laughed, bending and straightening in a virtual uncontrollable cloud-and-damburst of laughter, a self-immolation of laughter over which I had no control. (*GT,* 186)

His description of the scene recalls several of his own works. The back-to-back couple calls to mind the odd sexual position of his story "Backwacking," while sudden convulsive laughter at the discovery of a mask suggests the end of "Flying Home" where Todd's plane crashes in an Alabama field. Drawing from Constance Rourke's research into American humor, Ellison stresses the value of humor, particularly to deflate false self-images, an important part of his work that has received less critical examination than Ellison believes it should. By presenting an essay specifically on the value of laughter, Ellison emphasizes this important aspect of his view of life.

While in these autobiographical selections, Ellison uses his personal experiences to confirm the points about society and art, the last section of *Going to the Territory,* containing essays about literature, depends less on autobiography as the established critic takes the stage. The most important piece, "Society, Morality, and the Novel," written in 1957 but left out of *Shadow and Act* because of space limitations, remains one of Ellison's most important critical statements about literature's moral purpose. Ellison begins by defining the novel as a "form of communication," which depends on "action depicted in words" (*GT,* 242). Unlike poetry, concerned primarily with language, the novel concentrates on process and duration and seizes "from the flux and flow of our daily lives those abiding patterns of experience which, through their repetition and consequences in our affairs, help to form our sense of reality and from which emerge our sense of humanity and our conception of human value" (*GT,* 244).

Making sense of the process of life is especially important in America where change is inherent: "For in no other country was change such a given factor of existence; in no other country were the class lines so fluid and change so swift and continuous *and intentional*" (*GT,* 248). American literature at its best seizes flux, applies patterns, and affirms the moral principles to achieve stable change (another oxymoron): "The moral imperatives of American life that are implicit in the Declaration of Independence, the Constitution, and the Bill of Rights were a part of both the individual consciousness and the conscience of those writers who created what we consider our classic novels—Hawthorne, Melville, James, and Twain; and for all the hooky-playing attitude of the twenties or the political rebelliousness of the thirties, and the reluctance of contemporary writers to deal explicitly with politics, they still are." Ellison then examines how writers achieve "one of the enduring functions of the American novel" by "giving the American experience, as it unfolds in its diverse parts and regions, imaginative integration and moral continuity" (*GT,* 250). They achieve this goal by dramatizing the principles of the "great documents of state," which constitute "a body of assumptions about human possibility which is shared by all Americans—even those who resist most violently any attempt to embody them in social action" (*GT,* 251).

Although these abstract passages provide insight into Ellison's literary principles, they gave reviewers trouble. Dan Cryer in *Newsday* (27 July 1986) contrasted them to the autobiographical sections, noting that the "autobiographical anecdotes can light up an essay and make it sing. But alas, there is another Ellison, the *eminence grise* given to windy, pompous pronouncements on the most grandiose of themes." George Sim Johnston in *Commentary* (December 1986) reacted similarly: "Ellison is crisp and engaging when he addresses a concrete topic—his own past, for example, or jazz—but he tends to get windy when dealing with abstractions like culture and democracy." But John Edgar Wideman in the *New York Times Book Review* (3 August 1986) found that Ellison's essays reflect his reasoned wisdom: "The reader is impressed and delighted by the integrity of Mr.

Ellison's vision. His voice is assured, calm, wise. The first-person mode, the transcriptions of talk, give a relaxed, intimate tone to many of these essays. Mr. Ellison is remembering; he's lived more than 30 years with his classic, 'Invisible Man,' towering over his shoulder. But fame must have its compensation, not least the quiet power and authority he displays here." As Wideman notes, the Ellison of *Going to the Territory* is the seasoned novelist and critic looking back. Although the voice has changed, the issues that have compelled him throughout his life remain the same.

In 1957 Ellison commented on the difference between writing novels and writing nonfiction, noting the opposing abilities the two forms require of the writer. Fiction leads into the unknown and uncharted and calls for the writer "to play with the fires of chaos and to rearrange reality to the patterns of the imagination"; criticism "is held in by rules" (*GT,* 238). Thus, Ellison sees that the incessant process of freedom that has been his continuing theme is subject to more limitations in critical nonfiction than in imaginative creations that seek to liberate rather than civilize. Having adopted the Renaissance man ideal in the Oklahoma Territory, Ellison has chosen to spend his life functioning effectively in both realms, though many lack the flexibility to move between them.

Chapter Seven

Ellison's Achievement and Influence

When the Ralph Ellison Library was dedicated in Oklahoma City in 1975, Ellison spoke to family and friends at the ceremony and acknowledged his pride in his southwestern background ("my sense of possibility . . . came from Oklahoma") and his certainty of the library as a democratic force: "I have no doubt that within these walls other writers—black, white, Indian—will emerge. And, if so, it will be because the library is a place where a child or an adult can make a connection between the rich oral tradition which we have inherited from the past and the literary rendering of American experience that is to be found in the library. This function of language makes it possible for men and women to project the future, control the environment" (Anderson, 96). From the black community in which he grew up, people who "knew the historical time of day," Ellison had learned about "the power of language to make men truly free." To this goal he eventually dedicated his life.

Growing up a "brown nubbin of a boy" with a "heavy moniker" in Oklahoma City's Deep Second area during the twenties, Ellison carried his southwestern knowledge of language and possibility when he left the territory for Tuskegee Institute in Alabama in 1933, where he discovered the restriction and limitation of the Deep South. Then, with the great migration, Ellison went north to Harlem in 1936 and learned he had to chart new territory in the New York wilderness, where freedom merged with chaos.

Ellison planned to become a musician, but fate led him to a friendship with Richard Wright, to writing book reviews and short stories, to working for the Federal Writers' Project, and to literature as a craft and discipline. Avoiding a jim crow army in World War II, Ellison shipped out as a cook with the Merchant Marine and continued to write. Depressed and ill after an especially difficult mission taking war supplies across the North Atlantic during the Battle of the Bulge, he came back to the United States to recover and to write. Setting up in a friend's barn in Vermont, he suddenly typed: "I am an invisible man." Starting to destroy the page, he then reread it, began to wonder what kind of voice would speak such words, and set off down the path of writing what has become a twentieth-century American classic and probably the most important post-1950 American novel, *Invisible Man*. Selected by critics as "the most distinguished single work" published since World War II in polls, one by *Book Week* in 1965 and another by *Wilson Quarterly* in 1978, *Invisible Man* returned to the forefront of American critical thought as the century drew to a close. After attacks by proponents of the black aesthetic at the end of the sixties and the beginning of the seventies, the novel suffered a brief period of eclipse. But discussions of the constitution of the American canon reemphasized its importance. African American literary theorists who apply varieties of European literary theories to African American literature also underscored Ellison's stature.

The novel's strength derives from Ellison's integrative imagination. He draws from classical works in the European tradition, from major works in the American canon, from African American literature and folklore, from children's games and rhymes, and from the frontier mythology of his southwestern past. Although most of *Invisible Man* is set in Harlem, the narrative relies on frontier imagery associated with the duality between freedom and restriction often presented in American literature through the opposition between East and West.

Invisible Man received the Russwurm Award, the Certificate of Award from the *Chicago Defender,* and the National Book Award. Additionally Ellison has won a Rockefeller Foundation Award, the American Medal of Freedom, the Chevalier de l'Ordre des Artes et Lettres from France, the Langston Hughes medallion for contribution in arts and letters by City College in New York, and the National Medal of Arts. His numerous public appointments include vice-president of the American PEN club and the National Institute of Arts and Letters, trustee of the Citizens' Committee for Public Television and the John F. Kennedy Center in Cambridge, and member of the National Council on the Arts and the Carnegie Commission on Educational Television. He has lectured and taught widely, most notably as the Albert Schweitzer Professor of Humanities at New York University.

Since 1960 he has published eight excerpts of a work in progress with a working title, *And Hickman Arrives*. These eight stories total almost 150 pages of prose already in print, and Ellison's friends who have seen the manuscript of the second novel suggest that it is over 20 inches thick. Disturbing historical events interrupted his progress, particularly political assassinations similar to one portrayed in the novel: an attempted assassination of a famous racist senator who as a boy of indeterminate race had grown up with an African American itinerant preacher. Also a fire in his home in the

Berkshires in 1967 destroyed 368 manuscript pages. The published excerpts indicate that Ellison's second novel is a complex, carefully crafted
work concerned with themes of interest to Ellison throughout his career: the
spiral of history as the past boomerangs into the present, identity, resurrection, showmanship, amalgamation, and the positive and negative power of
language and narrative to transform. Like *Invisible Man,* Ellison's second
novel examines the dialectic of freedom and restriction. In *Invisible Man,*
Ellison dramatizes the restricted freedom language and democracy provide
for achieving wholeness; in the Hickman stories he is concerned with the
negative result of the same dialectic between freedom and restriction and
chaos from forgetting history.

Besides his fiction, Ellison has an established reputation as an essayist. In
1964 he published *Shadow and Act,* a collection of essays, reviews, and interviews from 1942 through 1964. The essays in *Shadow and Act* are important for revealing Ellison's background, particularly the effect of his
Oklahoma past, his interest in music, and his knowledge of classic American literature. A second essay collection, *Going to the Territory,* was published in 1986 and contains Ellison's essays written from 1964 to 1985, as
well as some essays left out of *Shadow and Act.* As an essayist, Ellison relies
on his personal experiences to present his continuing concerns: a regard
for history and the past, abhorrence of racial stereotyping, identity, the
power of art to transform, the richness of African American culture, and
amalgamation.

Ellison's Descendants

Ellison has had a profound impact on American literature, both mainstream and African American. The frontier paradigm of the innocent Adam
who becomes a messianic hero in *Invisible Man* reappears in numerous
post–World War II American novels written after 1952: Saul Bellow's
Henderson the Rain King (1959), Joseph Heller's *Catch-22* (1961), Ken
Kesey's *One Flew over the Cuckoo's Nest* (1962), William Styron's *The Confessions of Nat Turner* (1967), Kurt Vonnegut, Jr.'s, *Slaughterhouse-Five*
(1969), Tim O'Brien's *Going after Cacciato* (1978), and John Irving's *The
World According to Garp* (1979). Critical studies of this literature, such as
Marcus Klein's *After Alienation,* Ihab Hassan's *Radical Innocence,*
Jonathan Baumbach's *The Landscape of Nightmare,* Tony Tanner's *City of
Words,* and Jerry Bryant's *The Open Decision,* use Ellison to demonstrate
their varied theses and Ellison's connection to mainstream American litera-
ture. Additionally African American literary theorists such as Houston A.

Baker, Jr., in *Blues, Ideology, and Afro-American Literature: A Vernacular Theory* (1984) and Henry Louis Gates in *Figures in Black* (1987) and *The Signifying Monkey,* winner of the American Book Award for criticism (1988), use Ellison as a central figure as they trace literary themes or images and formulate literary theories.

Baker, applying Marxist and poststructuralist literary theories to African American experience, offers "suggestive accounts of moments in Afro-American discourse when personae, protagonists, autobiographical narrators, or literary critics, successfully negotiate an obdurate 'economics of slavery' and achieve a resonant, improvisational expressive dignity." Ellison's Trueblood episode is a centerpiece of Baker's theory of the "blues matrix at work" (Baker 1984, 13).

Gates, building from the African trickster figure, Esu-Elegbara, and the slave extension, the Signifying Monkey, as well as from Mikhail Bahktin, creates a literary theory of signifying. Signifying in black discourse has a variety of meanings, but it generally involves taking another person's language and improvising upon it to alter the meaning. In literature, African American writers draw from a previous writer's work, signify upon it, and create a new form. Ellison, for example,

in his fictions Signifies upon Wright by parodying Wright's literary structures through repetition and difference. . . . The play of language, the Signifyin(g), starts with the titles. Wright's *Native Son* and *Black Boy,* titles connoting race, self, and presence, Ellison tropes with *Invisible Man,* with invisibility as an ironic response of absence to the would-be presence of blacks and natives, while *man* suggests a more mature and stronger status than either *son* or *boy.* Ellison Signifies upon Wright's distinctive version of naturalism with a complex rendering of modernism.[1]

Ishmael Reed in turn signifies upon Ellison: "Whereas Ellison tropes the myth of presence in Wright's title of *Native Son* and *Black Boy* through his title of *Invisible Man,* Reed parodies all three titles by employing as his title [*Mumbo Jumbo*] the English-language parody of black language itself" (Gates, 221). And in Reed a "prologue, an epilogue, and an appended 'Partial Bibliography' frame the text proper, again in a parody of Ellison's framing devices in *Invisible Man*" (Gates, 223). While the line from Wright to Ellison to Reed is direct, Gates also finds elements of signifying from Hurston to Ellison to Alice Walker and Toni Morrison.

Keith E. Byerman in *Fingering the Jagged Grain: Tradition and Form in Recent Black Fiction* takes his title from Ellison and uses *Invisible Man* as a "paradigmatic work for more recent writers" such as "traditionalists" James

Alan McPherson, Ernest Gaines, Toni Cade Bambara, and Walker; Morrison and Gayl Jones, writers who "exceed the boundaries of realism"; and "experimentalists" Reed, Leon Forrest, and Clarence Major as direct descendants of Ellison, whose paradigm is a "dialectic of oppression and resistance." Ellison "created the literary space in which fictionists with a modern (and especially modernist) literary sensibility, an awareness of the totalitarian potential of oppressive systems, and an appreciation of the value of folk experience could operate successfully" (Byerman, 9–10).

Although Ellison can no more easily choose his literary descendants than he can his relatives, it is clear that many later American writers, black and white, count him as an influence. Coming from the territory where his geographical fate was to develop frontier attitudes about freedom, possibility, and amalgamation, Ralph Ellison has charted new frontiers in American literature in language that forces chaos to reveal its truth, blazing the trail for others to follow.

Notes and References

Chapter One

1. Ralph Ellison, *Going to the Territory* (New York: Random House, 1986), 198; hereafter cited in text as *GT.*

2. Robert B. Stepto and Michael S. Harper, "Study and Experience: An Interview with Ralph Ellison," in *Chant of Saints,* ed. Michael S. Harper and Robert B. Stepto (Urbana: University of Illinois Press, 1979), 458; hereafter cited in text.

3. Hollie West, "Growing Up Black in Frontier Oklahoma . . . From an Ellison Perspective," in *Speaking for You,* ed. Kimberly Benston (Washington: Howard University Press, 1987), 12; hereafter cited in text.

4. Ralph Ellison, *Shadow and Act* (New York: Vintage Books, 1953, 1964), xiii; hereafter cited in text as *SA.*

5. Jervis Anderson, "Going to the Territory," *New Yorker,* 22 November 1976, 55; hereafter cited in text.

6. John Hersey, " 'A Completion of Personality': A Talk with Ralph Ellison," in *Speaking for You,* 286; hereafter cited in text.

7. David L. Carson, "Ralph Ellison: Twenty Years After," *Studies in American Fiction* 1 (Spring 1973):17; hereafter cited in text.

8. Ron Welburn, "Ralph Ellison's Territorial Vantage," *Grackle* 4 (1977–78):6; hereafter cited in text.

9. Jimmie Lewis Franklin, *The Blacks in Oklahoma* (Norman: University of Oklahoma Press, 1980), 44.

10. Richard Kostelanetz, "Ralph Ellison: Novelist as Brown-Skinned Aristocrat," in *Master Minds* (New York: Macmillan, 1969), 38; hereafter cited in text.

11. Booker T. Washington, *Up from Slavery* (New York: Laurel Leaf Library, Dell, 1965), 156; hereafter cited in text.

12. Robert O'Meally, *Ralph Ellison: The Craft of Fiction* (Cambridge: Harvard University Press, 1980), 14–15; hereafter cited in text.

13. Robert Park and Ernest W. Burgess, *Introduction to the Science of Sociology* (Chicago: University of Chicago Press, 1919), 136.

14. See George Garrett, ed., *The Writer's Voice: Conversations with Contemporary Writers* (William Morrow & Co., 1973), 223; hereafter cited in text.

15. Michel Fabre, *The Unfinished Quest of Richard Wright,* trans. Isabel Barzun (New York: William Morrow, 1973), 145.

16. Allen Geller, "An Interview with Ralph Ellison," in *The Black American Writer, vol. 1: Fiction,* ed. C. W. E. Bigsby (Baltimore: Penguin Books, 1969), 154; hereafter cited in text.

17. Ann Banks, *First-Person America* (New York: Alfred A. Knopf, 1980), xx; hereafter cited in text.

18. Ralph Ellison, *Invisible Man*, 30th Anniversary ed. (New York: Random House, 1982), 194; hereafter cited in the text as *IM*.

19. Ellison was married once before, shortly after he arrived in New York, but he keeps the details of the first marriage private.

20. Quoted by Michael Fabre, "From *Native Son* to *Invisible Man*: Some Notes on Ralph Ellison's Evolution in the 1950s," in *Speaking for You*, 205; hereafter cited in text.

21. Ralph Ellison, "Introduction," *Invisible Man*, 30th Anniversary ed. (New York: Random House, 1982), xii–xiii; hereafter cited as "Introduction" in text.

22. Ralph Ellison, "A Special Message to Subscribers from Ralph Ellison," in *Invisible Man* (Franklin Center, Penn.: Franklin Library Limited Edition, 1980), n.p.; hereafter cited as "Message" in text.

23. John Corry, "Profile of an American Novelist," *New York Times Magazine*, 20 November 1966, 5, 179–85; reprinted in *Black World* (December 1970):117.

24. For a discussion of the history of Ellison's relationship with other black writers in the sixties and early seventies, see William Walling, " 'Art' and 'Protest': Ralph Ellison's *Invisible Man* Twenty Years After," *Phylon* 34 (June 1973):120–34; hereafter cited in text.

25. James Alan McPherson, "Indivisible Man," in *Speaking for You*, 18; hereafter cited in text.

26. Brent Staples, "In His Own Good Time," *New York Times Book Review*, 3 August 1986, 15; hereafter cited in text.

Chapter Two

1. Ralph Ellison, "Slick Gonna Learn," *Direction* (September 1939):10–11, 14, 16; hereafter cited in text.

2. Leonard Deutsch, "Ellison's Early Fiction," *Negro American Literature Forum* 7 (Summer 1973):55; hereafter cited in text.

3. Edith Schor, "The Early Fiction of Ralph Ellison: The Genesis of *Invisible Man*" (Ph.D diss., Columbia University, 1973), 45; hereafter cited in text.

4. Marcus Klein, *After Alienation* (Chicago: University of Chicago Press, 1964), 97–98; hereafter cited in text.

5. Ralph Ellison, "That I Had the Wings," *Common Ground* 3 (Summer 1943):30.

6. Robert Bone, "Ralph Ellison and the Uses of Imagination," in *Anger and Beyond*, ed. Herbert Hill (New York: Harper & Row, 1966), 91–92.

7. James E. Gray, "In Anticipation of *Invisible Man*: The Early Stories of Ralph Ellison" (Master's thesis, East Texas State University, 1987), 45.

8. Carter Harman, *A Popular History of Music.* rev. ed. (New York: Dell, 1969), 240–41.

9. Wayne Ude, "Forging an American Style: The Romance-Novel and Magical Realism as Response to the Frontier and Wilderness Experiences," in *The Frontier Experience and the American Dream,* eds. David Mogen, Mark Busby, and Paul Bryant (College Station: Texas A&M University Press, 1989), 57.

10. Ralph Ellison, "In a Strange Country," *Tomorrow,* 3 July 1944, 41–44.

11. Bernhard Ostendorf, "Ralph Ellison's 'Flying Home': From Folk Tale to Short Story," *Journal of the Folklore Institute* 13 (1976):186.

12. O'Meally, 1980, 70. See Richard M. Dorson, *American Negro Folktales* (Greenwich, Conn.: Fawcett, 1956), 178–80. O'Meally notes that Wright used a fragment of this tale in *Lawd, Today.*

13. Ralph Ellison, "Flying Home," in *Dark Symphony: Negro Literature in America,* ed. James A. Emanuel and Theodore L. Gross (Toronto: Free Press, 1968), 269; hereafter cited in text.

14. Susan L. Blake, "Ritual and Rationalization: Black Folklore in the Works of Ralph Ellison," *PMLA* 94 (1979):125; hereafter cited in text.

15. Joseph Trimmer, "Ralph Ellison's 'Flying Home,' " *Studies in Short Fiction* 9 (Spring 1972):181.

16. Ralph Ellison, "King of the Bingo Game," in *Dark Symphony,* 271–72; hereafter cited in text.

17. Although he does not mention this story, James R. Andreas in "*Invisible Man* and the Comic Tradition," in *Approaches to Teaching Ellison's "Invisible Man,"* ed. Susan Resneck Parr and Pancho Savery (New York: MLA, 1989), 102–3, points to Chaplin's influence on Ellison.

18. Eleanor R. Wilner, in "The Invisible Black Thread: Identity and Nonentity in *Invisible Man,*" *CLA Journal* 13 (1970):249, concludes that the thread is "the black identity that threaded its way, hidden, through all the oppressed past, the possession of those picaresque black men . . . who kept pride alive against a better day."

19. Pearl I. Saunders, "Symbolism in Ralph Ellison's 'King of the Bingo Game,' " *CLA Journal* 20 (September 1976):37, 39.

Chapter Three

1. Tony Tanner, *City of Words* (New York: Harper & Row, 1971), 50; hereafter cited in text.

2. Zbigniew Lewicki, *The Bang and the Whimper: Apocalypse and Entropy in American Literature* (Westport, Conn.: Greenwood Press, 1984), 46.

3. Berndt Ostendorf, "Ralph Waldo Ellison: Anthropology, Modernism, and Jazz," in *New Essays;* hereafter cited in text. Drawing from anthropological debate over Victor Turner's concept of liminality and Frederic Barth's boundary maintenance, Ostendorf points to Ellison's frontier past: "Ellison's sense of self, place, and time, as well as his particular cultural perspectives, are defined by the frontier paradigm, that

transitional space with its options and tensions between freedom and necessity, safety and danger, liberty and restraint, order and disorder" (99).

4. For an extended discussion of frontier mythology in post–World War II fiction, see Mark Busby, "The Significance of the Frontier in Contemporary American Fiction," in *Frontier Experience.*

5. Frederick Jackson Turner, "The Significance of the Frontier in American History," in *Selected Essays of Frederick Jackson Turner: Frontier and Section,* ed. Ray Allen Billington (Englewood Cliffs, N.J.: Prentice-Hall, 1961), 38.

6. D. H. Lawrence, *Studies in Classical American Literature* (1923; New York: Viking, 1964); Henry Nash Smith, *Virgin Land* (Cambridge, Mass.: Harvard University Press, 1950); R. W. B. Lewis, *The American Adam* (Chicago: University of Chicago Press, 1955); Leo Marx, *The Machine in the Garden* (New York: Oxford University Press, 1964); and Richard Slotkin, *Regeneration through Violence* (Middleton, Conn.: Wesleyan University Press, 1973), and *The Fatal Environment: The Myth of the Frontier in the Age of Industrialization, 1800–1890* (New York: Atheneum, 1985), have identified aspects of the frontier archetype.

7. Keith Byerman, *Fingering the Jagged Grain: Tradition and Form in Recent Black Fiction* (Athens: University of Georgia Press, 1985), hereafter cited in text, draws from the critical theories of such Frankfurt school theorists as Theodore Adorno, Herbert Marcuse, and Walter Benjamin and labels Ellison's method a "negative dialectic" because "the meeting of thesis and antithesis results not in synthesis but in disruption" (12). Byerman ties the importance of dialectic in African American literature to the tradition of call and response in African American culture.

8. Ursula Brumm, *American Thought and Religious Typology* (New Brunswick: Rutgers University Press, 1970), 23.

9. Richard Slotkin, *Regeneration through Violence* (Middleton, Conn.: Wesleyan University Press, 1973). Slotkin examines the similarity between the "warrior" and the Adam figure and the "shaman" and Christ and notes that both the hunter and the shaman have their counterparts in white mythology: "Indians were generally quick to notice the similarity between the laws of shamans like Quetzalcoatl and Deganawidah and the tenets of Christianity (especially those of Quaker Christianity). The spirit of the hunter likewise corresponded to the entrepreneurial spirit of the colonist-adventurers; the traders in furs and hides and land" (49).

10. Several critics have tried to explain why Ellison is so exact about the number of lights. Pancho Savery, " 'Not like an arrow, but a boomerang': Ellison's Existential Blues," in *Approaches to Teaching Ellison's "Invisible Man,"* notes that 1,369 is the "square of 37, Ellison's age when he finished the novel in 1951" (67). M. Celeste Oliver, "*Invisible Man* and the Numbers Game," *CLA Journal* notes that the numbers 3–69 are on the tank from which the narrator takes the incorrect black dope in the paint factory and says that in the numbers gambling game 3 6 9 symbolize "shit" or "the character's identity" (128). The numbers 3 9 6 are among the character's winning bingo in "King of the Bingo Game," for a prize of $36.90.

11. For a discussion of electricity as a metaphor for a morally neutral force, see Tanner, 52.

12. See Robert E. Abrams, "The Ambiguities of Dreaming in Ellison's *Invisible Man*," *American Literature* 49 (January 1978):592–603, and Eugenia W. Collier, "The Nightmare Truth of an Invisible Man," *Black World* 20 (December 1970):12–19.

13. R. W. B. Lewis, "The Ceremonial Imagination of Ralph Ellison," *Carleton Miscellany* 18 (1980):36.

14. This pattern—characters repeat events until they reach understanding—recurs in post–World War II fiction. James M. Mellard, "Catch-22: Deja Vu and the Labyrinth of Memory," *Bucknell Review* 16 (May 1968):29–44, reprinted in *Joseph Heller's Catch-22: A Critical Edition*, ed. Robert M. Scotto (New York: Dell Publishing Co., 1973), 512, discusses the emphasis on repetition or déja vu in Heller. When Ellison's narrator first enters the Chthonian and must press closely to an attractive woman, he "has the sense that I had somehow been through it all before" (228).

15. John F. Callahan, "Frequencies of Eloquence: The Performance and Composition of *Invisible Man*," in *New Essays*, 55–94, defines the narrator as a "failed orator" (87) (at the battle royal, at the old couple's dispossession, at Tod Clifton's funeral) who eventually discovers how writing allows him to shape his articulation and find an audience.

16. Houston A. Baker, Jr., *Blues, Ideology, and Afro-American Literature: A Vernacular Theory* (Chicago: University of Chicago Press, 1984), 5; hereafter cited in text.

17. Houston A. Baker, Jr., "To Move without Moving: An Analysis of Creativity and Commerce in Ralph Ellison's Trueblood Episode," *PMLA* 98 (October 1983):828–43; reprinted in *Blues*, 172–99.

18. Klein, 137, makes this point first. It becomes the focus of a chapter in Alan Nadel's study of Ellison and allusion in *Invisible Criticism: Ralph Ellison and the American Canon* (Iowa City: University of Iowa Press, 1988), 85–103; hereafter cited in text. Both Klein and Nadel point out that Mumford oversimplifies history and ignores slavery as he labels 1830–1860 the Golden Day of American history.

19. See R. W. B. Lewis's essay, "Days of Wrath and Laughter," for a discussion of the apocalyptic aspects of the novel, in *Trials of the Word* (New Haven: Yale University Press, 1965), 218–20.

20. Trudier Harris, "Ellison's 'Peter Wheatstraw': His Basis in Black Folk Tradition," *Mississippi Folklore Register* 6 (1975):123.

21. See Floyd Horowitz, "Ralph Ellison's Modern Version of Brer Bear and Brer Rabbit in *Invisible Man*," *Mid-Continent American Studies Journal* 4 (1963):21–27, reprinted in Joseph F. Trimmer, ed., *A Casebook on Ralph Ellison's "Invisible Man"* (New York: Thomas Y. Crowell, 1972), 273–80.

22. A good example of the innocent Robin and the scapegoat theme is Hawthorne's "My Kinsman, Major Molineux."

23. Leo Marx in *The Machine in the Garden*, 34–72, establishes "The Tempest" as a forerunner of the New World Garden myth, which contributed to the image of the American Adam and frontier mythology. See Slotkin, *Regeneration through Violence*, 16, for a discussion of Columbus's earthly paradise imagery in his first description of his discovery.

24. See Trudier Harris, *Exorcising Blackness* (Bloomington: Indiana University Press, 1984) for a discussion of castration in African American literature.

25. See Tanner, 59–63, for an excellent discussion of verbal freedom. Ellison's novel exemplifies Tanner's thesis: "there is an abiding dream in American literature that an unpatterned, unconditioned life is possible, in which your movements and stillnesses, choices and repudiations are all your own; and that there is also an abiding American dread that there are all sorts of invisible plots afoot to rob you of your autonomy of thought and action, that conditioning is ubiquitous" (15).

26. Carolyn W. Sylvander, "Ralph Ellison's *Invisible Man* and Female Stereotypes," *Negro American Literature Forum* 9 (1975):77.

27. Claudia Tate, "Invisible Women," in *Speaking for You*, 164.

28. Melvin Dixon, *Ride Out the Wilderness* (Urbana: University of Illinois Press, 1987), 87; hereafter cited in text.

Chapter Four

1. Leonard Deutsch, "*Invisible Man* and the European Tradition," in *Approaches*, 96–101; hereafter cited in text.

2. Douglas Robinson, *American Apocalypses: The Image of the End of the World in American Literature* (Baltimore: Johns Hopkins University Press, 1985), reprinted in *Ralph Ellison*, ed. Harold Bloom (New York: Chelsea House, 1986), 139.

3. Archie D. Sanders, "Odysseus in Black: An Analysis of the Structure of *Invisible Man*," *CLA Journal* 13 (March 1970):221.

4. Charles W. Scruggs, "Ralph Ellison's Use of *The Aeneid* in *Invisible Man*," *CLA Journal* 17 (March 1974):369.

5. Ronald J. Butler, "Dante's *Inferno* and Ellison's *Invisible Man*: A Study in Literary Continuity," *CLA Journal* 28 (1984):58; hereafter cited in text.

6. Marcia R. Lieberman, "Moral Innocents: Ellison's *Invisible Man* and *Candide*," *CLA Journal* 15 (September 1971):70, 79.

7. Joseph Frank, "Ralph Ellison and a Literary Ancestor: Dostoevski," in *Speaking for You*, 231–45.

8. Robert A. Bone, *The Negro Novel in America*, rev. ed. (New Haven: Yale University Press, 1965), 202.

9. See, for example, Jerry Bryant, *The Open Decision: The Contemporary American Novel and Its Intellectual Background* (New York: Free Press, 1979), 277–81.

10. Rudolf F. Dietze, "Ralph Ellison and the Literary Tradition," in *History and Tradition in Afro-American Culture*, ed. Gunter H. Lenz (Frankfort: Campus

Verlag, 1984), 122. Dietze devotes a chapter to Malraux and Ellison in *Ralph Ellison: The Genesis of an Artist* (Nuremberg: Verlag Hans Carl, 1982), 111–35.

11. Robert N. List, *Dedalus in Harlem: The Joyce-Ellison Connection* (Washington, D.C.: University Press of America, 1982); hereafter cited in text.

12. Lord Raglan in *The Hero: A Study in Tradition, Myth, and Drama* (1936; New York: Vintage, 1956), 174–75, identifies a 22-part pattern followed by mythic heroes.

13. John S. Wright, "The Conscious Hero and the Rites of Man," in *New Essays*, 161; hereafter cited in text.

14. Valerie Bonita Gray, *Invisible Man's Literary Heritage: Benito Cereno and Moby Dick* (Amsterdam: Editions Rodopi, N.V., 1978).

15. Mary F. Sisney, "The Power and Horror of Whiteness: Wright and Ellison Respond to Poe," *CLA Journal* 29 (September 1985):82.

16. Ralph Waldo Emerson, "Nature," in *Selections from Ralph Waldo Emerson*, ed. Stephen E. Whicher (Boston: Houghton Mifflin, 1957), 24.

17. Leonard J. Deutsch "Ralph Waldo Ellison and Ralph Waldo Emerson: A Shared Moral Vision," *CLA Journal* 16 (1972):160; hereafter cited in text.

18. David L. Vanderwerken, "Focusing on the Prologue and the Epilogue," in *Approaches*, 121.

19. Elizabeth A. Schultz, "The Illumination of Darkness: Affinities between *Moby Dick* and *Invisible Man*," *CLA Journal* 32 (December 1988):171–72.

20. Marvin E. Mengeling, "Whitman and Ellison: Older Symbols in a Modern Mainstream," in *Casebook*, 269.

21. Nadel, 133. Dietze in *Genesis*, 110, believes that the fog on the way to Liberty Paints is an allusion to lines from "The Waste Land": "Unreal City, / Under the brown fog of a winter dawn."

22. John Graham, *The Writer's Voice: Conversations with Contemporary Writers*, ed. George Garrett (New York: William Morrow & Co., 1973), 223.

23. Quoted in Robert G. O'Meally, "The Rules of Magic: Hemingway as Ellison's 'Ancestor,' " in *Speaking for You*, 249; hereafter cited in text.

24. Ralph Ellison, "Stormy Weather," *New Masses*, 24 September 1940, 20.

25. Gerald T. Gordon, "Rhetorical Strategy in Ralph Ellison's *Invisible Man*," *Rocky Mountain Review* 41 (1987):205.

26. William Faulkner, *The Sound and the Fury* (New York: Vintage, 1929), 367.

27. Michael Allen, "Some Examples of Faulknerian Rhetoric in *Invisible Man*," in *The Black American Writer*, 144–45.

28. See Dietze, *Genesis*, 67–110, for an analysis of Eliot's impact on Ellison. Dietze's discussion of Ellison's allusions to "The Love Song of J. Alfred Prufrock" are not as convincing as his comparison of "The Waste Land" and *Invisible Man*.

29. T. S. Eliot, *Selected Essays* (New York: Harcourt Brace Jovanovich, 1932), 4.

30. Ishmael Reed, Quincy Troupe, and Steve Cannon, "The Essential Ellison," *Y'Bird Reader* 1 (1978):156; hereafter cited in text.

31. Mary Ellen Williams Walsh, "*Invisible Man:* Ralph Ellison's Wasteland," *CLA Journal* 28 (1984):150–58.

32. As Robert List points out, the factory machine scene where the narrator is reprogrammed while he listens to "the opening motif of Beethoven's *Fifth*" (176) may have influenced Stanley Kubrick's *A Clockwork Orange*.

33. Martin Bucco, "Ellison's Invisible West," *Western American Literature* 10 (1975):237–38, points to this scene as one that shows how "Ellison's fluid attitudes, sense of freedom, and individual possibility flow not from the Old South but from promises inherent in the Old West."

34. Donald B. Gibson, "Reconciling Public and Private in Frederick Douglass' *Narrative*," *American Literature* 57 (1985):554.

35. Valerie Smith, *Self-Discovery and Authority in Afro-American Literature* (Cambridge: Harvard University Press, 1987), 2; hereafter cited in text.

36. Richard Kostelanetz, "The Politics of Ellison's Booker" in *Casebook,* 281–305.

37. W. E. B. Du Bois, *The Souls of Black Folk* (1903; New York: Signet, 1969), 45.

38. James Weldon Johnson, *God's Trombones* (New York: Viking Press, 1927), 21. Ellison also alludes to these lines in "Flying Home" when Todd's grandmother tells the child Todd that he is crazy to reach for a flying plane.

39. Houston A. Baker, Jr., *Singers of Daybreak* (Washington, D.C.: Howard University Press, 1974), 17–31.

40. Robert Stepto, *From Behind the Veil* (Urbana: University of Illinois Press, 1979), 164.

41. Ralph Ellison, "Recent Negro Fiction," *New Masses,* 5 August 1941, 22.

42. Wright Archive, Yale University, quoted in Fabre, "Evolution," 201; hereafter cited in text.

43. Constance Webb, *Richard Wright: A Biography* (New York: G. P. Putnam's Sons, 1968), 146.

44. Harold Bloom, *The Anxiety of Influence* (New York: Oxford University Press, 1973), 5; hereafter cited in text.

45. Joseph T. Skerrett, Jr., "The Wright Interpretation: Ralph Ellison and the Anxiety of Influence," in *Speaking for You,* 227; hereafter cited in text.

46. See William Goede, "On Lower Frequencies: The Buried Men in Wright and Ellison," *Modern Fiction Studies* 15 (1969):483–501, and Dietze, 1982, 33.

Chapter Five

1. Ralph Ellison, "Out of the Hospital and under the Bar," in *Soon, One Morning,* ed. Herbert Hill (New York: Knopf, 1963), 243; hereafter cited as "Bar" in text.

2. Melvin Dixon, "O Mary Rambo, Don't You Weep," *Carleton Miscellany* 18 (1980):99.

3. Kerry McSweeney, *Invisible Man: A Student's Companion to the Novel* (Boston: Twayne, 1988), 81.

4. Ralph Ellison, "Did You Ever Dream Lucky?" *New World Writing* 5 (April 1954):134–45; hereafter cited in text as "Lucky."

5. Ralph Ellison, "A Coupla Scalped Indians," *New World Writing* 9 (1956):225; hereafter cited in text as "Scalped."

6. Allen Geller, "An Interview with Ralph Ellison," in *The Black American Writer, Vol. 1: Fiction*, ed. C. W. E. Bigsby (Baltimore: Penguin Books, 1969), 158.

7. Ralph Ellison, "And Hickman Arrives," in *Black Writers of America,* ed. Richard Barksdale and Keneth Kinnamon (New York: Macmillan, 1972), 694; hereafter cited in text as "Hickman."

8. Ralph Ellison, "The Roof, the Steeple and the People," *Quarterly Review of Literature* 10 (1960):115; hereafter cited in text as "Roof."

9. Ralph Ellison, "Juneteenth," *Quarterly Review of Literature* 14 (1965): 262; hereafter cited in text.

10. Ralph Ellison, "Night-Talk," *Quarterly Review of Literature* 16 (1969): 317; hereafter cited in text as "Night."

11. Ralph Ellison, "Cadillac Flambé," *American Review* 16 (1973):251; hereafter cited in text as "Flambé."

12. Ralph Ellison, "It Always Breaks Out," *Partisan Review* 30 (Spring 1963):15; hereafter cited in text as "Breaks."

13. Ralph Ellison, "Backwacking: A Plea to the Senator," *Massachusetts Review* 18 (Autumn 1977):411–16, reprinted in Harper and Stepto, eds., *Chant of Saints*, 445–46.

14. Norman Mailer, *The White Negro* (San Francisco: City Lights Books, 1957), 4.

15. One cloudy detail concerns Severen's race. Clues indicate that these characters are black. Characters refer to Fats Waller and Louis Armstrong, and Tyree says about the ambergris, "Lissen here, y'all, that *there* is whale hockey; I don't care what that white man says!" (40). But Severen, even though he went to school with these other black boys, has blue eyes. Cliofus tells McIntyre: "But he just looked at me with a funny light in his blue eyes and that blue tie he was wearing gave them a deeper color than my own eyes could have remembered even if I'd recognized him." (35). Perhaps Severen, like Bliss, is of indeterminate race and grew up with blacks and will prove to be a double of Bliss.

16. Ralph Ellison, "A Song of Innocence," *Iowa Review* 1 (1970):39; hereafter cited in text as "Song."

Chapter Six

1. John S. Wright, "Shadowing Ellison," in *Speaking for You*, 66; hereafter cited in text.

2. John M. Reilly, "The Testament of Ralph Ellison," in *Speaking for You,* 51; hereafter cited in text.

3. Ralph Ellison, "Creative and Cultural Lag," *New Challenge* 2 (Fall 1937):91.

4. Ralph Ellison, "Negro Prize Fighter," *New Masses,* 17 December 1940, 27.

5. Ralph Ellison, "Practical Mystic," *New Masses,* 16 August 1938, 26; hereafter cited in text as "Mystic."

6. Ralph Ellison, "The Darker Brother," *Tomorrow* 4 (September 1943):55.

7. Ralph Ellison, "Escape the Thunder," *Tomorrow* 5 (March 1945):91. Other books about African American history and literature that Ellison reviewed from 1937 to 1944 are Louis Cochran's *Boss Man,* (Caldwell Idaho: Caxton, 1939), Walter D. Edmonds's *Chad Hanna,* (Boston: Little, Brown, 1940), Len Zinberg's *Walk Hard, Talk Loud* (New York: Bobbs-Merrill, 1940), and William Attaway's *Blood on the Forge* (New York: Doubleday Dovan, 1941). Additionally Ellison published two general surveys—actually the same essay with slight revisions—"Richard Wright and Recent Negro Fiction" in the Summer 1941 issue of *Direction* and "Recent Negro Fiction" in the 5 August 1941 issue of *New Masses.*

8. Ellison, "Recent Negro Fiction," 22; Ralph Ellison, "Richard Wright and Recent Negro Fiction," *Direction* 4 (Summer 1941):12; hereafter cited in text as "Recent."

9. Ralph Ellison, "The Magic of Limping John," *Tomorrow* 4 (December 1944):121.

10. Ralph Ellison, "Judge Lynch in New York," *New Masses,* 15 August 1939, 15.

11. Ralph Ellison, "A Congress Jim Crow Didn't Attend," *New Masses,* 14 May 1940, 8; hereafter cited in text as "Congress."

12. R. W. B. Lewis, "Ellison's Essays," in *Speaking for You,* 45.

13. Stanley Edgar Hyman, "Ralph Ellison in Our Time," in *Ralph Ellison: A Collection of Critical Essays,* 42.

14. Robert Penn Warren, "The Unity of Experience," in *Ralph Ellison: A Collection of Critical Essays,* 24.

Chapter Seven

1. Henry Louis Gates, *The Signifying Monkey* (New York: Oxford University, Press, 1988), 106; hereafter cited in text.

Selected Bibliography

PRIMARY WORKS

Novel

Invisible Man. New York: Random House, 1952. 30th Anniversary Edition, New York: Random House, 1982. Franklin Center, Penn.: Franklin Mint Corp., 1980.

Short Fiction

"Afternoon." *American Writing,* edited by Otto Storm and others, 28–37. Prairie City, Ill.: J. A. Decker, 1940.

"And Hickman Arrives." *Noble Savage* 1 (1960):5–49. Reprinted in *Black Writers of America,* edited by Richard Barksdale and Keneth Kinnamon, 693–712. New York: Macmillan, 1972.

"Backwacking: A Plea to the Senator." *Massachusetts Review* 18 (Autumn 1977): 411–16. Reprinted in *Chant of Saints,* edited by Michael S. Harper and Robert B. Stepto, 445–50. Urbana: University of Illinois Press, 1979.

"The Birthmark." *New Masses,* 2 July 1940, 16–17.

"Cadillac Flambé." *American Review* 16 (1973):249–69.

"A Coupla Scalped Indians." *New World Writing* 9 (1956):225–36.

"Did You Ever Dream Lucky?" *New World Writing* 5 (April 1954):134–45.

"Flying Home." In *Cross Section,* edited by Edwin Seaver, 469–85. New York: Fischer, 1944. Reprinted in *Dark Symphony: Negro Literature in America,* edited by James A. Emanuel and Theodore L. Gross, 254–74. Toronto: Free Press, 1968.

"In a Strange Country." *Tomorrow* 3 (July 1944):41–44.

"Invisible Man." *Horizon* 16 (October 1947):104–18.

"Invisible Man: Prologue to a Novel." *Partisan Review* 19 (January–February 1952):31–40.

"It Always Breaks Out." *Partisan Review* 30 (Spring 1963):113–28.

"Juneteenth." *Quarterly Review of Literature* 14 (1965):262–76.

"King of the Bingo Game." *Tomorrow* 4 (November 1944):29–33.

"Mr. Toussan." *New Masses,* 4 November 1941, 19–20.

"Night-Talk." *Quarterly Review of Literature* 16 (1969):317–29.

"Out of the Hospital and Under the Bar." In *Soon, One Morning,* edited by Herbert Hill, 242–90. New York: Knopf, 1963.

"The Roof, the Steeple and the People." *Quarterly Review of Literature* 10 (1960):115–28.
"Slick Gonna Learn. *Direction* (September 1939):10–11, 14, 16.
"A Song of Innocence." *Iowa Review* 1 (1970):30–40.
"That I Had the Wings." *Common Ground* 3 (Summer 1943):30–37.

Collected Nonfiction

Going to the Territory. New York: Random House, 1986.
Shadow and Act. New York: Vintage Books, 1953, 1964.

Uncollected Nonfiction

Banks, Ann. *First-Person America.* New York: Alfred A. Knopf, 1980. Collects various WPA pieces, including some of Ellison's.
Ellison, Ralph. "The Alain Locke Symposium." *Harvard Advocate* (Spring 1974):9–28.
"Anti-Semitism among Negroes." *Jewish People's Voice* 3 (April 1939):3, 8.
"Anti-War Novel." *New Masses,* 18 June 1940, 29–30.
"Argosy across the USA." *New Masses,* 26 November 1940, 24
"Big White Fog." *New Masses,* 12 November 1940, 22–23.
"Boston Adventure." *Tomorrow* 4 (December 1944):120.
"Collaborator with His Own Enemy." *New York Times Book Review,* 19 February 1950, 4.
"A Congress Jim Crow Didn't Attend." *New Masses,* 14 May 1940, 5–8.
"Creative and Cultural Lag." *New Challenge* 2 (Fall 1937):90–91.
"The Darker Brother." *Tomorrow* 4 (September 1943):55.
"Editorial Comment." *Negro Quarterly* 1 (Winter 1943):295–302.
"Escape the Thunder." *Tomorrow* 5 (March 1945):91.
"Eyewitness Story of Riot: False Rumor Spurred Mob." *New York Post,* 2 August 1943, 91.
Foreword to *There Is a Tree More Ancient Than Eden,* by Leon Forrest. New York: Random House, 1973.
"The Good Life." *New Masses,* 20 February 1940, 27.
"The Great Migration." *New Masses,* 2 December 1941, 23–24.
"Hunters and Pioneers." *New Masses,* 19 March 1940, 26.
Introduction to *Buying Time: An Anthology Celebrating 20 Years of the Literature Program of the National Endowment for the Arts,* edited by Scott Walker, xix–xxv. Saint Paul, Minn.: Graywolf Press, 1985.
"Javanese Folklore." *New Masses,* 26 December 1939, 25–26.
"Judge Lynch in New York." *New Masses,* 15 August 1939, 15–16.
"The Magic of Limping John." *Tomorrow* 4 (December 1944):121.
"Native Land." *New Masses,* 2 June 1942, 29.
"Negro Prize Fighter." *New Masses,* 17 December 1940, 26–27.

"New World A-Coming." *Tomorrow* 4 (December 1944):67–68.
"On Becoming a Writer." *Commentary* 38 (October 1964):57–60.
"Philippine Report." *Direction* 4 (Summer 1941):13.
"Practical Mystic." *New Masses,* 16 August 1938, 25–26.
"Recent Negro Fiction." *New Masses,* 5 August 1941, 22–26.
"Resourceful Human." *Saturday Review,* 12 July 1958, 25–26.
"Richard Wright and Recent Negro Fiction." *Direction* 4 (Summer 1941):12–13.
"Romance in the Slave Era." *New Masses,* 28 May 1940, 27–28.
"Ruling-class Southerner." *New Masses,* 5 December 1939, 27.
"Southern Folklore." *New Masses* 37, 29 October 1940, 28.
"A Special Message to Subscribers from Ralph Ellison." *Invisible Man.* Franklin
    Center, Penn.: Franklin Library Limited Edition, 1980.
"Stepchild Fantasy." *Saturday Review,* 8 June 1946, 25–26.
"Stormy Weather." *New Masses,* 24 September 1940, 20–21.
"TAC Negro Show." *New Masses,* 27 February 1940, 29–30.
"Transition." *Negro Quarterly, a Review of Life and Culture* 1 (Spring
    1942):87–92.

SECONDARY WORKS

Interviews

Carson, David L. "Ralph Ellison: Twenty Years After." *Studies in American Fiction* 1 (Spring 1973):1–23.
Cohen, Ted, and **N. A. Samstag.** "An Interview with Ralph Ellison." *Phoenix* 22 (Fall 1961):4–10.
Garrett, George, ed. *The Writer's Voice: Conversations with Contemporary Writers.* William Morrow & Co., 1973.
Geller, Allen. "An Interview with Ralph Ellison." In *The Black American Writer. Vol. 1: Fiction,* edited by C. W. E. Bigsby. Baltimore: Penguin Books, 1969.
Hersey, John. " 'A Completion of Personality': A Talk with Ralph Ellison." In *Speaking for You,* edited by Kimberly W. Benston, 285–307. Washington, D.C.: Howard University Press, 1987.
O'Brien, John. *Interviews with Black Writers.* New York: Liveright, 1973.
Reed, Ishmael, Quincy Troupe, and **Steve Cannon.** "The Essential Ellison." *Y'Bird Reader* 1 (1978):126–59.
Stepto, Robert B., and **Michael S. Harper.** "Study and Experience: An Interview with Ralph Ellison." In *Chant of Saints,* edited by Michael S. Harper and Robert B. Stepto, 451–69. Urbana: University of Illinois Press, 1979.
Welburn, Ron. "Ralph Ellison's Territorial Vantage." *Grackle* 4 (1977–78): 5–15.

Bibliography

Covo, Jacqueline. *The Blinking Eye: Ralph Waldo Ellison.* Metuchen, N.J.:
Scarecrow Press, 1974. Excellent bibliography of U.S., French, German, and
Italian criticism through 1971.

Collections

Benston, Kimberly W., ed. *Speaking for You: The Vision of Ralph Ellison.* Washington, D.C.: Howard University Press, 1987. Comprehensive collection with
essays by Frank, Burke, Fabre, Skerrett, Stepto, Reilly, O'Meally, John
Wright, Tate, and others and updated interviews with Hersey and
McPherson. Includes Ellison bibliography compiled by O'Meally.
Bloom, Harold, ed. *Ralph Ellison.* New York: Chelsea House Publishers, 1986.
Reprints 11 essays, including essays by Baker, Blake, and Stepto.
Gottesman, Ronald, ed. *The Merrill Studies in "Invisible Man".* Columbus:
Merrill, 1971. Contains eight essays, including essays by Bone, Horowitz,
Shafer, and Vogler.
Hersey, John, ed. *Ralph Ellison: A Collection of Critical Essays.* Englewood Cliffs,
N.J.: Prentice-Hall, 1970. Contains early reviews of *Invisible Man* and
Shadow and Act, eight essays (Bone, Rovit, Shafer, Vogler, Kent, and others),
and two interviews.
O'Meally, Robert G., ed. *New Essays on "Invisible Man".* New York: Cambridge
University Press, 1988. Good introduction by O'Meally, plus essays by
Callahan, Smith, Ostendorf, Schaub, and S. Wright.
Parr, Susan Resneck, and **Pancho Savery,** eds. *Approaches to Teaching Ellison's
"Invisible Man."* New York: MLA, 1989. In the Modern Library Association
series on teaching. Contains 16 short, original essays emphasizing pedagogy.
Good survey of criticism by Savery, and a bibliography.
Reilly, John M., ed. *Twentieth Century Interpretations of "Invisible Man."*
Englewood Cliffs, N.J.: Prentice-Hall, 1970. Contains 15 selections, including early reviews of *Invisible Man* and essays by Fraiberg, Glicksberg,
Jackson, and Horowitz.
Trimmer, Joseph, ed. *A Casebook on Ralph Ellison's "Invisible Man."* New York:
Thomas Y. Crowell, 1972. Important early collection. Also includes background selections from Washington, Du Bois, Locke, Garvey, and Eliot; essays by Ellison; eight critical essays; and study questions.

Special Issues of Journals

Carleton Miscellany 18 (1980).
CLA Journal 13 (March 1970).
Delta (Montpellier, France) 18 (1984).

Books

Dietze, Rudolf F. *Ralph Ellison: The Genesis of an Artist*. Nuremberg: Verlag Hans Carl, 1982. Examines various influences on *Invisible Man*. Excellent discussion of Eliot's and Malraux's importance.

Gray, Valerie Bonita. *Invisible Man's Literary Heritage: "Benito Cereno" and "Moby Dick."* Amsterdam: Editions Rodopi, N.V., 1978. Superficial discussion of Ellison and Melville.

List, Robert N. *Dedalus in Harlem: The Joyce-Ellison Connection*. Washington, D.C.: University Press of America, 1982. Poorly proofread and overstated analysis of Joyce's influence on Ellison; provides some insights despite its problems.

McSweeney, Kerry. *"Invisible Man": A Student's Companion to the Novel*. Boston: Twayne, 1988. Student guide to novel that makes a good distinction between narrator as character and narrator.

Nadel, Alan. *Invisible Criticism: Ralph Ellison and the American Canon*. Iowa City: University of Iowa Press, 1988. Interesting theoretical discussion of allusion, with good analyses of Twain, Melville, Eliot, and Lewis Mumford as influences.

O'Meally, Robert G. *The Craft of Ralph Ellison*. Cambridge: Harvard University Press, 1980. The most important work on Ellison to date. Contains a comprehensive discussion of Ellison's life, stories, essays, and *Invisible Man* and emphasizes the importance of folklore.

Parts of Books and Articles

Abrams, Robert E. "The Ambiguities of Dreaming in Ellison's *Invisible Man*." *American Literature* 49 (January 1978):592–603. Examines dreams.

Allen, Michael. "Some Examples of Faulknerian Rhetoric in *Invisible Man*." In, *The Black American Writer*, Vol. I, edited by C. W. E. Bigsby, 143–51. Baltimore, MD: Penguin Books, 1971. Faulkner's influence.

Anderson, Jervis. "Going to the Territory." *New Yorker*, 22 November 22, 1976, 55–108. A profile of Ellison that is important for Ellison's Oklahoma background; also reproduces his comments at the opening of the Ellison Library.

Baker, Houston A., Jr. *Blues, Ideology, and Afro-American Literature: A Vernacular Theory*. Chicago: University of Chicago Press, 1984. An important theoretical work influenced by poststructuralism and Marxism; contains an essay on *Invisible Man* originally published in *PMLA*.

_____. *The Journey Back: Issues in Black Literature and Criticism*. Chicago: University of Chicago Press, 1980. Presents a structuralist theory superseded by his later book.

_____. *Singers of Daybreak*. Washington, D.C.: Howard University Press, 1974. Collects seven essays on African American literature, including a comparison between Ellison and Johnson.

Blake, Susan L. "Ritual and Rationalization: Black Folklore in the Works of Ralph Ellison." *PMLA* 94 (1979):121–36. Attacks Ellison for making black folklore universal.

Bone, Robert. *The Negro Novel in America.* Rev. ed. New Haven: Yale University Press, 1965. An early survey of the African American novel that contains a good analysis of Ellison and Dostoyevski.

————. "Ralph Ellison and the Uses of Imagination." In *Anger and Beyond,* edited by Herbert Hill, 86–111. New York: Harper & Row, 1966. Reprinted in Hersey, Gottesman, Reilly, and Trimmer (see "Collections"). An excellent discussion of Ellison and jazz.

Bryant, Jerry. *The Open Decision: The Contemporary American Novel and Its Intellectual Background.* New York: Free Press, 1969. Discusses European philosophy, particularly existentialism, as a background for the post–World War II novel.

Bucco, Martin. "Ellison's Invisible West." *Western American Literature* (1975): 237–38. A brief note about the western motif in *Invisible Man.*

Busby, Mark. "The Significance of the Frontier in Contemporary American Fiction." In *The Frontier Experience and the American Dream,* edited by David Mogen, Mark Busby, and Paul Bryant, 95–103. College Station: Texas A&M University Press, 1989. Explores the frontier myth in Ellison and others.

Butler, Ronald J. "Dante's *Inferno* and Ellison's *Invisible Man:* A Study in Literary Continuity." *CLA Journal* 28 (1984):57–77.

Byerman, Keith. *Fingering the Jagged Grain: Tradition and Form in Recent Black Fiction.* Athens: University of Georgia Press, 1985. Uses Ellison's paradigm of the dialectic of oppression and resistance as a major influence on later African American writers, such as Gaines, Bambara, Alice Walker, Morrison, and Reed.

Callahan, John F. *In the African-American Grain.* Urbana: University of Illinois Press, 1988. A good discussion of African American literature that analyzes the *Invisible Man* narrator as "failed orator."

Clipper, Lawrence J. "Folkloric and Mythic Elements in *Invisible Man.*" *CLA Journal* 13 (March 1979):239. Compares Ellison and Lord Raglan and applies V. Propp's folktale pattern to *Invisible Man.*

Collier, Eugenia W. "The Nightmare Truth of an Invisible Man." *Black World* 20 (December 1970):12–19. Provides a discussion of dream imagery.

Cooke, Michael G. *Afro-American Literature in the Twentieth Century: The Achievement of Intimacy.* New Haven: Yale University Press, 1984. Discusses blues and signifying as masking techniques as novels move toward intimacy.

Corry, John. "An American Novelist Who Sometimes Teaches." *New York Times Magazine,* 20 November 1966, 55, 179–85. A profile of Ellison.

Deutsch, Leonard. "Ellison's Early Fiction." *Negro American Literature Forum* 7 (Summer 1973):53–59. An analysis of Ellison's early stories.

————. "Ralph Waldo Ellison and Ralph Waldo Emerson: A Shared Moral Vision." *CLA Journal* 16 (1972):160. Looks at Emerson's influence on Ellison as positive.

Dietze, Rudolf F. "Ralph Ellison and the Literary Tradition." In Ed. Gunter H. Lenz. 118–29. *History and Tradition in Afro-American Culture.* Frankfort: Campus Verlag, 1984. Analyzes various influences; especially good on Malraux.

Dixon, Melvin. "O Mary Rambo, Don't You Weep." *Carleton Miscellany* 18 (1980):98–104. Emphasizes Mary Rambo's character.

_____. *Ride Out the Wilderness.* Urbana: University of Illinois Press, 1987. Analyzes the importance of geographical images, such as the wilderness, underground, and mountain, in African American literature.

Dupre, F. W. "On 'Invisible Man.' " *Book Week (Washington Post),* 26 September 1965, 4. Discusses the poll selecting *Invisible Man* as the "most distinguished" post–World War II novel.

Fabre, Michel. *The Unfinished Quest of Richard Wright,* translated by Isabel Barzun. New York: William Morrow, 1973. Important biography that discusses Wright's relations with Ellison.

Gates, Henry Louis, Jr., ed. *Black Literature and Literary Theory.* New York: Methuen, 1984. Contains six theoretical essays and seven applications, including Baker's *PMLA* article on *Invisible Man.*

_____. *Figures in Black.* New York: Oxford, 1987. Uses signifying as a basis for a theory about African American literary tradition.

_____, ed. *"Race," Writing, and Difference.* Chicago: University of Chicago Press, 1986.

_____. *The Signifying Monkey.* New York: Oxford University Press, 1988. Extends earlier discussion of signifying. Winner of American Book Award.

Goede, William. "On Lower Frequencies: The Buried Men in Wright and Ellison." *Modern Fiction Studies* 15 (1969):483–501. Discusses Wright's story as influence.

Gordon, Gerald T. "Rhetorical Strategy in Ralph Ellison's *Invisible Man.*" *Rocky Mountain Review* 41 (1987):199–209. Discusses Hemingway's influence.

Harper, Michael S., and **Robert B. Stepto,** eds. *Chant of Saints.* Urbana: University of Illinois Press, 1979. A collection of essays, interviews, fiction, and poetry. Includes Callahan essay on Ellison and democracy and an Ellison essay, interview, and story.

Harris, Trudier. "Ellison's 'Peter Wheatstraw': His Basis in Black Folk Tradition." *Mississippi Folklore Register* 6 (1975):117–26. Traces Wheatstraw's background.

Horowitz, Floyd. "Ralph Ellison's Modern Version of Brer Bear and Brer Rabbit in *Invisible Man.*" *Mid-Continent American Studies Journal* 4 (1963):21–27. Reprinted in Gottesman, Reilly, and Trimmer (see "Collections").

Klein, Marcus. *After Alienation.* Chicago: University of Chicago Press, 1964.

Important early discussion of stories and *Invisible Man,* as well as an analysis of post–World War II fiction as a literature of accommodation.

Klotman, Phyllis R. "The Running Man as Metaphor in Ellison's *Invisible Man.*" *CLA Journal* 13 (March 1970):277–88.

Kostelanetz, Richard. "The Politics of Ellison's Booker." *Chicago Review* 19 (1967):5–26. Reprinted in Trimmer (see "Collections"). Analyzes Ellison's critique of Booker T. Washington.

————. "Ralph Ellison: Novelist as Brown-Skinned Aristocrat." *Master Minds.* New York: Macmillan, 1969. A profile of Ellison.

Lewicki, Zbigniew. *The Bang and the Whimper: Apocalypse and Entropy in American Literature.* Westport, Conn.: Greenwood Press, 1984. Uses Ellison to examine the theme of the subtitle.

Lewis, R. W. B. "The Ceremonial Imagination of Ralph Ellison." *Carleton Miscellany* 18 (1980):34–38. On Ellison's optimism.

————. *Trials of the Word.* New Haven: Yale University Press, 1965. Discusses apocalyptic images in *Invisible Man.*

Lieberman, Marcia R. "Moral Innocents: Ellison's *Invisible Man* and *Candide,*" *CLA Journal* 15 (September 1971):64–79.

Mengeling, Marvin E. "Whitman and Ellison: Older Symbols in a Modern Mainstream." *Walt Whitman Review* 12 (September 1966):67–70. Reprinted in Trimmer (see "Collections"). Points out Whitman echoes.

O'Meally, Robert G. "The Rules of Magic: Hemingway as Ellison's 'Ancestor.' " *Southern Review* 21 (1985):751–69. Reprinted in Benston (see "Collections"). A thorough discussion of Hemingway influence.

Ostendorf, Bernhard. "Ralph Ellison's 'Flying Home': From Folk Tale to Short Story." *Journal of the Folklore Institute* 13, no. 2 (1976):185–99.

Petesch, Donald A. *A Spy in the Enemy's Country.* Iowa City: University of Iowa Press, 1989. Stresses *Invisible Man* narrator's movement from solitude to community and resulting self-awareness, an important trend in modern black literature.

Robinson, Douglas. *American Apocalypses: The Image of the End of the World in American Literature.* Baltimore: Johns Hopkins University Press, 1985. A brief analysis of the Jonah image in *Invisible Man.*

Rovit, Earl H. "Ralph Ellison and the American Comic Tradition." *Wisconsin Studies in Contemporary Literature* 1 (1960):34–42. Reprinted in Hersey, Reilly, and Trimmer (see "Collections"). An early article exploring Ellison's humor and his connection with older American writers, such as Emerson and Melville.

Sanders, Archie D. "Odysseus in Black: An Analysis of the Structure of *Invisible Man.*" *CLA Journal* 13 (March 1970):217–28. Compares *Invisible Man* and *The Odyssey.*

Saunders, Pearl I. "Symbolism in Ralph Ellison's 'King of the Bingo Game.' " *CLA Journal* 20 (September 1976):35–39. A limited interpretation of the story.

Schafer, William J. "Ralph Ellison and the Birth of the Anti-Hero." *Critique: Studies in Modern Fiction* 10 (1968):81–93. Reprinted in Gottesman and Trimmer (see "Collections"). Notes rebirth imagery and points to the narrator's similarities to Joseph Campbell's mythic figure.

Schultz, Elizabeth A. "The Illumination of Darkness: Affinities between *Moby Dick* and *Invisible Man*." *CLA Journal* 32 (December 1988):170–200. A good discussion of the similarities.

Scruggs, Charles W. "Ralph Ellison's Use of *The Aeneid* in *Invisible Man*." *CLA Journal* 17 (March 1974):368–78. Compares Ellison's novel and *The Aeneid*'s themes of search for home, desire for reunification of shattered people, and source for Sybil's character.

Skerrett, Joseph T., Jr. "The Wright Interpretation: Ralph Ellison and the Anxiety of Influence." *Massachusetts Review* 21 (1980):196–212. Reprinted in Benston (see "Collections"). Applies Harold Bloom's theories to the relationship between Ellison and Wright.

Sisney, Mary F. "The Power and Horror of Whiteness: Wright and Ellison Respond to Poe." *CLA Journal* 29 (September 1985):82–90. Discusses Poe's influence.

Smith, Valerie. *Self-Discovery and Authority in Afro-American Literature.* Cambridge: Harvard University Press, 1987. An analysis of first person narrator/storyteller in *Invisible Man* and other African American literature.

Staples, Brent. "In His Own Good Time." *New York Times Book Review*, 3 August 1986, 15. A brief note on the publication of *Going to the Territory*.

Stepto, Robert. *From Behind the Veil.* Urbana: University of Illinois Press, 1979. Defines the two major types of black narratives as ascent and immersion and finds both patterns in *Invisible Man*.

Sylvander, Carolyn W. "Ralph Ellison's *Invisible Man* and Female Stereotypes." *Negro American Literature Forum* 9 (1975):77–79.

Tanner, Tony. *City of Words.* New York: Harper & Row, 1971. Major work on mainstream post–World War II fiction that connects Ellison with themes of fear of control and freedom of language.

Trimmer, Joseph. "Ralph Ellison's 'Flying Home.' " *Studies in Short Fiction* 9 (Spring 1972):175–82. Excellent analysis of this early story.

Walling, William. " 'Art' and 'Protest': Ralph Ellison's *Invisible Man* Twenty Years After." *Phylon* 34 (June 1973):120–34. Traces political reactions to *Invisible Man*.

Walsh, Mary Ellen Williams. "*Invisible Man*: Ralph Ellison's Wasteland." *CLA Journal* 28 (1984):150–58. Examines Eliot's influence.

Wilner, Eleanor R. "The Invisible Black Thread: Identity and Nonentity in *Invisible Man*." *CLA Journal* 13 (1970):242–57. Analyzes thread as image of tradition.

Index

Allen, Michael, 81
amalgamation, 4, 21, 41, 51, 52, 54, 60,
    62, 65, 98, 99, 105–7, 109, 113,
    120–22, 127, 130, 134, 142, 144; *see
    also* assimilation, synthesis, and
    syncretism
American Adam, 40, 42–43, 47, 50, 53,
    59–60
Anderson, Jervis, 9, 41, 84, 124, 140
Anderson, Sherwood, 9
Armstrong, Louis, 8, 30, 37, 44, 70, 79,
    113
assimilation, 4, 107; *see also*
    amalgamation, synthesis, and syncretism
autobiography, 122, 127, 128, 133, 135,
    137

Bahktin, Mikhail, 143
Baker, Houston, 48, 63, 86, 91, 143;
    *Blues, Ideology, and Afro-American
    Literature: A Vernacular Theory,* 48, 143
Baldwin, James, 18, 129, 132
Bambara, Toni Cade, 144
Basie, William "Count," 5, 51
Baumbach, Jonathan: *The Landscape of
    Nightmare,* 142
Bellow, Saul, 16, 100, 142; *Henderson the
    Rain King,* 142
Berry, Abner W., 17
biblical allusions, 43, 65, 66, 83, 97,
    103–5, 108, 109, 110
Bird, Charlie, 130
Blake, Susan L., 35, 62–63, 104
Blake, William, 116–17
Bliss (Senator Sunraider, the Hickman
    stories), 101–11, 131
Bloom, Harold, 71; *The Anxiety of
    Influence,* 90–91
blues, 5, 13, 31, 34, 44, 47–49, 51, 58,
    65, 69, 77–79, 84, 88, 90, 91, 96, 120
Bone, Robert, 31, 68
Breaux, Zelia N., 4, 5

Breton, André, 32
Bronte, Emily: *Wuthering Heights,* 3
Brown, Lloyd L., 17
Brumm, Ursula, 43
Bryant, Jerry: *The Open Decision,* 142
Bucco, Martin, 152n33
Burke, Kenneth, 45, 62
Busby, Mark, 148n4
Busoni, Ferruccio, 8, 134
Butler, Ronald J., 67
Byerman, Keith, 63, 144; *Fingering the
    Jagged Grain: Tradition and Form in
    Recent Black Fiction,* 143, 148n7

Cadmus myth, 108
Caldwell, Erskine, 137
Callahan, John F., 149n15
Campbell, Joseph: *The Masks of God,* 43
castration, 24, 25, 31, 52, 63, 99, 100
Chaplin, Charlie, 38, 83
Chase, Richard, 16
Christ, 41–43, 52, 57, 59–61, 63, 66,
    73, 83, 94, 95, 101, 102, 104, 105
Christian, Charlie, 4, 130
Christian, Edward, 4
Clifton, Tod (*Invisible Man*), 38, 42,
    54–56, 58, 60, 66, 67, 70, 79, 83
Clipper, Lawrence, 70
Coleman, Ermuel "Bucket," 4
Coleman, Lonnie: *Escape the Thunder,* 124
comic books, 65, 71
Connolly, Cyril, 16
Cooper, James Fenimore, 40, 65; *The Last
    of the Mohicans,* 3, 71
Crèvecoeur, J. Hector St. John de: *Letters
    from an American Farmer,* 121

Dante Alighieri, 63, 65, 67
Davis, Jefferson, 5, 107
Dawson, William L., 6, 7
Derrida, Jacques, 71
Deutsch, Leonard, 24, 27, 67, 69, 73

dialectic, 41, 63, 76, 117, 119, 130, 142, 144
Dietze, Rudolph, 69, 83, 91, 93, 150n10, 151n28
Dixon, Melvin, 62, 94–96; *Ride Out the Wilderness,* 62
Dobie, J. Frank: *Apache Gold and Yaqui Silver,* 98; *Coronado's Children,* 98
Dostoyevski, Feodor, 63, 65, 68, 90, 91; *Notes from Underground,* 68, 91
Douglass, Frederick, 4, 5, 30, 55, 65, 70, 82, 84, 85, 94, 95
Du Bois, W.E.B., 65, 85–86; *The Souls of Black Folk,* 85

Eliot, T. S., 8, 65, 69, 81–83, 90, 108, 111, 117, 126; *Family Reunion,* 82; *Four Quartets,* 82; "The Hollow Men," 111, 126; "The Love Song of J. Alfred Prufrock," 111; "The Metaphysical Poets," 81; "Tradition and the Individual Talent," 81; "The Waste Land," 8–9, 82–83, 108
Ellison, Fanny (McConnell), 14–16, 100
Ellison, Ida (Millsap), 1, 9
Ellison, Lewis Alfred, 1
Ellison, Ralph

LIFE:
Oklahoma background 1–3; reading 3–4; early education 4–6; musical training 4–5, 7; at Tuskegee Institute 6–10; move to Harlem 10–11; at the WPA 13–14; in Merchant Marine 14–15; composition of *Invisible Man* 15–16; Awards 17–18; attacks during 1960s, 18–20; Hickman stories 20, 100–102; achievement and influence 140–144

WORKS—STORIES:
"Afternoon," 22, 25–27
"And Hickman Arrives," 100, 102–5, 110
"Backwacking," 100, 115, 137
"The Birthmark," 12, 24–25, 31
"Cadillac Flambe," 111–13, 115

"A Coupla Scalped Indians," 32, 98–100, 118
"Did You Ever Dream Lucky?" 96–98
"Flying Home," 13, 23, 33, 34–37, 137
"In a Strange Country," 13, 23, 33–34
"It Always Breaks Out," 100, 112, 113–15, 116
"Juneteenth," 100, 107–9
"King of the Bingo Game," 13, 23, 37, 38
"Mr. Toussan," 27–29
"Night-Talk," 109–11
"Out of the Hospital and Under the Bar," 93–96
"The Roof, the Steeple, and the People," 105–7, 110
"Slick Gonna Learn," 23–24, 25, 37
"A Song of Innocence," 100, 116–18

NOVELS:
Invisible Man, 15–17, 39–92; frontier mythology, 39–44; American Adam 42–43; Prologue, 44–45; Battle Royal 45–46; college, 47–51; Trueblood episode, 47–49; paint factory, 51–54; Brotherhood 54–58; Tod Clifton's role, 55–56; Rinehart, 56–58; Epilogue, 58–60; themes, 60–61; characterization, 61; style, 61–62; structure, 62–63; symbol and image, 63–64; allusions and influences from European culture, 66–70; from American culture, 71–84; from African American culture, 84–92

NONFICTION:
"The Art of Romare Bearden," 134
"Beating that Boy," 128
"Brave Words for a Startling Occasion," 128
"Camp Lost Colony," 125
"Change the Joke and Slip the Yoke," 104, 129
"A Congress Jim Crow Didn't Attend," 125
"Creative and Cultural Lag," 123

Going to the Territory, 21, 76, 120,
    133–39, 142
"An Extravagance of Laughter," 134,
    136–37
"Harlem is Nowhere," 122, 131
"Hidden Name and Complex Fate,"
    128
"Homage to Duke Ellington on His
    Birthday," 134
"Judge Lynch in New York," 125
"The Little Man at Chehaw Station," 8,
    133, 134–35
"Living with Music," 130
"The Myth of the Flawed White
    Southerner," 19, 133
"The Novel as a Function of American
    Democracy," 134
"On Initiation Rites and Power," 133,
    135–36
"Perspective of Literature," 134
"Remembering Richard Wright," 90,
    134
Shadow and Act, 8, 18, 21, 31, 48,
    120, 123, 126–33, 134, 136, 137,
    142
"Society, Morality, and the Novel," 41,
    78, 80, 134, 137–38
"Sound and the Mainstream," 127, 130
"That Same Pain, That Same Pleasure,"
    127–28
"Twentieth Century Fiction and the
    Black Mask of Humanity," 77, 128
"What America Would Be Like
    Without Blacks," 133
"What These Children Are Like," 133
"The World and the Jug," 18, 129–30

Emerson, Ralph Waldo, 3, 65, 66, 70,
    72–73, 76, 77, 105, 113, 128;
    "Nature," 73; "Ode Inscribed to W. E.
    Channing," 73
existentialism, 68

Fabre, Michel, 87, 88
Faulkner, William, 32, 65, 79–81, 104,
    110, 114, 118; *Absalom, Absalom!,* 80;
    "The Bear," 80; *Go Down, Moses,* 80;

Intruder in the Dust, 126; *The Sound
    and the Fury,* 80, 118
Fauset, Arthur, 123
Fiedler, Leslie, 40, 76, 77
Fitzgerald, F. Scott, 9, 71, 104; *The Great
    Gatsby,* 51, 54, 71
Foley, Martha, 17
folklore, 13, 22, 27, 29, 32, 34–37,
    39, 47, 51, 65, 76, 83, 84, 95, 97,
    98, 121, 124, 125, 129, 133,
    141
Ford, Ford Madox, 9
Ford, John, 84
Frank, Joseph, 68
Franklin, Benjamin, 65, 71, 77;
    Autobiography, 71
freedom, 1, 2, 5, 11, 13, 21, 22, 27, 29,
    31, 38, 40–43, 45, 46, 54, 57–62, 80,
    87, 97, 98, 117–19, 121, 127, 130,
    132, 135, 137, 139, 140–42, 144; *see
    also* restriction
Freud, Sigmund, 9, 11, 32, 65, 70, 110;
    Totem and Taboo, 70
frontier mythology, 22, 39–43, 54,
    57, 60, 71, 76, 80, 84, 105,
    141
Frost, Robert, 45
Frye, Northrop, 71

Gaines, Ernest, 144
Gates, Henry Louis: *Figures in Black,* 143;
    The Signifying Monkey, 143
Gehrig, Lou, 25
Gibson, Donald B., 85
Goede, William, 91
Goodwyn, Frank: *The Magic of Limping
    John,* 125
Gordon, Gerald, 79
Grainger, Percy, 8, 134
grandfather (*Invisible Man*), 35, 45–46,
    49, 57, 59, 72, 94, 95, 129

Granger, Major General Gordon, 107
Gray, James, 31
Gray, Valerie Bonita: *Invisible Man's
    Literary Heritage: Benito Cereno and
    Moby-Dick,* 71, 74

Griffith, D. W.: *The Birth of a Nation*,
    66, 84
Guggenheimer, Mrs. J. Caesar, 16

Handy, W. C., 31
Hardy, Thomas: *Jude the Obscure*, 3
Harlem, 4, 9, 10–11, 13, 14, 15, 39, 49,
    56, 58, 63, 66, 122, 131, 140, 141
Harman, Carter: *A Popular History of
    Music*, 31
Harris, Trudier, 150n24
Harrison, Hazel, 8, 133, 134
Hassan, Ihab: *Radical Innocence*, 142
Hawthorne, Nathaniel, 25, 32, 36, 138
Hebestreit, Ludwig, 4
Heggen, Thomas: *Mr. Roberts*, 18
Heller, Joseph: *Catch-22*, 39, 142
Hemingway, Ernest, 9, 12, 26, 33, 65,
    69, 77–79, 90, 93, 124, 125, 131;
    Across the River and Into the Trees, 93;
    "In Another Country," 33; *The Sun Also
    Rises*, 78, 79
Herndon, Angelo, 14
hero, 15, 27, 34, 43, 50, 56, 57, 62, 64,
    67, 70, 71, 75, 80, 83, 95, 124, 125,
    142

Hersey, John, 100
Hickman, Alonzo Zuber (Hickman
    stories), 93, 100–111, 115, 117, 118,
    125, 131, 141, 142
history, 1, 2, 15, 28, 54–56, 62–63, 73,
    86, 102, 105, 108–11, 114, 117–19,
    120, 126, 131, 142
Homer, 110; *The Odyssey*, 63, 65–67, 69
Hopalong Cassidy, 71
Howe, Irving, 16–18, 65, 78, 129, 142
Hughes, Langston, 4, 8, 10, 11, 17, 65,
    68, 77, 124, 137; *The Big Sea*, 77, 124
humor, 3, 20, 22, 31, 46–48, 61, 96, 97,
    115, 128, 137
Hurston, Zora Neale, 65, 86, 87, 124,
    143; *Their Eyes Were Watching God*, 86
Hyman, Stanley Edgar, 129, 132

initiation, 22, 29, 34, 96–100, 107, 130,
    131, 133, 135

Irving, John: *The World According to
    Garp*, 142

Jackson, Mahalia, 130
jazz, 2, 4, 5, 8, 41, 65, 79, 82, 84, 98,
    101, 111, 116, 120, 121, 127, 130,
    131, 132, 138
Johnson, Hank, 126
Johnson, Jack, 26
Johnson, James Weldon, 4, 14, 65, 86,
    105, 152n38; *God's Trombones: Seven
    Negro Sermons in Verse*, 105; *The
    Autobiography of an Ex-Colored Man*,
    86
Johnson, Lyndon, 19, 133
Jones, Howard Mumford, 17
Jones, Leroi (Imamu Amiri Baraka), 17,
    130–32, 144; *Blues People*, 130, 131
Joyce, James, 9, 12, 65, 69, 70, 124;
    Finnegans Wake, 109, 110, 119; *A
    Portrait of the Artist as a Young Man*,
    69, 118; *Ulysses*, 69

Kazin, Alfred, 17
Kennedy, John F., 20, 101
Kennedy, Robert F., 20
Kesey, Ken: *One Flew Over the Cuckoo's
    Nest*, 142
Kierkegaard, Soren, 65, 68
Killens, John O., 17
King, Martin Luther, Jr., 20
Klein, Marcus, 29, 31, 34, 62, 149n18;
    After Alienation, 142
Klotman, Phyllis R., 71, 72
Kolatch, Myron, 129
Kostelanetz, Richard, 8, 19, 20, 85

Langbaum, Robert, 17
language, 28, 29, 34, 42, 44, 54, 60, 61,
    69, 75, 78–81, 100, 107, 108, 109,
    110, 112–18, 121, 122, 136, 138,
    140, 142–44
Lawrence, D. H., 4, 40, 70
Lewis, "Little Willie," 4
Lewis, R. W. B., 1, 4, 16, 40, 45, 49,
    127, 132, 149n19; *The American
    Adam*, 42

Lieberman, Marcia R., 67
List, Robert: *Dedalus in Harlem: The Joyce-Ellison Connection,* 69, 152n32
Locke, Alain, 8, 10, 11, 17
Lockridge, Ross: *Raintree County,* 18

magical realism, 32, 34, 36, 44, 62, 98, 100
Mailer, Norman: *The White Negro,* 116
Malcolm X, 20
Malraux, André, 10, 11, 19, 65, 68, 69, 90; *Man's Fate,* 10, 68; *The Psychology of Art,* 69
Marvell, Andrew: "To his Coy Mistress," 111
Marx, Karl, 9, 88
Marx, Leo, 150n23
Maupassant, Guy de, 3
McFarland, Mrs. L. C., 3
McKay, Claude, 4
McNeal, Edward "Crack," 4
McPherson, James Alan, 19, 102, 144
McSweeney, Kerry, 95
Mellard, James M., 149n14
Melville, Herman, 9, 32, 65, 71, 73–75, 76, 80, 114, 115, 120, 138; *Benito Cereno,* 71, 73–74, 114; *Moby Dick,* 39, 44, 71, 74–75, 118
Moon, Bucklin, 124; *Primer for White Folks,* 128
Morris, Wright, 16
Morrison, Toni, 143, 144
Moses, 70, 80, 83, 103, 104
Moton, Major Robert Russa, 7
movies, 65, 83, 84, 106, 110, 117
Moynihan, Daniel Patrick, 8
Mumford, Lewis: *The Golden Day,* 49
Murray, Governor "Alfalfa Bill", 9
music, 4–9, 11, 18, 31, 33, 34, 79, 83, 95, 116, 120, 121, 127, 130, 133, 134, 142
Myrdal, Gunnar: *An American Dilemma,* 131

Nadel, Alan, 71–74, 76, 77; *Invisible Criticism: Ralph Ellison and the American Canon,* 71

narrative, 4, 17, 39, 42, 44, 48, 57, 67, 84, 86, 87, 141, 142
narrator (*Invisible Man*), 7, 10, 13, 34, 35, 38, 42–47, 49–60, 62, 63, 66–77, 79, 80, 82, 83–86, 92–96, 113, 127, 129, 134, 143
New Negro Movement, 3, 124

O'Brien, Tim: *Going After Cacciato,* 142
Oedipal motifs, 50, 60, 63, 70, 94, 95
Oklahoma, 1–6, 9, 10, 12, 13, 18, 19, 22, 23, 25, 32, 43, 77, 89, 98, 101, 113, 115, 118, 122, 127, 130, 132, 133, 139, 140, 142
old veteran (*Invisible Man*), 49–51, 70
Oliver, M. Celeste, 148n10
O'Meally, Robert, 7, 9, 11, 24, 26, 27, 29, 51, 74, 79, 84, 95–98, 106, 107, 111, 113, 118
O'Neill, Eugene: *The Ice Man Cometh,* 104
Ostendorf, Bernard, 34, 35, 121, 147n3
oxymoron, 41, 58, 75, 134, 138; *see also* paradox

Page, Inman, 5, 133, 136
Page, Oran "Hot Lips," 3
paradox, 78; *see also* oxymoron
persona in nonfiction, 122, 132–33, 136, 139
Petri, Egon, 8, 134
Picasso, Pablo, 3
Pickford, Mary, 110, 111
Poe, Edgar Allan, 32, 47, 65, 72; *The Narrative of Arthur Gordon Pym,* 72; "The Philosophy of Composition," 72
Pound, Ezra, 9
Prescott, Orville, 16
Prokofiev, Sergei, 8, 134

racism, 19, 34, 36, 38, 107, 114–16, 121, 129
Raglan, Lord, 15, 64; *The Hero,* 70
Rambo, Mary (*Invisible Man,* stories), 13, 53, 61, 93, 95, 96
Randolph, A. Philip, 126
Randolph, J. D., 5–6
Ras (*Invisible Man*), 19, 56–58, 61, 63, 84

Redding, J. Saunders, 17
Reed, Ishmael, 89, 103, 143, 144
Reilly, John, 122, 127, 132
religion, 28, 109, 114
restriction, 1, 10, 27–29, 40–42, 44, 94,
    97–99, 113, 119, 130, 139–42; *see
    also* freedom
Richter, Conrad, 125
Rinehart (*Invisible Man*), 50, 55–61, 63,
    104, 105, 131
Robinson, Douglas: *American Apocalypses:
    The Image of the End of the World in
    American Literature*, 66
Rushing, Jimmy, 5, 51, 91, 130

Sanders, Archie D., 66
Savage, Augusta, 9, 11
Savery, Pancho, 148n10
Schor, Edith, 25, 27, 28, 29
Schott, Webster, 16
Schultz, Elizabeth A., 74–75
Schwartz, Delmore, 16
Scruggs, Charles W., 66–67
Seagrave, Dr. Gordon S., 16
Shakespeare, William, 65, 97, 114; *Julius
    Caesar*, 67, *The Tempest*, 55
Shaw, George Bernard, 3
Sisney, Mary F., 72
Skerrett, Joseph, Jr., 90, 91
Slotkin, Richard, 40, 148n9
Smith, Bessie, 133
Smith, Buster, 4
Smith, Lillian: *Strange Fruit*, 124
Smith, Valerie, 4, 85, 122, 124, 133
southwest, significance of, 1–5, 9, 19, 22,
    23, 39, 41, 43, 47, 93, 98, 105, 107,
    125, 127, 130, 136, 140, 141
Sprague, Morteza Drexel, 8
Stafford, Jean, 125
Steegmuller, Beatrice and Francis, 16
Stein, Gertrude, 9, 12, 124
Steinbeck, John: *The Grapes of Wrath*, 24
Steiner, George, 71
Stepto, Robert, 86, 87, 89, 109; *From
    Behind the Veil*, 86
Stern, Richard G., 5, 127, 128
Stravinsky, Igor, 3

Styron, William: *The Confessions of Nat
    Turner*, 142
Sullivan, Harry Stack, 11, 70
surrealism, 32, 62
Sybil (*Invisible Man*), 58, 61, 66, 67, 83,
    84
Sylvander, Carolyn, 61
syncretism, 96; *see also* amalgamation,
    assimilation, and synthesis
synthesis, 1; *see also* amalgamation,
    assimilation, and syncretism

Tanner, Tony: *The City of Words*, 39, 142,
    149n11, 150n25
Tate, Claudia, 61
Taylor, Frank, 16
Thoreau, Henry David, 40, 113
Toussaint L'Ouverture, 27
Trimmer, Joseph, 36
Trueblood (*Invisible Man*), 35, 37, 41, 45,
    47–49, 61, 63, 67, 70, 78, 96, 125, 143
Turner, Frederick Jackson, 1, 40
Turpin, Waters Edwin: *These Low
    Grounds*, 21, 123
Tuskegee, Alabama, 3, 6–10, 19, 34, 62,
    70, 81, 133, 134, 140
Twain, Mark, 9, 26, 29, 30, 65, 75–77,
    80, 81, 100, 112, 120, 133, 138; *The
    Adventures of Huckleberry Finn*, 22, 30,
    64, 76, 77, 98, 103; "The Celebrated
    Jumping Frog of Calaveras County," 112

Ude, Wayne, 32

Vanderworken, David, 73
Vico, Giambattista, 109
Virgil: *The Aeneid*, 66–67
Voltaire: *Candide*, 65, 67
Vonnegut, Kurt: *Slaughterhouse-Five*,
    142

Walker, Alice, 143, 144
Walling, William, 146n24
Walsh, Mary Ellen Williams, 83
Warren, Robert Penn, 132
Washington, Booker T., 6, 7, 10, 46, 65,
    85, 86, 105, 107, 126

Webb, Constance, 89
Welles, Orson: *Citizen Kane*, 83
West, Anthony, 16
Wheatstraw, Peter (*Invisible Man*), 35, 51, 58, 66, 70, 83
Whitfield, Owen, 125
Whitman, Walt, "When Lilacs Last in the Dooryard Bloom'd," 75
Wideman, John Edgar, 138
Williams, Lawrence "Inky," 4
Wilner, Eleanor R., 147n18
Winslow, Henry F., 17
WPA (Work's Progress Administration), 11, 13, 14, 25

Wright, John S., 70, 121
Wright, Richard, 8, 10, 12, 18, 19, 22, 24, 65, 78, 87–92, 95, 124, 128, 129, 133, 134, 140, 143; "The Man Who Lived Underground," 90, 91, 95; *12 Million Black Voices*, 88; *Black Boy*, 88–90, 118, 128, 143; *Native Son*, 17, 18, 87, 124, 143; *Uncle Tom's Children*, 12, 87, 124

Youngblood, Harry, 4

Zinberg, Len: *Walk Hard, Talk Loud*, 123
Zinn, Howard: *The Southern Mystique*, 133

The Author

Mark Busby, an associate professor of English at Texas A&M University, teaches post–World War II fiction, southwestern literature, and film. He received his M.A. degree from East Texas State University and his Ph.D. from the University of Colorado, Boulder, in 1977. He has published *Preston Jones* (1983) and *Lanford Wilson* (1987) in the Western Writers Series at Boise State University, coedited *The Frontier Experience and the American Dream* (1989), and is a contributing editor of *Taking Stock: A Larry McMurtry Casebook* (1989). He has published in *Western American Literature, MELUS, New Mexico Humanities Review, A Literary History of the American West,* and elsewhere.

Professor Busby has taught at East Texas State University, Indiana University-Purdue University at Indianapolis, the U.S. Army Adjutant General School, and the University of Colorado. At Texas A&M he received an Association of Former Students Distinguished Teaching Award for 1988–89.

The Editor

Warren French (Ph.D. University of Texas, Austin) retired from Indiana University in 1986 and is now an honorary professor associated with the Board of American Studies at the University College of Swansea, Wales. In 1985 Ohio University awarded him a Doctor of Humane Letters degree. The editor of the contemporary (1945–75) titles in Twayne's United States Authors Series, he has contributed volumes on Jack Kerouac, Frank Norris, John Steinbeck, and J. D. Salinger. His most recent publication for Twayne is *The San Francisco Poetry Renaissance, 1955–1960.*